Soviet Politics,
Political Science
and Reform

by the same author

Soviet Political Elites: The Case of Tiraspol
(Martin Robertson, 1977)

Soviet Politics, Political Science and Reform

Ronald J. Hill

Martin Robertson / M. E. Sharpe, Inc.

First published in 1980 in the United Kingdom by Martin Robertson & Company Ltd, 108 Cowley Road, Oxford OX4 1JF.

ISBN 0 85520 331 5 (U.K. case edition)

Published in the United States by M. E. Sharpe Inc., 901 North Broadway, White Plains, New York 10603.

ISBN 0 87332 156 1 (U.S. case edition)

Library of Congress Catalog Card Number 79-55751

Typeset by Pintail Studios Ltd, Ringwood, Hampshire.
Printed and bound in the United Kingdom by
Richard Clay Ltd at The Chaucer Press, Bungay, Suffolk.

Contents

Preface

My main aim in writing this book is to bring to the attention of Western readers a body of scholarly writings by Soviet specialists that is virtually unknown outside the USSR but that, in my view, merits our discerning awareness.

The idea for such a survey originated in Moscow, during a study trip in the summer of 1975, when I was fortunate in coming across — frequently by following up footnotes in monographs and scholarly journals — a mass of somewhat obscure published writings, many of which contained to my mind surprising, even startling, criticisms of aspects of the Soviet political system. Few of these, to my knowledge, had been noted by Western scholars, and their very existence seemed to question basic Western assumptions about the nature of political and scholarly argument in the Soviet Union, the ability of Soviet social science to present challenging and critical opinions, and the capacity of that society to generate reformist ideas. For it must be emphasized right at the outset that I am dealing, not with illegal, *samizdat*, dissident literature (that genre is well established in translation in the West), but with books and articles published with the *imprimatur* of Glavlit, the government censorship system. The names of the authors are not well known. Frequently they work in provincial universities and institutes; often their works are published in the provinces, by local publishing houses, and in small — occasionally minute — editions; or the ideas and analytical data are presented to professional colleagues in conference papers, sponsored, as often as not, by the party and state authorities of a province or an autonomous republic. Some of the ideas have been echoed by party officials, or incorporated in policy statements and new legislation. Such literature forms the basis of this book, which I hope will be of interest to those readers who, like myself, are

vii

attempting to understand and evaluate developments in Soviet political life.

While of course accepting complete responsibility for any errors of judgement or interpretation, I wish to record my gratitude for the help and support of various institutions, colleagues and friends. This book would have been impossible without the valuable assistance of the staffs of three Moscow libraries: the Lenin Library, the Gorky Library, and the Law Faculty Library of Moscow State University. I am equally indebted to the British Council, which sponsored my trip to Moscow in May–July 1975, and to the Graduate Studies Committee of Trinity College, Dublin, for financial support. I am grateful to the editors of *Government and Opposition* for permission to include in chapter 2 material that appeared in that journal in Autumn 1976. I wish to record my appreciation of the interest, encouragement and hospitality offered to me by Professor Georgi Barabashev, of Moscow State University. Professional colleagues in Britain have been extremely helpful on a number of occasions with their critical comments on various chapters, and no less for their encouragement: among them, Archie Brown deserves special mention. The final draft was expertly typed by Mary Cotter. Finally, my warmest appreciation must again go to my wife, for her forbearance and her tolerance of the abandonment that writing this book has entailed.

Translations from Russian texts are my own.

R. J. Hill
August 1979

Glossary of Russian Terms

aktiv   the most politically active members of an organization, or associated with an institution

apparatchik   party or state bureaucrat

buro   executive committee of a CPSU committee

central committee   authoritative body of CPSU, elected by congress

CPSU   Communist Party of the Soviet Union

glasnost'   openness, publicity

IGPAN   Institute of State and Law, USSR Academy of Sciences

ispolkom   executive committee of local soviet

Komsomol   Young Communist League

obkom   provincial committee of CPSU

oblast   province (administrative unit below republic)

oblispolkom   executive committee of provincial (oblast) soviet

partiinost'   ideological and party commitment; party-mindedness

plenum   full (plenary) session of CPSU committee

podmena   substitution, supplantation (see chapter 6)

politburo   buro of central committee (= political buro) raikom   district committee (especially of CPSU)

raiispolkom   executive committee of district (raion) soviet

raion   district (administrative unit below oblast; also urban district or borough within large cities)

RSFSR   Russian Soviet Federative Socialist Republic

samizdat   illegally published, dissident writings

soviet   elected council, organ of state power

Supreme Soviet   republican or all-USSR parliamentary institution

Soviet Politics,
Political Science
and Reform

CHAPTER 1

The Development of Political Science, and the Need for Political Reform

In 1958 and 1961 Gordon Skilling visited the Soviet Union 'in search of political science' (Skilling, 1963). His quest was only moderately successful, for, despite the existence of a 'Soviet Political Sciences Association' and the presence in a variety of different institutions of scholars working within what in the West would be recognized as political science, there was no such formally recognized academic discipline in the Soviet Union.

Almost two decades later, little has changed. There is still no recognized 'political science' in the USSR; and the Soviet Political Sciences Association, host in August 1979 to the eleventh world congress of the International Political Science Association, consists of scholars working in relevant areas in law faculties, economics institutes, institutes of philosophy and so forth, who publish in journals of law, philosophy, economics and history – there is no *Soviet Political Science Review*. Such is the parlous state of a scholarly discipline whose ancestry has been traced back to Aristotle (Blondel, 1969, p. 31).

In the intervening years there have occasionally been signs of an impending breakthrough in securing the status of political science – along with other social sciences such as sociology, which, according to one observer, 'has – for all practical purposes – won the battle for legitimation and recognition as an independent academic discipline within the Soviet Union' (Weinberg, 1974, p. 14). (Not everyone would accept this judgement, however: see, for example, Theen, 1972, for a pessimistic view

1

of the situation of all social sciences.) In the mid-1960s a lively debate on the future of political science was conducted in the Soviet press. In January 1965, in *Pravda*, Professor F. M. Burlatskii called for the establishment of a separate discipline of political science as a 'further differentiation of Marxist–Leninist social science'. It would have its 'own angle of vision' (*ugol zreniya*), namely 'the study of the mechanism of leadership of society in its dynamics, that is, the study of how it functions, and what is necessary for its improvement and development'. Moreover – and this is the phrase that was accorded most significance by Western commentators (e.g. Powell and Shoup, 1970, p. 576; Theen, 1972, p. 66) – Burlatskii boldly asserted that genuine political science 'presupposes the formulation of questions the answers to which are not known in advance' (Burlatskii, 1965). The article concluded by inviting readers' comments, and five months later *Pravda* carried an editorial summary of reactions, implying by its comments that whatever one called this discipline, there was certainly a need for research into those aspects of society ('O razrabotke problem...', 1965).

Pravda was not the sole vehicle for discussing this important issue, and Burlatskii's call was echoed, sometimes even more explicitly, by other scholars around the country. At a conference in Irkutsk, for example, V. Ye. Chirkin argued for proper courses in political science in the country's higher educational establishments, in a paper significantly entitled 'On the systems analysis of the political organization of society' (Chirkin, 1967). The conference papers, as published (Petrov, 1967), show a remarkable concern for methodology and for defining the aims of their particular branch of knowledge (ostensibly, legal science); indeed, the methodological awareness and concern of Soviet writers in the 1960s are reminiscent of the similar, perhaps exaggerated, preoccupation with method that characterized Western political science at the height of the 'behavioural revolution'. A similar call for a value-free political science is contained in A. Ye. Lunev's contribution to the same symposium: he wrote of the need to devise a research methodology that would permit 'a scientific conclusion'. He continued:

> This conclusion will reflect the objective state of affairs if it is free of any preconceptions. Genuine objectivity in conclusions will be achieved only through a scientific – genuinely scientific – approach to analysing practice and the facts of life; what is needed is not the 'collection' of illustrations and examples, but the *establishment*, relying on scientific methods of research, of a genuine picture of life, for the confirmation or negation of a suggested hypothesis. [Lunev, 1967, pp. 96–7]

The question had also been debated, with an introductory paper by Burlatskii, in February 1965, at a general meeting of the Soviet Political Sciences Association; and the divisions of opinion came out clearly in the 'lively' debate, which involved 20 of the 160 participants in the meeting (as reported in Tadevosyan, 1965). Those in favour of a separate discipline (including G. Kh. Shakhnazarov, later president of the Association) argued that there were many important areas of social and political life that were not being properly researched by the disciplines of legal science, economics, scientific communism, and so forth. Moreover, although the areas proposed for inclusion under the new discipline were to some extent studied by historians, lawyers and philosophers, their work tended to be restricted in its scope to historical description or analysing the legal aspects of government activity. The new science would have certain concrete areas and methods, including examination of the sociological aspects of political matters. Opponents, led by B. M. Chkhikvadze, proposed simply extending the scope of *legal science* to cover those areas not satisfactorily covered to date. Tadevosyan himself, although clearly unfavourable towards 'political science', allows for the possibility of a new science arising where scientific communism and legal science meet: however, like economics, it would be explicitly an *applied* science, and he preferred to call it 'concrete politics' (*konkretnaya politika*) (Tadevosyan, 1965, pp. 165–6).

Since then the discipline has perceptibly developed, and the late 1960s also witnessed many calls for the adoption of experimental methods in social science research. The most explicit statement along these lines was made by A. A. Golovko. Speaking at a conference in Minsk, in February 1970, on improving the structure and functioning of local soviets, he stated that this could be achieved only on a scientific basis, 'and science is unthinkable without experiments' (Golovko, 1970, p. 16). Over three years earlier, in November 1966, he had extolled the virtues of the experimental method, citing experiments in the administrative structure in Belorussia in the 1920s and 1930s, and proposing that law faculties should have 'laboratories' of specialists trained to conduct research and experiments (Golovko, 1966). Other writers to promote the use of such experiments include Safarov (1964), Nikitinskii (1967) and Perttsik (1970, p. 98).

Nikitinskii captures the optimistic mood of political scientists in the second half of the 1960s: 'In the last decade, legislative activity has come to rest on a scientific basis, which has led, in particular, to the perfecting of legislation on the basis of the experimental testing of the corresponding legal norms.' Legal science had only recently woken up to the idea of experimentation, and in his enthusiasm he suggested a Statute on Legal Experiment, which would formalize and legitimate the practice (Nikitinskii, 1967, pp. 26–7). Whether such a statute would achieve Nikitinskii's aim is an open question: in practice, it might neutralize the researcher's freedom to engage in such research. Nevertheless, the mood of optimism was shared by other writers, for example Kazimirchuk, who saw good prospects for the development of numero-mathematical methods, and for the establishment of research teams, well trained, properly equipped with computers, and adequately funded, to replace the one-man research 'by eye' and 'by intuition' (Kazimirchuk, 1967, pp. 44–5).

Indeed, there were grounds for hopefulness. Despite the lack of statistical and other data, which some scholars openly deplored (e.g. Barabashev and Sheremet, 1965b, p. 154; Lepëshkin, 1965a, p. 14; 1965b, pp. 131–2), the party authorities themselves were moving towards recognizing the place of the social sciences in a society that was supposedly building communism. At the twenty-third party congress, in 1966, Leonid Brezhnev himself stressed the importance of the social sciences. His speech contained a highly significant passage about the nature of these disciplines: so significant, indeed, that (as Theen perceptively noted – 1972, p. 64, n. 3) it was deleted from all subsequent versions of the report, including even the official stenographic record of the congress. The passage read as follows:

> It is necessary to put an end to the notion, current among part of our cadres, that the social sciences have merely a propagandistic significance, and are called upon to explain and comment upon practice. [*Pravda*, 30 March 1966, p. 9]

Brezhnev went on to equate the role of the social sciences with that of the natural sciences. The deletion of the quoted passage suggests that it was felt, on reflection, that the party secretary had gone too far in freeing social science from its explicitly political role. Nevertheless, the central committee issued a major statement on the role and importance of the social sciences. Although political science as such was not mentioned, the defined research fields in the spheres of philosophy, scientific communism, party history and legal science left plenty of scope for political research; the promise of better training for social scientists, better teaching of the social sciences, and the encouragement to produce 'new conclusions, generalizations and recommendations having serious theoretical and practical significance' – all this seemed to give the go-ahead for a blossoming of the social sciences, albeit within the framework of helping to build communism (*Spravochnik partiinogo rabotnika*, 8, pp. 245–57, esp. p. 248).

This seemed to represent a recognition by the authorities that the social sciences, including legal science (which for many purposes we may take as a synonym for political science) were advancing to a new stage of maturity, out of the moribund state into which they had been allowed (or forced) to decline under

Stalin. The problem, as defined by Burlatskii, was that 'commentating' (*kommentatorstvo*) was 'an extremely widespread illness here'; in the field of legal science it meant 'the interpretation of laws and other legal norms: at best it systematizes laws and gives illustrations'; moreover, there was not enough linkage between the social scientists and the practical legislators and administrators. 'Is it not obvious', he asked rhetorically, in a reference to Khrushchev's ill thought-out reforms, 'that, if the restructurings that have taken place in the government apparatus had been more based on a scientific analysis, it would have been possible to avoid many negative consequences?' Equally obvious, at least to Burlatskii, was that the social sciences should be developed to perform a new role – that of working closely with the legislators in order to ensure that society is run rationally, scientifically (Burlatskii, 1965). Lepëshkin, a few weeks after the appearance of Burlatskii's article, firmly asserted that legal science had moved a long way from its extremely limited role in the era of the 'Stalin–Vyshynskii cult', when the discipline became simply a commentary on new legislation and original ideas were damned as 'deviations from Marxism–Leninism'. Already, wrote Lepëshkin, the legal profession was introducing less dogmatism and quotation-brandishing (*tsitatnichestvo*), although still not enough attention was being paid to certain questions, including ways of rationalizing the political structure and democratizing the forms and methods of its activities (Lepëshkin, 1965a, pp. 6–7).

There is a clear sense of optimism in this writing, and much other writing in the same vein, and the political authorities were showing signs of interest. The same expectancy was shared in the West. Churchward (1966a) saw a movement 'Towards a Soviet Political Science'; Powell and Shoup (1970) felt sufficiently confident to write of 'The Emergence of Political Science in Communist Countries', including the Soviet Union; and Theen (1971) saw positive signs in a Soviet critique of American political science, noting that in other instances Soviet criticism of a Western 'bourgeois' phenomenon had foreshadowed its adoption in the Soviet Union. At that stage – the beginning of the 1970s – there seemed to be enough straws in the wind to indicate that we were 'witnessing the "birth pangs" of Soviet political science' (Theen, 1971, p. 702).

A more recent writer, Moshe Lewin (1975), directly associates the development of political science (and, indeed, other social sciences) with the economic reformers and reforms of the mid-1960s. He writes of reformist ideas gradually unfolding, and moving 'from the more strictly economic to the larger socio-political aspects'; he refers specifically to the 'spillover from "economics" to "politics" ' (Lewin, 1975, p. 190), and later suggests that criticisms of the directly political aspects of society, and 'elements of programs for change and of alternative models' were available 'scattered through various writings, *mainly of economists*' (p. 215; emphasis added). Hence, Lewin's interpretation of Soviet intellectual development in the 1960s leads him to the conclusion that 'a great debate was thus initiated, and out of it Soviet political science was born' (p. 336).

In fact, the evidence in the present book suggests that such an interpretation is mistaken. The chronology of the publication of 'political science' research extends at least to the early 1960s, and some of the intellectual basis for work produced in the 1960s and 1970s was laid in the late 1950s. It seems clear that reformist political science and reformist economics were contemporaneous phenomena in Soviet society, and probably stimulated each other: just as 'the renaissance of economics' began about 1957–8 (Lewin, 1975, p. 134), the process of de-Stalinization involved a new awakening, and new searching, in other branches of the social sciences; this led to the adoption of fresh ways of asking questions, fresh means of seeking answers, and, inevitably, fresh answers, incorporating fresh views of Soviet reality, frequently contradicting long-standing 'official' pictures, produced by the propagandists. Such, in essence, was the course of development of Soviet sociology (Weinberg, 1974, pp. 10–12) and criminology (Solomon, 1978, pp. 19–64); and, as will become clear, political science in the early 1960s was not backward in adopting concrete sociological methods, including surveys and statistical and quantitative analysis, to examine the functioning of the political (i.e., essentially, state) institutions. Lewin correctly points out that the great economic debate, and the reforms introduced in the second half of the 1960s, and somewhat watered down and even reversed a few years later, were part of a much broader intellectual challenging in Soviet society, which must have been exciting and exhilarating for those engaged in it. There is, for instance, something endearing in the proud references to analysis by Ural-4 computer in empirical works published in the 1960s (for example, Kalits *et al.*, 1965, p. 65; Perttsik, 1967b, p. 17, n. 2; Kazimirchuk and Adamyan, 1970, p. 111; Pavlov and Kazimirchuk, 1971, p. 180, n. 2), rather reminiscent of the similar phase in quantification in Western political science. Since the late 1960s, such methods have been adopted for studying the performance of the party itself.

Yet, despite the optimism of a decade or so ago, and the excitement that prevailed a few years before that (when, for example, Perttsik could publish a list of pioneering lawyers who had used sociological methods in their work: Perttsik, 1967a, p. 134), 'political science' has failed to gain acceptance as a distinct and separate discipline. The reasons for this are not difficult to identify. Any profession that uses the word 'political' is by definition politically sensitive, and likely to be even more closely guarded by the party ideologues than other disciplines. The nature of the ideology, and the party's claims of a 'special relationship' with it, leave very little room for free and open inquiry into the political system. The ideology prescribes a conceptual framework, based on a specific interpretation of Marx's and Lenin's views on class, history, progress and the role of the workers' party, and writers on social matters have to express themselves within this framework. Furthermore, through its long dominance the communist party has established its own customary ways of viewing political processes, using distinctive vocabulary, which further restricts political analysis. An excellent example is in the work of Farukshin, who discusses the Western functionalist conceptual framework and explicitly rejects such concepts as 'political recruitment', preferring the concept 'selection and placement of cadres' – which is how the party itself sees this aspect of its own role (Farukshin, 1973, pp. 58–61). Clearly, when the 'correct' conceptual framework is prescribed by the political authorities (who also have indirect control over all publication, and over the careers of scholars and academics), the creative importation of social science concepts is somewhat circumscribed.

In fact, just as the economic reform and reformers were challenged and – with perceptible success – opposed by the 'conservatives', so political science has failed to win acceptance, in the face of opposition from party ideologists supported by conservative academics (Churchward, 1973, pp. 120–1). Political science has been a victim of the general reversal of progressive trends characteristic of the mid-1960s. The 1970s have been marked by the re-assertion of the centrality of the party and its role in guiding the society towards communism, through the stage of development defined as 'mature' socialism. It is a fact of life for political scientists, as for all other professions, that society is directed by the party of which the majority of them are members. This is one of the ground rules – indeed, the basic ground rule – of all scientific and creative endeavour in the USSR. In this situation, we should not be at all surprised if Soviet political scientists fail to produce and publish critical analyses and interpretations of the party's role: it would be astounding if they did. Public opinion research, too, has perforce had to be treated with the utmost caution by social scientists, because the statistically valid results of polling might cast doubts on – even contradict – the official assertions of monolithic unanimity in support of the party and its policies.

Must we then dismiss the notion of Soviet political science? It is easy to argue that this 'discipline' is subordinated to the needs of the party. There are abundant statements, by politicians and political scientists alike, to the effect that 'the conditions of the development of socialist society demand a strengthening of the links between science and the practice of communist construction' (Barabashev and Sheremet, 1975, p. 9), or that 'the confrontation of views [among social scientists] must be based on our general Marxist–Leninist platform. It is important that the principles of party-mindedness in science be consistently maintained, and that the right-opportunist and leftist views of our foreign ideological opponents be given a decisive rebuff'; this speaker (M. V. Zimyanin, secretary of the CPSU central committee) added that 'scholastic theorizing' and 'isolation from life' were impermissible (*XXV s"ezd KPSS i zadachi kafedr obshchestvennykh nauk*, 1977, p. 15). There is clearly no room here for the 'value-free' science of politics that was the supposed aim of an earnest generation of Western political scientists in the 1950s and 1960s. A similar view, expressed in perhaps more scientific language, was presented by academician Yegorov, secretary of the philosophy and law section of the Academy, at a conference of the section in March 1976:

> When we speak of research at the junctions of different sciences, particularly the natural and social sciences, we must ..., most importantly, not forget that the strength of our science is in its Marxist–Leninist methodology. Individual methods of research, including the latest, must be worked out on its basis and in close communication with it. [Quoted in I. N. Smirnov, 1976, p. 151]

But political engagement does not necessarily disqualify scholars in a particular field from identifying themselves as a discipline or a science, as the members of the Caucus for a New Political Science have shown in America. Indeed, much of the argument about the 'scientific' nature of 'political science' is peculiar to speakers of English, for whom 'science' has implications not shared by the equivalent word in other languages. The Russian *nauka* is far less stringent, implying simply a coherent and linked body of knowledge (Kneen, 1978, p. 181). In practice, the stipulation of *partiinost'* – party-mindedness, ideological commitment – ensures a certain basic perspective in the writings of Soviet specialists, and to some extent limits what may be investigated and what may be said. But it may also facilitate the publication of moderately critical ideas which could never appear in print if they derived from the pen of a 'dissident'.

There is an obvious 'applied' quality in much of their work: they are, at the behest of party and government, attempting to solve specific problems, and thereby to improve the functioning of the system. Brezhnev himself asserted at the twenty-fifth party congress (1976) that the need for 'further creative elaboration of theory' is not diminished, but rather increases, with the need to work out the implications of attaining the stage of 'mature' socialism (cited in I. N. Smirnov, 1976, p. 151). Perhaps scholars have very little choice in the matter; but, be that as it may, the fact is that many Soviet social scientists accept this role. V. N. Kudryavtsev, director of the Institute of State and Law of the Academy of Sciences (IGPAN), told an audience of scholars in 1976 that the task of legal scientists consisted in working out a strategy for research in the field of state and law, democracy and legality, 'taking our lead from the decisions of the twenty-fifth CPSU congress' (cited in Smirnov, 1976, p. 155); while Chkhikvadze mentioned the need to work out the theory of the political system of socialism, the problems of the all-people's state, and to busy themselves with preparation of the draft new Constitution (cited in Smirnov, 1976, p. 156) – all tasks that stemmed from the party's current ideological conceptual framework.

Some may regard this as an improper or inappropriate aim for a scholarly discipline; but such a view could rightly be held as simply reflecting bourgeois liberal values: the Soviet view is that all human activity should be directed towards improving the lot of mankind, and that goes for those who in another society might occupy an ivory tower. How far Soviet scholars adhere to this aim will be seen in this book; how far they are influential in bringing about the desired improvements is more problematical, but an attempt will be made to assess this in chapter 8. At the very least, however, it can be said that the idea of 'scientific' political science may not contribute towards the best use of the talents of members of the profession – a point that was tellingly made by the British minister of education, Mrs Shirley Williams, in an illuminating address to the 1977 conference of the United Kingdom Political Studies Association: where, she asked, is the political science profession's analysis of the phenomenon and problems of devolution within the unitary state, an item that had been on the British political agenda for some years? Soviet political scientists would have turned urgently to the task, as they have to the task of analysing a whole variety of issues raised by the political leadership.

Churchward perceptively wrote of the characteristics of Soviet political science in his essay, 'Towards a Soviet Political Science'. It would, he stated, be 'closely tied to existing marxist theory', which was now becoming far more sophisticated and far less dogmatic than it had been since Stalin's day. It would 'clearly be under close party control, and the party [would] exert a major influence on the orientation of research programs'. It would be normative, 'directed towards assisting the realization of the party objective of communism' (Churchward, 1966a, p. 71). Its content, and where it might most comfortably be accommodated, were still open questions. By 1976 the disciplines embraced by 'political science' had come to comprise historical materialism, scientific communism, sociology, political economy, the general theory of the state and law, and the science of constitutional law (*Time, Space and Politics*, 1976, p. 5); there has also been an attempt to establish 'party construction' as an independent discipline (see Kadeikin *et al.*, 1974, p. 3).

I believe the most remarkable aspect of the whole trend in the development of Soviet social science is that it implies a public recognition by the political leaders that the system does not operate as perfectly as it was said to do during the period of their own political training. This new recognition might be explained simply – and slightly cynically – by saying that they have had plenty of direct experience of an inadequate set of political institutions, customs and practices; yet it needs to be borne in mind that their political training taught them to present a particular, monolithic façade, and to bluff their way through, hiding behind a massive propaganda picture: the indications of a partial return to 'Stalinist' methods demonstrate that the effects of that training have not been entirely eradicated. Yet, from the mid-1950s onwards, party and government statements have repeatedly referred to the need for 'further democratization' in the political system, 'further development of the principles of socialist democracy'. In programmatic documents such as the 1961 CPSU programme and the 1977 USSR Constitution, the need for such developments has been openly acknowledged by the political leadership, thereby implicitly recognizing the existence of deficiencies and imperfections, some of which have been more explicitly identified, and certain steps taken to overcome them (see chapter 8). Moreover, occasional statements by politicians imply that the party does not always know in specific terms what is best for people – again an admission that would have been unthinkable up to a generation ago (see chapter 5). Social scientists are called upon to identify and investigate problem areas, and to make proposals for eliminating them, in the cause of 'developing socialist democracy'.

Political science today leads a shady existence, spread among a variety of defined disciplines and operating in a range of different institutions. There are certainly people in the Soviet Union who happily consider themselves to be 'political scientists' in conversation with Western colleagues in that profession. Their work is loosely coordinated by the Soviet Political Sciences Association, which is affiliated to the International Political Science Association, under UNESCO auspices, and which has now resumed active participation in that body's work, an involvement that first began in 1955 (Churchward, 1966a, p. 67). The tenth IPSA congress, held in Edinburgh in August 1976, was attended by a twenty-seven-member Soviet delegation, led by P. N. Fedoseev, vice-president of the USSR Academy of Sciences. At its own symposia and conferences, the Soviet association has discussed such questions as the subject of political science and its place in the system of social sciences; the main trends in political science in the developed capitalist countries; political activity in socialist society; socialist statehood and communist public self-government; political culture; peaceful coexistence and socio-political development (*Time, Space and Politics*, 1976, p. 6).

Meanwhile, Soviet 'political scientists' continue to pursue their theoretical and empirical research, publish their results, and attend scientific conferences where ideas and opinions are exchanged. Many understand foreign languages, and significant numbers travel abroad to conferences and for extended study periods, thereby gaining familiarity with the work of Western scholars and an acquaintance with Western political science literature, more of which is also becoming available in Soviet libraries. This has an enriching effect on the content of Soviet political science, by introducing fresh concepts and methods of analysis and research. For example, the concepts of system, function, political culture, interests and public opinion are now frequently to be found in the works of Soviet scholars, as will become clear.

All of this represents an enormous development from the situation of only a few years ago – a generation at most. It is justified by political scientists themselves and by their patrons among the political leadership by the argument that, as society develops, so the need for changes in the political system becomes apparent; as the standards of education, experience and 'culture' develop, so does the people's capacity for involvement and participation. There is therefore a perpetual need for reviewing the present system and seeking ways to develop it to meet new requirements – a task in which specialists have an important place (Tikhomirov, 1975, p. 237). Moreover, the increasingly rapid development of technology, with its potential impact on the political system, also provides social scientists of all disciplines with an object for serious and careful study, to assist the party itself in understanding, and thereby controlling, these novel processes (Tikhomirov, 1975, chapter 5). This need for reliable methods of predicting trends, as a means of helping the party to adopt sound policies, has been well expressed by V. V. Kopeichikov, who concludes:

> The joining together of politics and science is one of the characteristic features of the society of developed socialism. Their linking ... is a property above all of the activity of the communist party and the Soviet state, and of those

relationships in which they participate. [Babii *et al.*, 1976, p. 26]

And so, in Shakhnazarov's words, 'In addition to organizing research work on pressing problems requiring scientifically-based solutions, the Party exercises general guidance of the social sciences'; one of the methods used is 'recommendation on topical directions of research' (Shakhnazarov, 1974, p. 67).

The 'political sciences' thus seem to have found a role in Soviet society. Moreover, scholars are securing that position by arguing for the synthesis or integration of all branches of knowledge, including legal science, biology, economics and so forth (see Berg *et al.*, 1971, p. 93). 'Legal science cannot be an exception to this general law in the development of contemporary science', writes A. R. Shlyakhov, since 'at the junctions of the natural, technical and legal sciences new branches of knowledge are now already being formed', and he predicts that legal science will more and more use the methods of the natural and technical sciences, particularly computer technology and mathematical methods (see Shebanov, 1972, p. 268).

Yet, for all the positive signs, there still remains a certain ambivalence, ambiguity or diffidence in Soviet political scientists' attitude towards their profession, symbolized perhaps by a reluctance to employ the term 'political science' in Russian (*politicheskaya nauka*). The term was virtually unknown in the Soviet Union in the early 1960s, although it was at least understood by scholars and students at the end of the decade (Theen, 1971, p. 691, n. 4). Today the plural 'political sciences' is preferred. This ambivalence is also revealed in the existence of two distinct terms for the practitioner of the art: *politolog*, literally 'politologist', a word introduced about 1968 (Churchward, 1973, p. 182, n. 38), and sometimes used in English translations from Soviet texts (e.g., *Time, Space and Politics*, 1976, p. 25); and the Slavonic-root word *gosudarstvoved*, meaning 'student of the state', which perhaps more accurately defines the scope of the work of the majority of their number.

The question of terminology is one of the issues raised in *Pravda*'s response to Burlatskii's 1965 article. A whole variety of alternatives to Burlatskii's 'political science' had been proposed, including, in addition to those mentioned already, *gosudarstvovedcheskie nauki* – 'the sciences dealing with the study of the state', a phrase even more cumbersome than *gosudarstvovedenie*, 'the study of the state'. *Politologiya* ('politology') is also used. *Pravda* quite rightly pointed out that the stress on the *state* was restricting, and 'political system' was a wider concept. It particularly noted the importance of the party and other institutions in Soviet political life, and concluded that, in the final analysis, terminology is not what matters: the main thing is that a certain range of topics should be subjected to thoroughgoing analysis. It ended with an implied warning: the development of sociological research had been long held up by wrangling over terminology ('O razrabotke problem . . .', 1965).

Yet the matter still remains unresolved, and it applies more broadly to the social sciences, where that term's literal translation (*obshchestvennye nauki*) coexists alongside the word *obshchestvovedenie*, 'the study of society' (see, for example, *XXV s"ezd KPSS i zadachi kafedr obshchestvennykh nauk*, 1977, pp. 127, 138). In the case of political science, the use of the two terms may reflect different opinions about the scope of the discipline, and specifically whether the party is a proper subject for scientific analysis. Also, the Slavonic-root terms may be employed specifically to distinguish Soviet social or political science from the bourgeois variety, implied in the use of foreign terminology: in other words, a form of socialist one-up-manship.

Despite all this, however, the work of Soviet scholars should be taken seriously. Very little can be gained by writing off Soviet political science as 'in the service of the party': after all, as Soviet writers and many Western writers have cogently argued, the gist of much Western writing on politics is that 'democracy' – understood as liberal democratic theory and practice, and specifically that pertaining in the United States of America – is the 'natural' political system for the human race, towards which all societies are likely to (and should) develop. More specifically, Western political science writings on the Soviet political system often have a clear, if not overtly acknowledged, political aim and content (White, 1975). This point, of course, has not been left unmade by Soviet writers (for example, Shakhnazarov, 1974, pp. 27–9; Marchenko, 1973, chapter 2); the mistake made by some of them – if indeed it is a 'mistake' – is to assume that all Western students of Soviet politics and social life are tied in with what one such writer refers to as 'the publishing and propaganda machine of the bourgeois world' (Shapko *et al.*, 1977, p. 271).

Yet, leaving aside the crude and unsophisticated 'revelations' and 'exposures' characteristic of this type of writing, there are three reasons why the work of serious Soviet scholars merits attention. First, they have access to research material that is not available to Western researchers; they perform kinds of research – say, into attitudes towards certain types of issue, or into the functioning of institutions – that are impossible for Western scholars to undertake. Second, in approaching their task with an essentially 'applied' attitude – setting out to identify problems and propose solutions – they are bound to make criticism and put forward suggestions that can help us, as well as Soviet politicians, in evaluating various parts of the political system. Third, their analyses and interpretations (and changes and developments therein) given an idea of how the system is perceived by those who work within it. In so far as those who run the system do so on the basis of their perceptions of it, we have a means of gaining insights into the political culture, particularly of the leadership. It is interesting to note the changes in perspective over the past decade or so, as the purely institutional approach has given way to a far more sophisticated picture, derived from the application of fresh concepts (see chapter 8).

A further consideration to bear in mind is the nature of the literature. Although one can identify some individual scholars who are bolder in their analysis and in their proposals for reform than some of their colleagues, and some who stick with well-worn approaches and methods of analysis, one does not meet consistency among all the writings of individual scholars. This is partly because they write for a variety of different readerships, and adjust their style and content accordingly. There are, perhaps, three basic types of political literature in the Soviet Union: first, the 'official' literature, as identified, for example, by Imashev (Aimbetov *et al.*, 1967, p. 79), including the speeches and writings of politicians, together with official handbooks and commentaries on, say, various institutions; second, 'propagandistic' literature, written in a popular style, for home or foreign consumption, and designed to present the accepted view, revealing no secrets, no serious problems; and, third, 'heavy' political science, published by academic or provincial presses or in specialist journals, often by scholars whose work also appears in more popular format or in the periodical press. This literature tends to be more revealing, more realistic in its assessment of the functioning of the system, more willing to discuss problems in a serious manner. It relies much less on pure *assertion*, more on the results of detailed study, backed up with argumentation and judgement. There is also a concern for methodology that immediately raises such work to a level of respectability that few would accord the unsophisticated accounts.

I believe that Soviet scholars have undertaken serious political research, aimed at pinpointing problems and their causes and proposing ways of eliminating them. In doing so, they have raised issues that could not have been broached a generation ago, and they have thereby encouraged the political leadership at least to face up to certain realities about Soviet politics – particularly the malfunctioning of institutions – that were perhaps barely and inadequately perceived hitherto. Furthermore, the presentation of challenging facts, the application of fresh concepts and the promotion of suggestions for reforms in the system may well have had their impact on the way Soviet politics is viewed within the country, and have affected the way the system operates (see chapter 8).

This book, however, is intended to be less about Soviet political science as a professional discipline, and more about the discipline's content and its role: how it sees Soviet politics, what areas are regarded as needing reform, and the results of Soviet investigations. By examining aspects of Soviet politics through the work of scholars whose task is to seek ways of making the system work better, I hope that the English-speaking reader will gain an awareness of a body of more or less influential literature, and insights that otherwise might not be accessible.

THE NEED FOR POLITICAL REFORM

There are two major reasons why any political system might need reform: either because of malfunctioning of the system at present, or because structural changes in the social and economic environment (the base) render the political system (part of the superstructure) incapable of resolving new problems. The two are not entirely separate: a system that functions adequately at one stage of development may cease to perform competently, with no appreciable difference in the performance of the institutions and individuals who make up the system. Marxists and non-Marxists may disagree on how far reform is capable of bringing a political system into line with developments in socioeconomic relations in class society, and whether revolution is necessary for bringing about radical change. Soviet scholars are faced with a different set of circumstances that govern the way in which they discuss reform. The word 'reform' is itself suspect; although it has been used in the context of institutional changes in the economy, in the political sphere an endorsement of the concept might be construed as supporting reform in any society, and thereby diverting attention from the allegedly inevitable role of revolution as the engine of history. Hence the common references in the Soviet literature to 'perfecting' (even 'further perfecting') and developing the system: both words have a very positive ring about them.

But what kind of arguments in favour of reform can be put forward by Soviet scholars? Since official claims have always asserted that the Soviet Union is the most democratic country in the world, what scope is there for political reform?

Soviet writers make use of both types of argument in calling for change. As for the malfunctioning of the system, the present generation of scholars has inherited the phrase, introduced by

Khrushchev at the twentieth CPSU congress in 1956, 'cult of the personality of Stalin', which came to sum up all that was wrong in the way the political system operated. This concept launched the anti-Stalin campaign in the latter 1950s and gave the first impetus to the searching analysis of the way the political institutions operated. The 1956 congress authorized the drawing up of the new party programme, adopted five years later, which encouraged scholars to examine various ways of developing soviet democracy, and drew specific attention to the need to introduce democratic principles in the way the administration operated (see *KPSS v rez.*, vol. 7, p. 182; vol. 8, pp. 274–80). The identification of weaknesses in the operation of the system has therefore been an important element in Soviet political science writings. In the early 1960s, it was still possible to refer to the personality cult as the reason for the weaknesses; later it became necessary to ascribe some weaknesses to Khrushchev's wilfulness in tampering with the system. But whoever might be held responsible for the problems, the implication in the writings of scholars and the speeches of politicians is always that the current leadership is doing its utmost to overcome them. On a different tack, P. P. Ukrainets (1976, p. 82), turned for support to Lenin, drawing attention to his 'insistent demand' 'to perfect the government apparatus constantly, to study the effectiveness of its work attentively, conforming to the demands of real actuality, to alter its structure if there is a need for this'.

The more sophisticated trend in the 1970s, however, when the Brezhnev leadership had been so long in command that it was no longer plausible to blame weaknesses in the system on former leaders, has been to argue the case for reform in socioeconomic terms – a line of argument that not only sounds reasonable and rational, but is also fully compatible with Marxist teachings about the relationship between substructure and superstructure. The argument has been put forward, fully or in part, by many scholars and was used in justification for introducing the 1977 Constitution: why, asked Brezhnev, have we had to devise a new Constitution? And he gave his answer:

Because, comrades, over four decades in our country, profound changes have taken place in the whole of our society.... Great, fundamental changes have affected all sides of social life.... Such are the basic reasons and premises for the creation of a new USSR Constitution. [Brezhnev, 1977a, pp. 34–5]

In less rhetorical language, scholars express the same idea, and go on to state that improving the governmental system is not a once-off affair, but 'a dynamic process of resolving the practical problems of communist construction' (Kerimov, 1973, pp. 26–7).

Other writers, fixing on the concept of 'democratization' (usually identified as involving the masses in the political process), speak of the importance of public opinion in government, once there exists an educated and informed population (Safarov, 1975b, pp. 131–2), or of needing to develop various forms of participation (Babii *et al.*, 1976, p. 451).

But whatever the specific angle from which a Soviet writer approaches the question, the general argument is the same: as society becomes more and more complex, sophisticated, diverse, professional, highly educated and experienced, the more it needs a system of political institutions and practices that permit modern techniques of management and government to be combined with fuller application of the democratic principle of participation. The call in the 1970s has been for enhancing the role of all political institutions: party, state, and public organizations; this will eventually (although Khrushchev's rash twenty-year timetable has been quietly dropped) give way to 'communist self-administration'.

It is within the context of such a vision of the political system that this book needs to be read. The work of Soviet scholars is closely tied in with implementing this long-term aspiration, their task being to identify weaknesses in the present system, or to examine problems identified by the political authorities, to whom they are expected to make proposals for reforms. It is, of course, possible to take a cynical view of the whole process, and declare that such fanciful utterances are intended to blind the Soviet masses to their essentially subject position in the system: this view will be fully discussed in chapter 9. My working proposition, however, is that those Soviet scholars with whom I am concerned are earnest in their endeavours, and that they believe there is some chance that their views will be sympathetically received.

The items discussed in the following chapters roughly follow the chronology of their appearance in the literature: it is noteworthy that the almost exclusively institutional preoccupations of the early 1960s have recently given way to more theoretical concepts, such as information, opinion, function and role. To the extent that how a system is perceived by the actors in it affects how it functions, this seems to indicate a move towards a much more sophisticated perception of political life in the present-day USSR.

CHAPTER 2
The Electoral System

Perhaps surprisingly, elections have been one aspect of the Soviet political system at which Soviet scholars have levelled much criticism in the past. The surprise stems from the fact that these essentially ritualistic exercises have long been consigned by Western observers to a place on the very fringes of Soviet political life. The absence of electoral competition; the meaningless electoral statistics; the banal commentaries of the mass media: these and other features have led to the almost universally held conclusion that Soviet elections are at best an amusing charade, and at worst downright dishonest.

The official picture of the Soviet electoral system is of a perfect, or at least near-perfect, participatory democratic process, in which popular representatives are chosen by an almost unanimous population. Nevertheless, the system as operated does present a number of problems, of a political and philosophical nature, which have been openly discussed by Soviet political scientists, in their professional journals, in books and pamphlets, and at learned conferences, since at least the early 1960s.

The general aim of Soviet writers on the topic has been to follow up the call of the twenty-second party congress (1961), expressed in the party programme, to 'perfect the forms of popular representation and develop the democratic principles of the Soviet electoral system' (*KPSS v rez.*, vol. 8, p. 274), a formulation that implies a recognition, on the side of the party leadership of that time, that the system did have scope for improvement. The task of political scientists is to identify the points of weakness, and propose ways of overcoming them. A leading writer on constitutional and political affairs, A. I. Kim, gave a suitable justification of this role at a conference in 1967.

He pointed out that the electoral law was already thirty years old, and had been formulated in a previous stage of socialist development, that is during the stage of 'building socialism', which has been superseded by the phases of the 'state of the whole people' and the 'unfolding building of communism' (and now by 'developed socialism'). Kim added the comment that 'experience has shown that some norms and institutions of the electoral law do not answer to the demands of today, and it is necessary to bring them into correspondence with the tasks of building communism' (Kim, 1967, p. 118).

Another writer, T. M. Pal'gunova, indicated that the electoral laws and the Constitution were in conflict: she referred to article 96 of the 1936 USSR Constitution, which stated that representation ratios in local soviets are regulated by the Constitutions of the union republics, whereas these Constitutions stated that the ratios were to be established by electoral statutes (Pal'gunova, 1969, pp. 148–9). This example shows, and a further survey of the literature confirms, that the Soviet political science profession has not been backward in identifying areas for development and improvement in the way the system operates. As A. Aimbetov and his associates wrote in 1967, certain aspects of the electoral system 'have so far been researched far from adequately, or their interpretations in the official literature seem arguable or debatable' (Aimbetov *et al.*, 1967, p. 79).

In this chapter, three areas will be specifically dealt with:
1 electoral choice: the number of candidates with which the voters are faced on election day;
2 the method of balloting, and the related topic of the secrecy of the ballot;
3 popular participation in the selection of candidates.

ELECTORAL CHOICE

Perhaps the major criticism of the Soviet electoral system, from a Western standpoint, is the lack of choice offered to electors. There has never been a contested election to the soviets, at least not under the present electoral law: since 1937 all candidates have campaigned under the aegis of the 'block of communists and non-party candidates', one candidate to a constituency, and electoral success is all but guaranteed. In terms of liberal democracy, which defines choice as an essential element in a democratic system, this is obviously a denial of democracy.

Soviet writers, not unexpectedly, reject this argument, saying that the democratic character of elections is measured not by how many names appear on the ballot paper, but rather by the overall level of participation by the electorate in the total process of selecting representatives: that is, not simply by what happens on election day (Shabanov, 1969b, p. 145; Tikhomirov, 1975, p. 30). Another common line of argument is that the level of democracy depends on 'which party directs the elections and organizes them, whose interests it represents and expresses in the election programme, whom it supports, and, finally, what the elected organs of state power are like' (Lashin, 1975, p. 35). According to the widely held view reflected in the scholarly literature, there are no competing social forces and parties representing different conflicting classes, vying with each other for support; hence, for some writers, to allow two or more candidates to stand would represent an 'artificial atomization of votes' and 'playing at democracy': there is no need for competing candidates in a society where fundamental interests are identical and are expressed by the single communist party (Gorkin, 1957, pp. 13–14; Kotok, 1963, p. 37; Kim, 1965, p. 185).

There are other Soviet justifications for this continued lack of choice, including a fear that a change in the system would lead to political rivalry (at best) or hostility (at worst) among the workers' collectives who sponsor different candidates: the supposed monolithic unity of the populace would thus be shattered. And since the regime depends for its legitimacy partly on the myth of unanimity (and elections are claimed to demonstrate its existence), this kind of change would have unacceptable political implications: an argument along these lines was put in an interview by Professor K. F. Sheremet. In any case, the elaborate selection procedures are said to ensure that only 'the best of the best' are nominated, and there is a feeling that 'it would indicate a lack of confidence in the candidate if you were to nominate two men for the same post. It would mean you think one of them is not good enough for the office. We don't want to insult our candidates' (Mote, 1965, p. 29).

Nevertheless, the question of contested elections has been widely discussed in Soviet political science literature since the early 1960s, as some Western scholars have noted (e.g., Frolic, 1970, p. 688; Lewin, 1975, p. 239; Gélard, 1975, p. 201).

Soviet writers and Western scholars alike have pointed out that the electoral statutes are phrased in such a way as to provide for more than one candidate. The instructions to the voters (to cross out the names of those candidates for whom they do not wish to vote) suggest the possibility of a contest, and this may have been in the minds of the drafters of the present electoral law (Carson, 1956, p. 52). The fact that in practice only one candidate has ever been allowed to run in each constituency is in reality a political *custom*, as N. A. Kudinov pointed out at a conference in 1970. Kudinov conceded that this custom does not contradict Soviet law; yet at the same time, it 'does not permit this law to be utilized in full measure. This custom', he concluded, 'in our opinion, does not contribute to the development of the electors' activity and the improvement of the body of deputies. Nor does it correspond to the level of political maturity of the people' (Kudinov, 1970, p. 155). Similar points have been made by other writers, notably N. Arutyunyan (1969) – then chairman of the Armenian supreme soviet presidium – and A. I. Kim (1967, p. 127).

In fact, the question of contested elections had been a topic of lively debate among specialist writers, and even the public, as the editor-in-chief of the journal *Sovetskoe gosudarstvo i pravo* (Soviet State and Law) stated, in an article that summed up the current state of the discussion among Soviet political scientists. He repeated the virtually mandatory caution that the level of democracy in an electoral system is not measured solely in terms of the number of candidates, and concluded: 'none the less, this question is not of secondary importance, and its correct resolution in our conditions has important significance for the development of the democratic principles of the Soviet electoral system' (Lepëshkin, 1965a, p. 12).

Some writers have recognized that, irrespective of devotion to a particular ideology and political programme, there might be other legitimate grounds on which the voters might prefer one candidate to another – their maturity, energy or experience, for example. Therefore, despite the careful assurances that the electoral system is already democratic, the general implication of much of the literature is that some kind of choice would allow the voters a greater say than they have at present in selecting a representative who might represent their interests and aspirations more satisfactorily; or (as it is sometimes expressed), the voters would be given a choice over who they thought could more competently work to carry the party's policies into practice (Strashun, 1973, p. 46).

In arguing the merits of such a proposal, Soviet writers can cite the experience of other socialist countries. B. A. Strashun, a specialist on the electoral system of socialist states, has pointed out that a limited degree of electoral choice has taken place in five socialist countries without damaging the socialist system (Strashun, 1973, p. 46; see also Kim, 1967, p. 127). The point is stressed that to allow competing candidates does not imply allowing competition between different political programmes or platforms: rather, electors would be asked to assess the 'personal and business' qualities of the competing candidates – 'their desire, readiness and capability to express the will of their constituents and represent their interests in the representative organs of power' (Strashun, 1973, p. 46). Thus, the basic feature of the system, whereby each candidate, whether a party member or not, is given the party's support and campaigns as a member of the 'block of communists and non-party candidates', would not be altered. The party would endorse a number of candidates as suitable for election in a given constituency, and let the voters decide the issue, choosing on the basis, for example, of youth and dynamism versus wisdom and maturity. Such a modest form of contest might well enliven Soviet election campaigns, which would then become much more interesting events. The count would have more point than at present, and if they felt so inclined Soviet political scientists could import the dubious science of psephology.

Nevertheless, there are still serious obstacles before even this degree of choice becomes available to Soviet voters. Quite apart from fears of undesirable political consequences (including, perhaps, a tendency for electoral candidates to canvas for votes, and thereby build up bases of independent political support among their constituents), inertia encourages the perpetuation of the present system, not to mention the reputations of politicians and scholars who have steadfastly defended current practice. In the past, much effort has been put into justifying the system, including attempts to demonstrate that the scrupulousness of selection procedures really does produce 'the best' possible candidates. Examples of candidates being asked to withdraw shortly before election day can be (and are) used to justify making no change, by arguing that the voters, who are involved at every stage of the campaign, can have a full say in the debate, and get rid of unsuitable candidates at various stages. Moreover, the fact that some candidates are actually defeated at the polls – despite all the care supposedly taken in selection – is used to support the view that the system gives the electorate enough opportunities to reject the candidates, without going so far as to offer a choice; indeed, it has even been argued that the final ballot is essential, and that the practice common in some bourgeois countries of declaring single candidates 'elected unopposed' is undemocratic (Kravchuk, 1966, p. 13): that is a fair point.

Not all those who have discussed this question have come out directly for or against a contested election: some have proposed what look like compromise procedures. For instance, Kim suggested in 1967 that there was no need to specify the number of candidates who shall stand (one, two or several), arguing that this question could safely be left to the electors, participating at the nomination stage (Kim, 1967, pp. 126–7). In a different vein,

Pal'gunova suggested that, at least at village level, the voters should be presented with a list of candidates for the complete soviet, rather than being asked to endorse a single candidate for a constituency of perhaps a mere thirty or fifty voters. This, she argues, would probably raise the level of responsibility on the part of village deputies, who would now be answerable to a larger number of citizens; it would also cut down on the amount of paperwork involved in running village elections. Such a proposal, she points out (without giving precise details), was made in the Latvian supreme soviet during its fourth term of office (the late 1950s) (Pal'gunova, 1969, p. 155).

The next logical stage would be to permit the nomination of more candidates than there were places, in multi-member constituencies. This proposal has not, I believe, appeared in print, but it has been discussed, for example in a graduate seminar that I attended in Moscow university in May 1975. In the seminar, Professor G. V. Barabashev, after repeating the now familiar idea that the concept of electoral choice is not alien to socialist systems, added that in the USSR this question was still at the level of an *experiment*. So far, no experiment has actually taken place. However, this is perhaps the most likely development, as recommended by Kim (1967, p. 130).

Meanwhile, the question of contested elections remains essentially unresolved. It is now customary in books and pamphlets to remind readers that the law does not restrict the number of candidates (e.g., Shchetinin, 1974, pp. 37–9; Pal'gunova, 1977, p. 59). It is doubtful, however, whether this can be interpreted as an *encouragement* to nominate more than one candidate per constituency, since the same sources go on to explain how representatives of the nominating bodies normally get together and decide which of the several candidates is to go forward. Nor does it seem likely that the public is being subtly prepared for a change in the system with which they are familiar. It seems more probable that this is intended to 'explain away' the lack of choice in the present system, on the grounds that if it were not acceptable 'the people' could insist on their right to nominate more than one candidate and ensure a choice on election day. The plain fact is that the whole process is closely supervised and coordinated by the party, which monitors nomination, approves of candidates and scrutinizes the balloting (see Hill, 1976b): 'the people' have not the power to alter the traditional custom, even if they wish to do so in some cases. That is the essential point that Soviet writers consistently refuse to acknowledge, even when they discuss the party's role in elections.

METHOD OF BALLOTING AND SECRECY OF THE BALLOT

Contested elections would be the most dramatic break from traditional practice, and doubtless the change most acceptable to Western critics. Yet there are other, seemingly minor, changes in the system that might be made, but that have generally not been considered by Western commentators, even though they have potentially considerable significance. One of these concerns the method of voting.

It is clear on examining the stages of the campaign that the voting system is heavily weighted in favour of achieving a unanimous endorsement of the official candidates, thanks to the system of 'inertia voting'. A positive vote – an endorsement of the candidate, the system, and the way of life – is cast by simply placing the unmarked ballot paper into the box. It requires greater physical effort and, more significantly, considerable psychological effort to break away from the behaviour pattern of one's neighbours and colleagues, enter a polling booth and (supposedly in secret) delete the candidate's name. Even accepting that a voter might wish to discriminate, by accepting some candidates (say, at *oblast* level) and rejecting others (say, in his village); and accepting too that the record suggests that some voters use the occasion to write patriotic slogans on their ballots (see, e.g., 'Bol'shoi den' stolitsy', 1975) – nevertheless, observers point out that a tiny fraction of all voters do in fact enter the polling booths. Churchward has written of one elector in fifty (Churchward, 1966b, pp. 449, 451); a Soviet political scientist mentioned 'less than 10 per cent'.

Soviet specialists are aware that this makes a mockery of the secret ballot, and they would like to remove this particular pressure to conform. The view expressed by, for example, Ye.I. Kozlova, that 'the Soviet electoral system provides the correct reflection and expression of the will of the Soviet people in the voting' (Kozlova, 1972, p. 25), does not find unanimous support among her professional colleagues. One writer goes so far as to assert that

> the custom that has received widespread circulation, of voting without going into the booth to fill in the ballot paper, contradicts the Soviet constitution and the electoral laws, which envisage secret voting. Open voting, at first glance, may seem like a manifestation of patriotism, but in reality it is an infringement of Soviet democracy. [Kudinov, 1970, p. 155]

The fullest discussion of this particular issue appears in the work of Yu. V. Shabanov (1969b, pp. 163–4). After pointing out that the secrecy of the ballot, which is guaranteed by law and technically provided for with the erection of the booths, is infringed by the voters themselves, Shabanov asks rhetorically: 'Can this be avoided, and the role of the individual expression of the electors' will be raised?' His answer is that it is possible, and he proposes modifications to the mechanics of vote-casting.

Interestingly enough, he does not suggest that the use of the booths be made compulsory; rather, he suggests a rearrangement of the furniture in polling stations. Since the booths are normally placed to one side, against a wall, the voter has to make a detour – in full view of all present – on the route from the table where the ballot papers are issued to the boxes where they are cast in the act of voting. Shabanov's proposed solution is to arrange the polling stations so that the voter cannot avoid going into the booths to 'study' the ballot papers, as he puts it. The precise physical layout is not described, and an obvious objection can be put forward to Shabanov's suggestion: namely that Soviet voters might adopt a 'formal approach' to this question, perfunctorily passing through the booths, and those who did take advantage of the arrangement in order to 'study' the ballot papers might distinguish themselves in any case.

However, there is a second and potentially more effective way of ensuring the 'strengthening of the individual expression of the electors' will'. Shabanov proposes that the electors should be required to mark the ballot paper in some way, by answering such questions as 'for' or 'against', 'yes' or 'no'. This would, in his phrase, require the elector to 'work' with the ballot papers in the polling booth (Shabanov, 1969b, p. 164). The idea that the voters should be asked to mark the ballot paper was also insisted on in relation to the institution of a consultative referendum on draft bills, another reform that was under discussion in the 1960s (Kotok, 1964, p. 178).

This kind of modification would obviously make it easier for dissident voters to make use of their rights in entering the booths to cross out the names of unpopular candidates, since to do so would not attract attention. Shabanov's own comment is that such an apparently small change will 'lead to the development of the activeness of the masses, evoke in each citizen the desire to express his own opinion, and perfect in people the sense of being rulers of the country, whose voice is listened to, and whose opinions must be taken into account' (Shabanov, 1969b, p. 164). Such a comment is very revealing about the present level of political efficacy felt by Soviet citizens at election time.

The kind of change envisaged by Shabanov, in abolishing 'inertia voting', may contain an element of window-dressing. It might, though, lead to a greater incidence of candidate rejection at the polls, particularly in the middle range (town and rural district soviets): at present, rejections are almost completely confined to the village level (Gilison, 1968, p. 820). This in turn might lead to greater care being exercised in selection, to take into better account the likely acceptability of candidates to the electors in the constituencies where they are to stand, without going to the lengths of offering them a direct choice. A further effect might be increased confidence and authority among those candidates who were still overwhelmingly supported by the electorate.

That would depend, however, in large measure on the conduct of the initial selection process.

SELECTION PROCEDURES

Soviet writers stress the selection stage of the campaign as the phase at which the electors have a major say in the promotion of their future candidates. Thus, for Kim, 'the preliminary discussion of candidatures, with the participation of a wide public, makes easier for the voters the expression of their will in the secret ballot, and contributes to the formation of genuinely representative organs of state power' (Kim, 1965, p. 185). In this, the Soviet system is said to be superior to Western systems, where the crucial stage of the selection of candidates is normally carried out in secret by party caucuses and selection committees. In the lavish prose of Pal'gunova:

> The Soviet electoral system is the most democratic in the world. One of the manifestations of its democratic nature is the fact that the direct organization of the elections and the exercise of control over the strict observation of the electoral laws is performed by the workers themselves through the electoral commissions created by them. [Pal'gunova, 1969, p. 151]

In fact, there is abundant evidence that, in the USSR too, the total campaign is initiated and monitored, if not completely controlled, by the party authorities, with the local *raikoms* (district committees) playing a leading role (Hill, 1976b). Even so, by ignoring the details of the party's role, or interpreting it simply as one of leading, guiding or persuading, Soviet scholars can point to a number of potentially democratic principles in the nomination process, which give the electors themselves an opportunity of involvement at the selection stage. These include participation in the selection of electoral commissions, and involvement in their membership; participation in nomination meetings, at which various candidatures are discussed and nominations for election candidates formally made; meetings with candidates in the constituencies, at which 'mandates' or instructions (*nakazy*) are given, which formally bind the deputy during his term of office (see chapter 5). Moreover, even at this stage registered candidates have in the past been required to withdraw (for figures, see Gorkin, 1957, p. 14). Gorkin writes approvingly of this practice. He fails to mention that it contradicts the electoral law, which states explicitly that 'all registered candidates ... are subject to obligatory inclusion on the ballot papers' (*Polozhenie o vyborakh ...*, article 87).

Such arguments, spurious though they may be, are used to support claims of widespread popular involvement in the various stages of the campaign, and the view that this ensures that truly 'the best of the best' are selected to run for election, people whose acceptability has been proven in the course of the campaign. The tiny number of cases where the candidate is rejected indicates the validity of this interpretation, in the eyes of Soviet observers, and also proves the necessity of going through the final stage of balloting: this demonstrates that it is *not* all tied up in advance, and the electors presented with a *fait accompli* (Kravchuk, 1966, pp. 10–14).

Not all scholars in the Soviet Union are equally satisfied, however, that the system is effective in achieving a sufficiently representative body of deputies. Even a comparatively conservative writer, the constitutional lawyer S. S. Kravchuk (1966, p. 10), has called for the election of deputies 'who really can express the interests of the people, the interests of their constituents, and be worthy of their trust'; while Kim (1967, p. 125) has argued that the practice of largely restricting nomination to meetings of workers' collectives has 'some shady sides'. In particular, the only interests that can be properly taken into account are the interests of the electors as *members of the work-unit* to which they belong; their interests as *residents*, perhaps of a different constituency from that in which they work, or that to which their factory nominates a candidate, cannot be fully taken into account. This point has been thoroughly researched by other writers, notably A. T. Leizerov, who argues forcefully the political weaknesses involved in separating nomination from representation (Leizerov, 1964; 1974a, pp. 98–110). Frequently the result is that the workers of a given factory are asked to nominate someone they scarcely know to a constituency where neither their factory is situated, nor they themselves are resident. This naturally poses the interesting question: to whom are these particular deputies answerable: their nominating institution, or their constituents?

Some writers attempt to justify the custom whereby nominations are made almost exclusively at meetings of workers' collectives (see, e.g., Tikhomirov, 1975, pp. 30–1). However, in elaborating the second 'shady side' of this custom, Kim (1967, p. 125) points out that it effectively debars a considerable section of the electorate from taking part, thereby undermining the validity of the standard defence of the system. Those whose 'franchise' is reduced in this way include housewives and pensioners, and Kim quotes figures from the 1959 Census to illustrate the magnitude of the problem; Leizerov, too, points out (1974a, p. 103, footnote) that in Belorussia one elector in six or seven is a pensioner.

Several suggestions have been made for overcoming these difficulties. V. A. Nemtsev, for instance, proposed modifying the timetable of an election campaign (Nemtsev, 1968, p. 31). At present, nomination is followed by registration, after which the adopted candidates meet their electors in the constituencies. By that time, (despite examples of candidates being forced to withdraw), it is mostly too late for the electors to influence the selection; particularly since a delicate balance has been achieved in the social composition of the deputies, to fit in with centrally prescribed 'norms' for the representation of certain characteristics such as age, sex, party membership and occupation: to start 'tinkering' with the body of candidates at a late stage would involve great difficulties in preserving the appropriate balance (see Jacobs, 1970, pp. 66–7; 1972, pp. 503–4; Hill, 1973). Nemtsev suggests that the public meetings should take place *before* registration, thereby permitting the voters to assess the favoured candidates before they are finally selected for inclusion in the ballot and endorsed on election day. These public meetings might then become less formalistic than at present, and would serve the purpose of 'primary' elections: a preliminary examination of the 'field' by those voters whose sense of interest or public duty brought them to the meeting. That sense might even be enhanced.

A second approach to the problem has been to suggest that the constituencies be based on places of work, that is based on the 'production principle', rather than on the territorial principle as at present. This proposal, first put forward in recent times in 1961 (Burlatskii, 1961, p. 46), has the qualified support of a number of writers, including Nemtsev, Kim, Leizerov, Perttsik and Pal'gunova, and was apparently favoured by Lenin. Its advantages, as expounded by Nemtsev, are that it would help to strengthen the links between the deputies and their constituents, and between the soviet executive committee and the industrial management; the level of activity of deputies would be raised, since they would be under the direct control of their electors at their place of work; and the nominating collective's sense of responsibility towards 'its' deputy in the performance of his duties would also be enhanced; moreover, the possibility would be opened for deputies' groups to operate at the place of work, perhaps more effectively than in territorially based constituencies (Nemtsev, 1968, p. 33).

If the enterprise were large enough to support more than one constituency, either there could be constituencies based on workshops or departments, or two or three names could appear on the ballot papers, and all employees at the enterprise would vote for deputies to represent all the constituencies based there. If a given enterprise were too small to support a constituency, production–territorial constituencies could be formed by including the inhabitants of streets adjacent to the enterprise (Nemtsev, 1968, pp. 34–5; also Perttsik, 1967b, pp. 17–19). It has also been suggested that the voters should be asked to elect two deputies – one from the place of work, and one from the residential district (Shabanov, 1969b, pp. 164–5).

Even so, Kim's point that the nomination process denies participation by non-workers would still be valid. Kim argues (and is, in fact, supported by Nemtsev and others) that what is needed is a combination of production-based and territorially-based constituencies; a modification in the law regarding nomination is also proposed. Kim suggests that meetings of

electors in territorially based constituencies should be em-
powered to nominate candidates for their own constituency.
Here, he argues, non-workers could take part, and specific local
interests, not associated with the production collective, would be
primarily taken into account; the interests of electors as workers
would be accounted for in nominating to the new, production-
based constituencies. Thus, the whole range of legitimate objective interests of the electors — as workers and as residents —
would be represented in the selection process and (presumably)
also in the body of newly elected deputies. Kim also proposes
that both kinds of nomination meeting — in factories or in
residential districts — should have a fixed quorum (Kim, 1965,
pp. 179–80; 1967, pp. 124–6).

There are problems, however, in operating such a dual
system, which in any case is less directly applicable in rural
areas, where place of residence and place of work are virtually
identical (Nemtsev, 1968, p. 37). There might be difficulties in
defining the constituency boundaries, or drawing up the lists of
voters, since obviously in a single-vote system no voter should
be included on more than one voting list. Also, as noted by
Nemtsev, different members of a family might vote in different
constituencies. Residential constituencies might have electoral
rolls consisting almost entirely of pensioners, housewives,
students and perhaps writers and other 'self-employed' workers.
Some workers might object to having to visit their work-place
on a Sunday in order to vote, and the practice of splitting up the
electorate in this way would operate against the custom of
making voting a great social event in which families and groups
of neighbours or friends vote together. This approach would also
involve changing the ratios of representation: in the production
constituencies this would be based on the number of electors,
not on the number of inhabitants, as in the present territorial
constituencies (Pal'gunova, 1969, p. 151). As Nemtsev
indicated, this is a complex question, which requires further
study by lawyers, economists, sociologists and practical
workers; he suggested holding an experiment at the next elections (in 1969) (Nemtsev, 1968, p. 38).

To my knowledge, no such experiment has actually taken

place. However, a great deal of detailed calculation by Leizerov has revealed the potential for such a change in Minsk and other cities in Belorussia. He concluded that only a proportion of factories could support constituencies, so that (as Kim later recommended) a mixture of production-based and territorially-based constituencies would have to remain (Leizerov, 1964, pp. 68–72; 1974a, pp. 101–2). To date, however, production-based constituencies have not been formed; housewives and pensioners remain deprived of their right to take part in nomination; and one writer has been prepared to reject the whole idea as unworkable and, in any case, irrelevant (Starovoitov, in Sheremet, 1976, pp. 96–7).

Other aspects of the electoral system have been discussed in the literature: the question of how to handle by-elections, when deputies die in office or leave the area towards the end of a term (Nemtsev, 1968, pp. 26–7; Kim, 1965, pp. 189–91; Leizerov, 1974a, p. 88); lack of clear legal guidance, leading to undesirable practice, in cases where candidates fail to secure election (Kravchuk, 1966, pp. 11–14); philosophical distinctions between electoral law and electoral system (Kim, 1965, pp. 11, 23); the party's role in the electoral system (Kim, 1965, pp. 23–4, 127–8; Shabanov, 1969a, pp. 25–33). In drawing a distinction between the concepts of 'electoral law' and 'electoral system', Kim stresses the leading role of the party in directing elections, pointing out that 'many relationships embraced by the electoral system are brought into existence by organizational and political norms contained in cpsu decisions.' As an example, he cites the party programme's requirement that there should be a turnover of one-third among deputies at each election: this is a part of the electoral *system*, but not of electoral *law* (Kim, 1965, chapter 1). Much of the uncritical Soviet comment is clearly based on analysis of electoral law, rather than of the electoral system.

The discussions outlined above give a picture of the variety and the provocative nature of some of the comments that have been made. Moreover, the electoral system is still the object of critical comment and suggestion, not to mention a degree of speculation, in the 1970s. Strashun, for example, in a monograph on the representative system, suggested *inter alia* that the age limit for voting should be reduced to sixteen or seventeen, because young people are now maturing earlier (Strashun, 1976, p. 151); this suggestion was dismissed as 'dubious' by one reviewer, since political maturity is a somewhat different concept from physical maturity, and the two processes do not necessarily coincide (Stepanov, 1977, p. 74). Strashun has also referred to the great cost of mounting frequent campaigns (Strashun, 1976, p. 181) – an impeccably democratic reason for holding elections less often! Tikhomirov, in analysing the likely impact of modern technology on political life, raises the possibility of machine-voting as computer technology is placed at the disposal of the political system (Tikhomirov, 1975, p. 260); also Strashun, 1976, p. 181; Sheremet, 1976, p. 102). In his faintly amusing discussion of the appropriate season for holding campaigns (the amusement stems from the seriousness with which the author holds forth), N. G. Starovoitov (who elsewhere commented favourably on the shift of election dates from March to June) refers to difficulties caused to certain electors by summer elections, particularly those on holiday, geological prospectors, fishermen, pastural herdsmen, river boatmen and others. He ignores the fact that all voters are eligible to receive a certificate allowing them to vote anywhere in the country; he also seems unaware that the 'problem' that he has identified is not borne out by the official turnout figures of close on 100 per cent: nevertheless, he comes down on the side of autumn elections (in Sheremet, 1976, pp. 95–6). He also supports the creation of constituencies according to the number of voters, rather than of electors (p. 97); on contested elections he is extremely cautious, but puts forward the proposition that several candidates might be nominated, all but one of whom would be eliminated in the widespread public debate during the campaign: in that connection, he refers to 'formalism' and 'haste' in some of the meetings between candidates and electors (pp. 98–100). Finally, Starovoitov called for new electoral legislation, to be introduced at republican level, as 'a worthy continuation of the CPSU's measures for the all-round development and improvement of socialist democracy in the period of developed socialism' (p. 103).

Writing in 1975, V. M. Terletskii stated that questions of further improving the electoral system 'are to be found at the centre of the CPSU's attention' (Babii *et al.*, 1976, p. 441); and, introducing the draft 1977 Constitution, Brezhnev himself spoke of the need to draft a new all-union electoral law (Brezhnev, 1977a, p. 41).

A general electoral statute is still awaited, but in the wake of the new Constitution a statute for Supreme Soviet elections was introduced (*Zakon . . . o Vyborakh*, 1978). Alas for the pundits, this statute contained practically none of the contentious proposals that have been put forward in the literature, and largely confirmed the long-standing practices. Meanwhile, however, Soviet scholars have been devoting attention to the product of the electoral system: the deputies who are elected, and the soviets of which they are members.

CHAPTER 3
The Deputy and His Role

The identity and role of the deputy has been much studied in the
USSR. Beginning in the early 1960s with the work of Perttsik in
Siberia and Leizerov in Belorussia, scholarly studies of deputies
have been undertaken in different parts of the country (and still
are being undertaken), and sophisticated analyses of their composition and role activity have been published. The general tenor
of comment has been to say that the deputies are doing a good
job, but they could do it better: they could be more *representative* of their constituents, and more *responsive* to their
interests and needs. The research has revealed a range of restric-
tions, based either on the law or on political custom and
practice, that seriously reduce the effectiveness with which the
deputies can perform their representative role. The proposals for
reform are intended to rectify the identified weaknesses, by
strengthening deputy–elector relations, and generally enhancing
the position of the deputy in the system: in short, to *pro-
fessionalize* the role of the deputy.

THE SOCIAL COMPOSITION OF DEPUTIES

The official view for decades has been of a perfectly representative system, closely dependent on the supposed democratic
nature of the electoral procedures discussed in the previous
chapter. The careful screening of all potential deputies through
the elaborate nomination and selection procedures, in which
the voters themselves have a chance for full participation,
supposedly guarantees that the body of deputies is fully
representative of the voters and their interests, a point that was

41

stressed in the 1961 party programme (see *KPSS v rez.*, vol. 8, p. 274). Moreover, much of the official literature is couched in terms that evidently assume that the 'elected representative of the people' truly does possess the power, influence and authority to reach policy decisions on behalf of those he represents.

Yet much of the specialist research and analysis reveals many serious weaknesses in the nature and effectiveness of the representative system, beginning with the social composition of the body of deputies.

Attention has been paid to this question by Western scholars. It has long been clear that the deputies are carefully selected in order to conform to certain criteria of 'representativeness'. The selection procedure is 'guided' by the party authorities, to ensure that the whole range of social characteristics is present in appropriate numbers to provide for adequate representation, and also to maintain general political control for the party. Soviet writers stress the *breadth* of representation, since this gives the various social groups an opportunity to put forward their views in the debates. Not only the rapturous commentaries of the *Pravda* and *Izvestiya* editorial-writers, but also serious scholars present an impressive array of descriptive statistics, which show how 'representative' the soviets are (e.g., Lepëshkin, 1967, pp. 243–51; Kotok, 1963, pp. 38–43; Tikhomirov, 1975, p. 129). Western writers also indicate that the soviets are composed 'so as almost perfectly to replicate the ethnic, sex, and other demographic differences in society' (Azrael, 1970, p. 207).

However, some specialists have expressed misgivings about claims made on the basis of such an unsophisticated use of statistics. In 1964, for instance, M. A. Shafir reported research on rural soviets in Tula oblast, and complained that there were very few young deputies, and scarcely any workers from the fields of culture and the provision of services and facilities: out of almost 2000 medical workers in the villages, only 273 were deputies in the village soviets; out of 2100 cultural and educational workers, only 208 were deputies; there were 101 deputies in trade and public catering out of 7055 such workers; in many village soviets there were absolutely no deputies working in medical institutions or cultural and service establishments. It is obvious, commented Shafir, that when the general basic task of village soviets is now to provide such facilities, there should be more of these workers among the deputies (Shafir, 1964, pp. 26–7).

A. A. Bezuglov, an expert on the legal position of deputies, repeated the commonly expressed official satisfaction with the breadth of representation of various social groups, giving figures from official statistics to demonstrate the point (Bezuglov, 1973, pp. 18–19). Yet he added that 'It is important, in particular, to examine the influence that the quantitative and qualitative composition of the representative organs has on their success in expressing completely, correctly and with objectivity the will of the people' (p. 21).

In fact, the claims of broad and quasi-proportional representation of group interests can be upheld only by examining the social composition in terms of single variables: when the distribution of different characteristics is cross-tabulated, there is a clustering of characteristics, such that one can identify two types of deputy, 'weak' and 'strong'. The weak (the majority of deputies) tend to be younger, not party members, frequently women, in low-status occupations, probably with inferior educational attainments, and they acquire relatively little experience as representatives before being replaced by similar individuals; the strong tend to be older, male, party members in prestigious occupations, and presumably also better educated, whose experience of representative functions is enhanced by longer service on soviets following re-election, which is frequently repeated (Hill, 1973; 1977, chapter 4).

In Soviet writings, V. A. Kim and G. V. Nechitailo, for example, imply that various groups should be represented by their own members, and state explicitly that the best people to represent the interests of the younger generation are the young themselves (Kim and Nechitailo, 1970, p. 45). But the clearest statement of the need for representativeness in the social composition of deputies is to be found in a paper by Kazimirchuk and Adamyan, who assert that 'deputies of local soviets should, as representative organs of the whole people, reflect the structure of the population. . . .' (Kazimirchuk and Adamyan, 1970, p. 114). Moving beyond the level of single-variable analysis, they take a more searching look at the distribution of characteristics by combining and cross-tabulating selected variables, in particular the age distribution of women deputies; they find that they predominate among deputies under forty, whereas among the over-forties women account for a mere 15 per cent. The level of women's participation in Armenia compared unfavourably with other republics, and their age structure was not consistent with that of the total population (Kazimirchuk and Adamyan, 1970, pp. 113–14). Applying their criterion that the composition of the deputies should reflect the distribution of various social groups within the population, they propose the 'correction' of the composition of deputies not only on specific individual variables (e.g. by bringing in more young deputies), but also with respect to combinations of variables: 'it is obvious that this composition must be corrected in respect of both age and sex. This applies particularly to deputies over 35 years of age' (p. 114).

There seems to be a radical implication in the assumption of these two authors. If the principle of close correspondence between population distribution and the social composition of the body of deputies were to be extended, there would be a need for considerable adjustment in selection procedures. Although Kazimirchuk and Adamyan do not go so far, this might involve changes in the electoral system itself – quite distinct from the kind of modifications discussed in the previous chapter.

DEPUTY–CONSTITUENCY LINKS

The social identity of deputies is only one dimension of the degree of representativeness in Soviet local government. Moreover, despite the radical implications of Kazimirchuk and Adamyan's assumption, one might argue that striving for a close correspondence between population and representatives is irrelevant: it would make the statistics look attractive, but would not guarantee that the even more carefully selected individuals could perform representative functions adequately. Nor would it guarantee that the deputies would even maintain links with their constituents, once the latter had endorsed their candidature on election day. We saw above the frequent separation of the place of nomination from the location of the constituency. A further, comparable, problem arises, also with considerable frequency: deputies often neither live nor work in their constituency; and sometimes they neither live nor work in the district where the nominating collective is situated. This practice is common at parliamentary level in most countries, including the USSR, especially where ministers and other members of government are concerned; it is less common at local level, and may be less acceptable.

This is certainly the opinion of Leizerov, who presented a detailed argument, backed with carefully prepared statistics from Minsk and other Belorussian cities, at a conference of young scholars in 1964; that the problem had not been solved a decade later is indicated by the inclusion of the argument, supported by updated statistical data, in the same author's Belorussian-language monograph on the electoral system (Leizerov, 1964; 1974a, pp. 99–110). The proposal had been made that as a rule candidates should be resident in their constituency, so that they would normally live among their constituents; Leizerov agreed with this, adding that, as of 1964, the number of candidates who did so was insignificant (Leizerov, 1964, p. 69; also 1974a, p. 103). He gave abundant statistical evidence to illustrate the point (1974a, pp. 107–8).

Leizerov pointed out that such arrangements greatly complicate the question of the effective representation of constituents' interests, and inhibit the work of deputies' groups and other formal and informal working arrangements among deputies and their soviets. He concludes: 'it must be acknowledged that such a situation is not to be regarded as normal' (1964, p. 70). After all, it is clear that only a deputy who lives in his constituency is likely to know it and his electors well;

he therefore will be more active in carrying out his functions as a representative: Leizerov gives examples of such deputies in Borisov town soviet, who were more active in the sessions of their soviet and in the work of the permanent commissions, were more energetic in fulfilling their electors' requests, and reported to their constituents on the work of the soviet and its executive committee more frequently than other deputies who did not have this personal link of involvement through residence (Leizerov, 1974a, pp. 104–5).

Research in eastern Siberia in the early 1960s revealed a serious problem to be overcome: not only did considerable numbers of deputies live or work away from their constituency (Perttsik, 1968b, p. 11), but (presumably partly as a result of this) only a part of the electors could name the deputy for whom they had voted (Perttsik, 1967b, p. 17). So voters with problems tended not to go for help to their own official representative; instead, they ignored constituency boundaries and approached whichever deputy they knew best, or was more active, or received constituents in his 'surgery' in the most convenient place (Perttsik, 1968b, pp. 8–9).

For Leizerov the argument is clear-cut: the normal practice should be at least to select a resident in the *district* where the constituency is situated; he cited a book by R. A. Safarov, published in 1961, in support (Leizerov, 1974a, p. 108). Perttsik also supports the proposal for deputies to be drawn from among people living in the constituency, disagreeing with Kim, who suggested that such a restriction would impede the electors in their choice (see Kim, 1967, pp. 123–4).

Moreover, Perttsik adds, his inquiries have revealed that public opinion is ready for this (Perttsik, 1968b, pp. 11–12; also Kravchuk, 1966, p. 14).

A further aspect of this question is the allocation of deputies to their constituencies for re-election at the end of a term of office. Several writers – notably Leizerov, A. V. Moshak and Kim and Nechitailo – have pointed out that the usual practice is for the deputies selected for a further term to stand in a different constituency each time (Leizerov, 1974a, p. 106; Moshak, 1971,

p. 95; Kim and Nechitailo, 1970, pp. 41–3). In exhibiting this tendency, local soviets differ from the supreme soviets, where deputies normally continue to represent the same locality for many years.

It is clear that this mobility is connected with the separation of nomination from endorsement, the basic question (discussed in chapter 2) of the divorce between nominating bodies and electorate. In that situation, a deputy who satisfies the *electors* may still fail to be re-nominated; yet a deputy who fails to perform any useful role as a *representative* may nevertheless be nominated for re-election by his trade union organization or workers' collective, at the instigation of the local party authorities.

Leizerov appears to want a change in the practice of frequent mobility without a change in the law as the mechanism for regulating it, arguing that a legal requirement that (for example) a deputy should run only where he has previously served would constitute an interference in the rights of the voters to choose their representative (Leizerov, 1974a, p. 106; also Kim, 1967, pp. 123–4). Kim and Nechitailo spell out the advantages of repeated election in the same constituency, in terms of the deputy's familiarity with the constituency and its constituents, awareness of individual and collective interests, contacts with individuals and public committees – features that can be strengthened and enhanced to the mutual benefit of electors and representatives alike. They also point to the positive side of mobility: giving deputies an awareness of different problems and interests, and broader experience of the problems that arise in the given soviet's territory. The authors say that the advantages and disadvantages of re-allocating a representative to a new constituency must be carefully considered in each case, and this provides 'wide possibilities for the manifestation of wisdom and initiative on the part of public organizations'; however, they make their preference clear: 'the more correct resolution of this question would be a repeated promotion of a candidature in their former constituency' (Kim and Nechitailo, 1970, pp. 41–2).

Firmer still is the proposal of Moshak: deputies should normally be required to run for re-election in their previous constituency, so that the electors can really pass judgement on them through the ballot-box – an interesting attempt to give solid meaning to the electoral process, but not without its irony in view of the criticisms of the procedures for the ballot. Moreover, Moshak suggests, deputies should be allowed to stand in a different constituency only in special circumstances, and then only if the former constituents have given a positive evaluation (Moshak, 1971, p. 95).

Of the proposals discussed here, Moshak's is the most radical in its implications. First, it should (as was the author's intention, and also that of the other writers, particularly Kim and Nechitailo) tend to raise the level of efficiency and effectiveness with which deputies attend to their constituents' needs and requirements. It might also – and this could be one important reason why the current practice is still the norm – lead to a deputy's building up a base of personal political support among the electorate, something that has little point, even if it is not impossible, under present arrangements. That, in turn, might lead to a development in the role of the electors in selecting the individual whose name will be presented to them for electoral endorsement. This would also have implications for the position of the deputies as representatives, and would affect the level of competence with which they approach their task, and how much they achieve in office.

THE DEPUTY'S ROLE PERFORMANCE

The performance by deputies of their duties has been thoroughly researched by Soviet writers. Surveys and analysis by Leizerov, Perttsik, Kazimirchuk and others have established wide variations in the level and forms of political participation among deputies, and identified the salient influencing factors. Studies have been undertaken in different parts of the country since the early 1960s, and indeed are still being undertaken. In 1968, for example, it was reported that sociological work on the activities of deputies was being done in the Estonian Academy of Sciences, at the Belorussian State University, at Kharkov University, in the Ukraine, and in Siberia, at Irkutsk University (Perttsik, 1968b, p. 5); in May 1975 a Moscow University graduate student defended a thesis on deputies in the Primorskii *krai*, on the Pacific coast.

The early work using quantitative analysis of survey results was done in eastern Siberia, by Perttsik and a group of associates attached to the informal Laboratory of Experimental Political Science at Irkutsk University. The project, embarked on in 1961, involved a questionnaire survey of electors and deputies, a separate survey of deputies about their time budget, and an experiment in the structure of local government. The first results were presented to a conference in Irkutsk in 1967 and published in professional journals and newspapers beginning in the same year (Perttsik, 1967a; 1967b; 1968a; 1968b).

The kind of questions investigated by Perttsik indicate the aims of this work:

– How much time is needed to carry out a deputy's duties?
– What forms of deputy's work produce the best results?
– Which factors assist and which interfere with the organization of a deputy's activities in the soviet and in the constituency?
– What is the optimal way of organizing the deputy's work in the soviet and the constituency?
– How and in what direction should the electoral laws be improved? (Perttsik, 1968b, p. 5).

The applied nature of the research comes out clearly here: the establishment of the facts as the basis for proposing improvements. A similar approach was adopted in Estonia by Kalits, Laumets and Shneider (1965); in Belorussia by Leizerov (1970a; 1970b; 1974a; 1977); in Armenia by Kazimirchuk and Adamyan (1970); and countrywide by the editors of the monthly journal for deputies, *Sovety deputatov trudyash-chikhsya* ('O chëm rasskazala anketa', 1966). The results of Estonian and Armenian research were combined by Pavlov,

Kazimirchuk and their associates in a 1971 book on government, sociology and law (Pavlov and Kazimirchuk, 1971). Some of this work – for example, time budget analysis and opinion sampling – coincided with similar work in general sociology in the USSR (see Weinberg, 1974, pp. 54–9, 82–107).

The time factor

This research revealed wide discrepancies in the amount of time devoted by deputies to their duties. Pavlov and Kazimirchuk and their associates report that, of 4320 deputies of local soviets at various levels in the hierarchy, 41.8 per cent spent 1–5 hours a month, 29.5 per cent spent 6–10 hours, 13.6 per cent spent 11–15 hours; 1.6 per cent of deputies spent over 40 hours a month, or about one and a half hours daily; the mean was 9.8 hours (Pavlov and Kazimirchuk, 1971, pp. 182–4). Perttsik found that city soviet deputies, for example, spent 2–4 hours working as members of standing commissions, up to 4 hours in carrying out assignments given by the soviet, and 2–3 hours on constituency work; all deputies believed they needed at least 7 hours a week to perform their duties adequately (Perttsik, 1968a; 1968b, p. 16). In the *Sovety* readership survey, 69 per cent of deputies felt they had *no* problem over shortage of time, and one replied that an honest deputy, anxious to make his mark by serving the people, would always find enough time; but 27 per cent did complain of insufficient time ('O chëm rasskazala anketa', 1966, p. 42) – an indication that they were dissatisfied with their performance as deputies.

Pavlov and Kazimirchuk go into the factors that influence the amount of time spent by deputies and find a variety of influences at work. More time was spent by deputies of urban district soviets (an average of 14.8 hours a month); by deputies with higher educational attainment; by older deputies, particularly those aged between forty and sixty; by industrial and other leaders; by men; and by party members (Pavlov and Kazimirchuk, 1971, p. 185, Table 15).

The Armenian study of 1968 found that 48.9 per cent of

deputies considered attendance at sessions and meetings to be the most time-demanding activity: the authors of the report were not entirely happy about this 'exaggerated attention to the holding of sittings and sessions', adding that 'this form of activity must not swallow up almost all the deputy's time' ('Effektivnost' deputatskoi deyatel'nosti', 1969, p. 111).

This question was again raised in the course of the nationwide discussion of the draft Constitution in the summer of 1977. Two female deputies complained of the ever-increasing burden of work involved in effectively fulfilling the deputy's role, particularly the problem of assimilating information in preparation for the sessions, which left too little time for working with constituents in carrying out the decisions of the soviet. They proposed reducing the frequency of sessions in order to lighten the load (Slepneva and Mineeva, 1977; see chapter 4 below).

The sessions

Even so, participation in the session – the 'basic organizational and legal form of work of local soviets' (Moskalev, 1975, p. 18) – is a central part of the deputy's role, and several writers have gone on to examine this forum, by looking at participation levels among deputies; again, wide discrepancies have been found. The more sophisticated investigators have correlated participation – normally defined as speaking in a debate – with other variables such as age, sex, education, party membership, occupation, term of office, presence of non-deputies and so forth. The most detailed account is that of Leizerov, first presented to a conference at the Belorussian University in 1970, and published in amended form later in the same year (Leizerov, 1970a; 1970b). He is explicitly concerned with 'the factors that influence the activity of deputies'; the twenty pages of tables in his conference paper contain a wealth of statistical information supporting the author's conclusions, which may be summarized as follows.

1 Purely on grounds of time available, few deputies can have

a chance to speak in a year – or, indeed, during their term of office.

2 Level of educational attainment correlates with frequency of participation in sessions – deputies with higher education speak more often. The general improvement in educational standards in the country, reflected in a similar trend among deputies, augurs well for continued improvement in the quality of debate.

3 Women speak less frequently than men, and are rarely elected to chair sessions or act as secretary. This can be explained by the burden of domestic duties, which has also been noted by other writers, specifically Kazimirchuk (Pavlov and Kazimirchuk, 1971, p. 187; Kazimirchuk and Adamyan, 1970, p. 114). Leizerov comments: 'All this negatively influences the possibilities of women to participate in political life, and particularly in the activities of the soviets' (Leizerov, 1970a, p. 82) – a stark admission that the constitutional guarantees of political equality are not so firm in practice.

(On this precise point, G. N. Manov refers to 'the factual inequality of men and women in utilizing their budget of free time', as one of a range of factors that 'negatively influence the political and socio-psychological climate of mature socialist society', adding that 'these factors will not disappear of their own accord' (in Tikhomirov, 1975, p. 278).)

4 Younger deputies speak less frequently than older deputies; if re-elected, their participation increases. For Leizerov, this reflects the political inexperience of the young, an interpretation that is supported by indications that those who already have experience of, say, Komsomol committee work more quickly come to grips with their duties as deputy.

5 Various officials play a dominant role in the debates (about 60 per cent of contributions, according to more recent calculations – see Maslennikov, 1977, p. 88). They possess debating skills, experience of public life, and also information, all of which equip them to play a leading role. Apart from officials, the most active deputies are medical workers, teachers, and various technical specialists. Leizerov's solution to the problem of

domination by officials is to extend the duration of the debates, to allow more deputies to speak.

6 The level of activity declined from the first to the second year of a two-year term of office, a finding in line with other research results (e.g., Perttsik, 1967b, p. 19).

7 The key variable, however, is the general level of experience and social skill, which is too little taken into account when election candidates are being selected. This, Leizerov argues, is an important reason why the sessions are so poor, a point that was forcefully expressed by N. Arutyunyan in 1969:

> not all deputies can handle their mission equally well. Much here depends on the ability quickly to get used to the new sphere of work, on the experience of previous activity, on organizational habits, and finally on the level of knowledge, breadth of vision and erudition.... Why do sessions occasionally turn out lifelessly? Why do some permanent commissions function at half strength? If you look at the deputies of these soviets, the answer will be clear. Among them are people whom no force can make speak. At best, they merely attend the sessions of the soviet or the sittings of the commissions. They are conscientious workers, they enjoy the respect of their work-mates, ... but they cannot fully work in the soviet, because they have little experience of organizational work, or simply do not have the inclination for public activity. [Arutyunyan, 1969, p. 1]

8 A final significant factor influencing participation in debates is the presence of non-deputies, whose involvement makes for more open debate and brings in their professional experience, but obviously affects the ordinary deputies' chances of speaking. Leizerov cites several authors who have pointed out the dangers of inviting too many guests, and elsewhere has suggested that the question of their participation should be defined in legislation on the soviets (Leizerov, 1970b, p. 103).

In a study of rural soviets, Leizerov makes similar points, adding that the details of the agenda items also affect participation (Leizerov, 1974b, pp. 57–8): indeed, by 1977 he was arguing that this was the major consideration (see the review of this latest monograph, by Maslennikov (1977), who calls, however, for greater methodological sophistication in analysing participation).

Some of these points have also been made by other writers, notably Pavlov and Kazimirchuk, who thoroughly analyse the frequency, duration and content of speeches, and conclude that frequency of speaking correlates with educational level, age, occupation, party membership and sex (Pavlov and Kazimirchuk, 1971, pp. 195–204).

Other sides of the deputy

While participation in the debates of the soviet sessions is one of the important aspects of the deputy's role, there are others, perhaps of no less significance, in which he may have greater opportunities for playing a positive part in local politics and administration, for instance the frequency with which electors approach their deputy at a regular 'surgery'. Pavlov and Kazimirchuk found that 20.8 per cent of deputies had 11–20 visits per year; 12.3 per cent had 21–30 visits; and 13.1 per cent received over 40 petitioners. The authors' assessment is that this is a positive phenomenon. Yet they also point out that 7.2 per cent of deputies received no electors with problems, most of them in rural towns and settlements. Further figures reveal somewhat disappointing levels of contact between working-class and peasant deputies and their constituents, indicating a need for support in carrying out this function (Pavlov and Kazimirchuk, 1971, p. 199); in other words, these writers see the problem as one of inadequate training among the deputies. It might, however, reflect a lack of socialization among the electors (implying they are unaware of this side of the deputy's role), or an unwillingness, or even disdain, on their part for these representatives of what they perceive as an unsympathetic political system: such an implication could not, of course, even be considered by a Soviet writer.

A further dimension of the deputy's role is the duty to fulfil the so-called electors' mandates (*nakazy*). This question will be more fully discussed in chapter 5, but here it is perhaps appropriate to mention one survey, which revealed that 24 per cent of respondents succeeded in carrying out their mandates; 57 per cent did not always do so; and 19 per cent completely failed to fulfil them. In other words, as the writer stresses, 'only a quarter of deputies reply with confidence that all is in order'. The results are disturbing, a 'somewhat sore point' ('O chëm rass-kazala anketa', 1966, pp. 43–4).

The work of deputies in the permanent commissions has also been paid much attention, and certain problems have been identified. Zhilin reveals a particular problem for rural deputies: they tend to be dispersed among many farms and villages, so that arranging meetings of the commissions is not so easy as in the towns; moreover, at the time he was writing (1966), travel expenses were not reimbursed (Zhilin, 1966, p. 59): that obviously placed a burden on deputies, or on their farms, or (more likely) drastically reduced the effectiveness of these bodies.

MEANS OF IMPROVEMENT

Soviet research confirms long-standing Western evaluations of the soviets and deputies. There are serious hindrances to their functioning as representative bodies, supposedly reflecting the various interests existing in society, and to their taking authoritative decisions on matters of local or national importance. Yet there remains an underlying assumption that this is precisely the kind of role they should be playing. We have seen some specific proposals for enabling the deputies and soviets to fulfil that role. Apart from institutional modifications, and changes in long-established habits surrounding the convening and conduct of sessions, much of the research points towards greater care being paid to the deputies themselves, both at the selection stage and during their term of office. Deputies must not only possess the sociological qualifications for a representative role (including a high level of educational attainment, in view of the increasing complexity of public issues), but they must also have the capacity for getting on with people, and the inclination to devote their time and energies to the task of being a deputy (see Manov, in Tikhomirov, 1975, pp. 278–9, for a description of what is required).

One important ingredient in the successful deputy is obviously willingness and enthusiasm for the task, a characteristic that is typical of youth. Yet researchers repeatedly emphasize the need for *maturity* and *experience*, two qualities frequently lacking not only among the young, but among many newly elected deputies of all ages. As a Moldavian village soviet chairman put it in 1972:

> I well remember how I was first elected to the soviet. In the beginning I even lost my head; I didn't know where to start, how to set about it. Because then I knew neither the rights nor the obligations of a deputy. I am certain that almost every newly elected deputy experiences the same. [Gondrya, 1972]

The most radical (reactionary?) proposal for overcoming this was, the suggestion that only persons who already had some experience of public work should be eligible for selection as deputies. This was justified on the grounds that 'the soviet is a school of political activity, and the person will more successfully graduate through it who already has a definite experience of public work' (Lott, 1964, pp. 87–8). However, this suggestion was dismissed as 'organically alien to the nature of socialist democracy', and aimed at restricting the voters' freedom of choice in whom they nominate and elect (Aimbetov *et al.*, 1967, pp. 101–2). Yet a similar notion, expressed in perhaps a more acceptable formulation, was put forward by Ukrainets, who urged that election candidates' involvement in party, Komsomol, trade union and other public organizations be taken into account in the selection procedures, since prior schooling in other institutions can help to give the appropriate experience (Ukrainets, 1976, p. 51).

A different approach is hinted at, and rejected, by Strashun. Citing Kim's explanation that the minimum age for election to the supreme soviets was raised in 1946 'in connection with further raising the role and significance of the soviets' (Kim, 1965, p. 122), Strashun points out the logic of this argument: 'as the role of the soviets is further raised, it is necessary also to raise further the age limit for their deputies' (Strashun, 1976, p. 150). Obviously that would contradict democratic principles; however, it does reveal a conflict in the minds of Soviet specialists between the aim of *democratic participation* and the aim of *raising the effectiveness* of representative institutions, which is also not unconnected with democratization.

A reasonable alternative is to provide training facilities for deputies, to teach the rules of debate and other formalities, and develop the skills required in their new position. Feelings of incompetence and inadequacy must be replaced by 'the habits of politicians actively participating in the asking, discussion and adoption of serious decisions of state' (Pavlov and Kazimirchuk, 1971, p. 196), and Imashev suggests setting up training schools attached to all local soviets (in Aimbetov *et al.*, 1967, p. 102). Other writers have stressed the need for more careful training, particularly when the level of turnover amounts to approximately 50 per cent every two years (see, e.g., Burkauskas, 1966, p. 119; Arutyunyan, 1969, p. 3; Perttsik, 1968a). More recently, a conference on deputies, held in Yaroslavl in May 1975, paid particular attention to the need for legal training, and proposed the establishment of a permanent commission of local soviets, charged with organizing the deputies' work. A draft statute for such a commission for Yaroslavl city soviet was appended to the published conference report; and other means were proposed towards the same end, including seminars and legal consultancies, and the development of a minimal body of legal knowledge for deputies to acquire (Gorshenev and Kozlov, 1976, pp. 127–8; 130–2).

A frequently cited proposal aimed at overcoming several of the present difficulties is to double the term of office in local soviets to four years. Nemtsev, in particular, pointed out (1968, pp. 30–1) that this would give deputies a chance to get to know their constituents and acquire the experience necessary for effective action. He added that elections every two years take up a great deal of effort, require considerable funds, and lead 'willy-nilly' to a certain degree of formalism. Moreover, in his estimation public opinion was inclined towards a four-year term. Shafir had earlier pointed out (1964, p. 27) that many local leaders were already making this proposal, which also found strong support from Imashev (Aimbetov *et al.*, 1967, p. 101); Frolic too quotes two Soviet commentators (Safarov and an unidentified Moscow official) who express the same view (Frolic, 1970, p. 688 and n. 29).

Not all commentators shared these sentiments, however. Kravchuk put forward several arguments against, in 1966: young voters would have to wait longer before being given a chance to vote; bearing in mind the rapid movements of population and extensive building programmes across the country, including the growth of new towns, it is essential to keep the representation as full and up-to-date as possible. Moreover, such a change would not correspond to the trend of history, towards the participation of ever-more citizens in government: lengthening the term would reduce the number who could become deputies over a long period (Kravchuk, 1966, pp. 15–16). Pal'gunova agrees that this would not enhance the democratic nature of the soviets, and cites other writers who favour this position (Pal'gunova, 1969, p. 156).

For Bezuglov, the question is not so simple. True, longer terms would mean that fewer citizens would gain this experience. Yet efficiency is lowered under current arrangements, for the reasons advanced by Nemtsev; the cost of elections is also a factor to bear in mind, a point also made by Strashun (1976, p. 181, footnote); so is the custom of planning in five-year periods. The long-term trend has been to extend the term of office, but Bezuglov cautiously concluded that the matter needed further careful study (Bezuglov, 1971, p. 22; 1973, pp. 45–8).

Finally, Leizerov took up the question. He gave a line-up of scholars who had taken a stand on the issue, with 'heavyweights' on each side: *for* a four-year term – Safarov, Kotok, Makhnenko, Golovko; *against* – Azovkin, Manokhin, Kravchuk, and

Kozlova. He himself proposed a compromise: pointing out that the question was referred to at the twenty-third party congress (1966) by M. S. Solomentsev (then first secretary of the Rostov *obkom*), Leizerov's solution is a three-year term (Leizerov, 1974a, pp. 86–7).

For the present, though, further discussion of the issue has been pre-empted by the 1977 Constitution, which extended the term of supreme soviets to five years, and of local soviets to half that period (article 90). However, that fails to solve all problems (see chapter 5), so it seems unlikely that the matter is resolved once and for all.

A further issue is the feedback between deputies and electors, through meetings where deputies report back on their success in fulfilling their mandates, and generally on the work of the soviet. Most writers hold that this is very important, but it is far from universal: in 1964 81.1 per cent of deputies reported back to their constituents; at village level the rate was 83 per cent, but this fell to 75 per cent in town soviets and 67 per cent in urban districts (Kravchuk, 1966, p. 19). Sometimes formal reports (*otchëty*) are replaced simply by 'meetings with electors', although 'a meeting compels no one to do anything' (Kravchuk, 1966, p. 22): it may be useful for information purposes, but it is a relatively weak and useless forum. Even the formal accounting meeting has its weaknesses: often very few electors turn up, one deputy speaks on behalf of several, or a whole group of deputies present a collective account; records are not kept, and so this aspect of the deputy's work is not properly monitored; and deputies tend not to regard this duty as a normal part of their work, seeing it instead as a kind of campaign (Kravchuk, 1966, p. 22). Bezuglov discussed this question in 1968, pointing out that a number of questions relating to these *otchëty* are not clear in law. For instance, who should call the meetings: the deputy himself? the collective that nominated him? the electors who endorsed him? Or, before whom should the report be made: again, his electors, or those who nominated him? The Constitution states firmly, 'the electors' – but the literature and common practice are ambiguous: some deputies report to their party organization, the trade union, or the Komsomol branch. For Bezuglov, a report can be regarded as a formal *otchët* only when a certain proportion of the electors have witnessed it; it must contain information about the deputy's own activities and those of the soviet, although Bezuglov does not support (for example) Leizerov in prescribing a specific format (Leizerov, 1974a, p. 115). On the basis of the reports, electors should judge their deputy's performance and the performance of the whole soviet; expressions of dissatisfaction must be discussed at future sessions of the soviet, and may be the basis for instigating proceedings for the recall of the deputy and revocation of his mandate (Bezuglov, 1968a, p. 104).

There are many reasons why a deputy might not perform his duties as well as he, or his electors, or a political scientist, might wish. Indeed, attempts have been made to find out how satisfied they are with their own performance, and how it might be improved. In the Armenian study, 1306 deputies out of 3327 respondents (40 per cent) said they had no serious difficulties in their work ('Effektivnost' deputatskoi deyatel'nosti', 1969, p. 113); the Estonian study found under a quarter without difficulties (Kalits *et al.*, 1965, p. 68, Table 1). Among those with problems, lack of time was a major source of dissatisfaction, often coupled with an overburdening of public duties: an average of 9.1 per cent in the Estonian study noted this problem; 40 per cent of Perttsik's respondents had two or more extra assignments, including 8 per cent who were deputies of soviets at several levels, often simply on account of their official position; the *Sovety* article cites examples of this tendency for obligations to pile on top of one another ('O chëm rasskazala anketa', 1966, p. 46). This problem of overburdening deputies was also noted by a party plenum in the Moscow oblast, and party primary organization secretaries were specifically requested to take the matter in hand (Paputin, 1970, p. 207; that, indeed, accurately reveals how things tend to get done in the Soviet system). Perttsik suggested that permanent commission chairmen should be given one or two days off work each month, without loss of pay, in order to deal with their obligations (Perttsik, 1967b, p. 19;

1968b, p. 15); ordinary deputies suggested for themselves a free day a week in which to attend to their obligations as deputy ('O chëm rasskazala anketa', 1966, p. 46); the idea of time off for deputies was supported by Shabanov (1969b, p. 99). Others suggested that time could be saved if deputies were permitted to jump the queue when seeking an interview on official business ('O chëm rasskazala anketa', 1966, p. 46).

The dominant theme is that the deputy must perform his representative functions more effectively, in a more businesslike, serious, indeed professional, way. In large measure, according to some writers, the way forward lies in adjusting the 'subjective' factors that influence the deputy's behaviour – his personal qualities, skills and capacities, which can be improved by more careful initial selection – and by giving appropriate training to newly elected representatives. 'Appropriate' may well be the operative word here: courses for deputies introduced in many areas recently have tended to cover 'traditional' questions (unspecified), but few have dealt with new methods and techniques of government, 'although the current importance of such questions is obvious' (Tikhomirov, 1975, p. 243). Others stress the need for structural changes, accompanied perhaps by changes in attitude on the part of those in controlling positions (Shabanov, 1969b, p. 101), in order to ensure that deputies can take proper advantage of their knowledge and enthusiasm. The attempt to use the law to regulate behaviour and standardize political practice also comes across strongly.

Whatever the specific proposals, there is general agreement on the need to revitalize the role of the deputy, and to redefine it in the era of 'developed socialist society'. All this seems to presuppose a very different, and developing, range of duties for the representative in Soviet politics. Indeed, one writer in the provincial press referred to the role of deputy as 'a political profession, very important and responsible', adding that 'it must be learnt, it must be practically mastered, as any other from the list of human professions' (Mel'nikov, 1975). Another writes of deputies exercising 'the complex art of governing', which can be learnt, in part, through conferences, seminars, courses of instruction and so forth, arranged by party and state bodies (Ukrainets, 1976, p. 78). The Western scholar, B. Michael Frolic, in this connection quotes a Moscow deputy who predicted that 'It won't be long before our deputies will be full-time members of the city government' (Frolic, 1970, p. 688). In that case, payment would have to be made to deputies, a question raised by Shabanov (1969b, p. 99), who asserts that this would not contradict the process of democratizing the work of the soviets. Later, however, he calls for the flat-rate expenses payment for supreme soviet deputies to be abolished, and for legal provision to be made for reimbursing only those expenses incurred (Shabanov, 1969, p. 161, n. 1).

The more fanciful suggestions for professionalizing the role of public representative have certainly not been taken up by the politicians, although there is evidence that greater attention is being paid to the deputy selection process, and higher expectations are now placed on the deputies in fulfilling their role. To a considerable extent, however, they are restricted by structural and other weaknesses in the representative institutions themselves. This will be discussed in the next chapter.

CHAPTER 4

Local Government Reform

Official views of the soviets and their apparatus have always extolled their virtues as institutions created by the working class in the excitement and fervour of revolution: they were originally conceived as coordinating committees in 1905 and again in 1917; Lenin and the Bolsheviks campaigned in 1917 under the slogan 'All Power to the Soviets', and with success: it was the Congress of Soviets that formally endorsed the revolution on 25 October 1917. Since then, their structure and role have been formalized and transformed, so that they are now constitutionally the organs of state power throughout the country, and their executive bodies have legal responsibility for administration. Still, however, they are presented as the instruments through which the Soviet people genuinely rule their affairs. Thus, in 1971 Leonid Brezhnev spoke of the soviets as 'the basis of the socialist state and the fullest embodiment of its democratic character ... the organs of popular power ... which manage the affairs of all our State of the Whole People from the bottom to the top' (*XXIV s"ezd*, vol. I, p. 102). In rather more flamboyant language, the then prime minister of Moldavia wrote of the soviets in 1967 as

> a superior form of state organization, the political basis of the USSR; ... the most all-embracing mass organizations of the toilers, expressing their will, the genuinely democratic and authoritative organs of the very masses, providing them with the possibility of actively participating in the government of the state. [Diorditsa, 1967, pp. 13–14]

Such extravagant assertions would seem to leave little, if any, room for improvement in the work of the soviets. Yet Soviet

63

scholars have found weaknesses that indicate that their functioning is not so perfect as the propagandists and some political
leaders would have the world believe. And in 1966, Brezhnev
himself said that 'improving the activity of the soviets must take
place on the basis of their further democratization' – a clear
admission that there was scope for improvement (*XXIII s"ezd*,
vol. I, p. 91).

Indeed, the political authorities themselves, in the wake of the
twentieth party congress in 1956, set about eliminating 'the consequences of the personality cult' in the work of the Soviet state
apparatus, and initiated 'a process of democratization and
further improvement of the Soviet state apparatus [which] continued in subsequent years' (Vasilenkov, 1967, pp. 10–11).
Beginning with an authoritative statement on 22 January 1957,
entitled 'On Improving the Activity of the Soviets of Toilers'
Deputies and Strengthening their Links with the Masses' (text in
KPSS v rez., vol. 7, pp. 237–48), the party and state
authorities have periodically issued statements concerning
different aspects of the work of local soviets. The soviets were
discussed at the twenty-second, twenty-third, twenty-fourth and
twenty-fifth party congresses, and since the late 1960s new
statutes are being introduced to re-define the legal rights and
obligations of soviets at different levels, and to regularize aspects
of the institutions and their deputies that were previously
unregulated (see Hill, 1972).

These developments have been accompanied – and to some
extent influenced – by the work of Soviet scholars, which is
likely to expand, possibly shifting its emphasis as these developments continue. Their work has adopted several approaches,
including the theoretical (e.g., devising ways of assessing the
efficiency of local soviets); legal (examining the legal position of
various aspects of the system, and proposing legislative amend-
ments in order to achieve certain aims); and behavioural (including the work of deputies, discussed in chapter 3).

Three specific areas have been the subject of research,
comment and debate: the competence of local soviets, and their
relations with the central authorities; the work of the sessions;

and the relationship between the soviet and the administrative apparatus.

THE COMPETENCE OF LOCAL SOVIETS

A number of scholars have devoted attention to elucidating the legal position of local soviets, a reflection, no doubt, of the fact that many Soviet political scientists were legally trained and work in law faculties or similar institutions. For example, Kravchuk edited a collection of essays, 'Questions of the Development of the Soviets at the Present Stage' (1966), and a further collection specifically focusing on 'Legal Problems of the Further Perfection of the Representative Organs of State Power' (Kravchuk, 1973); in 1974, the Institute of State and Law brought out a similar collection, entitled 'Legal Questions of the Work of Local Soviets' (Tikhomirov and Sheremet, 1974). All three books contained contributions by the country's leading specialist on the competence of local soviets, K. F. Sheremet. His interest in the subject goes back at least to the mid-1960s (Sheremet, 1965), and he has written a scholarly monograph and a popular brochure on this question (Sheremet, 1968a; Sheremet and Kutafin, 1976).

At a time (1966–8) when the process of devising a new set of statutes on local soviets was being initiated, Sheremet was concerned that the new legislation should spell out with far greater precision than hitherto the areas within which the different levels of soviet would have exclusive competence to decide issues, without interference from higher bodies or from their own executive organs. The whole concept of 'competence' was a new one in Soviet thinking about the local government institutions: the statutes referred to the 'rights and obligations' of soviets, an approach that for Sheremet had 'exceedingly undesirable consequences' (Kravchuk, 1966, p. 75). Existing statutes were completely inadequate in dealing with 'competence': for example, some laws on local soviets stated that the executive committees decided all questions except those subject to decision by the soviet sessions – yet failed to specify what those questions were; in the Uzbek village soviets statute, the question was completely omitted (Sheremet, 1968a, pp. 62–3).

Sheremet proposed significantly widening the scope for debate by the soviet sessions, at the expense of the executive bodies. For him, the characteristic feature of developments in Soviet statehood was the raising of the role of the soviets, which, legally, were not the representatives of central power in the localities, but constitutionally established institutions of popular power (Sheremet, 1968b, pp. 90, 92–3). In particular, their economic role must be strengthened, by permitting them to discuss and resolve a wider range of matters, even when there is only one possible decision (Sheremet, 1968a, p. 112 *et seq.*): after all, one-fifth of the total state budget is expended through the budgets of local soviets (Sheremet, 1968b, p. 92, n. 8). Similarly, a number of powers granted to executive committees *vis-à-vis* deputies (e.g., calling by-elections, revoking a deputy's mandate, granting permission for the arrest or prosecution of a deputy) should be either handed over to the soviets themselves or otherwise brought under the legal control of the full soviet (Sheremet, 1968a, pp. 118–20). (Sheremet points out that prosecution of a deputy does not mean automatic revocation of his mandate: that must follow conviction only, and until arrested he has the right to continue to fulfil his functions as a deputy: 1968a, p. 120.)

All this is in line with the general trend towards revitalizing local soviets, and stimulating their initiative and effectiveness. Moreover, since 90 per cent of all soviets were at the village level, and these embraced three-quarters of all deputies, particular significance attached to raising the role of these soviets in the system (Sheremet, 1968b, p. 93). Some specific weaknesses of village soviets had been spelled out by M. A. Shafir (1964). He pointed out that some village soviets had completely ceased to deal with questions about the development of agriculture, or matters of labour discipline on the farms, or the extension of successful farming practices; and an important reason for this lack of attention to perhaps the very stuff of rural administration was that these soviets had so few powers to do anything positive: one significant result of a questionnaire, administered to village and *raion* soviets and workers in the *raiispolkom* apparatus, was the repeated response: 'transfer powers from the raion organs to the village soviets' (Shafir, 1964, p. 24). Others recommended relieving the local soviets of certain administrative tasks, such as collection of taxes and agricultural products (which took up 70–80 per cent of their time), and allowing them to devote their energies to serving the people. Shafir puts forward the sensible proposal that, instead of the soviet chairman and secretary doing the quarterly rounds of all villages – all households! – to collect taxes, these should be deducted from workers' pay and transferred to the state in a lump sum; taxes in kind and fixed-price procurements should be collected directly by the procurement agencies through the farms. Clearly – as Shafir stated – the new statutes on village soviets must significantly widen their powers (1964, p. 25), a point echoed by the head of the legal department of the Azerbaidzhan supreme soviet presidium (Rasulbekov, 1964, p. 121).

In view of the parlous state of village soviets, which scarcely seemed to be fulfilling their functions at all, two writers, L. Karapetyan and V. Razin (1964, p. 159; cited in Kravchuk, 1966, pp. 31–4; and in Lepëshkin, 1965, p. 6), suggested abolishing village soviets altogether and handing over their functions to the collective and state farms. Lepëshkin summarily dismisses the proposal, pointing out that the idea had already been rejected in the 1930s. Kravchuk discusses the argument at greater length. The proposal, as summarized by Kravchuk, was, first, to abolish village soviets in places where several soviets existed on the territory of a single farm; their paid apparatus would then be abolished, and its functions taken over by the inhabitants on a voluntary basis. It is fair to add that this proposal was made at a time when Khrushchev was desperately attempting to cause the state to 'wither away', by transferring some of its functions to 'voluntary' organizations, such as trade unions: as such, the proposal was an obvious candidate for rejection after Khrushchev's political demise. Kravchuk asked the question, revealing a touching concern for legal niceties, what authority would abolish the paid apparatus, when the organ of state power in the locality had already been abolished in the first phase?; and he said that much administration was already being done on a voluntary basis. More serious is the point that Karapetyan and Razin looked on village soviets as really part of the administrative apparatus for agriculture. Kravchuk makes the legal position clear, however:

> Village soviets have never been any link in agricultural production, and their activity was never restricted only to questions of agricultural production. Therefore to decide the question of their future only from the viewpoint of agricultural production is manifestly incorrect. [Kravchuk, 1966, p. 32]

The two authors had proposed extending the powers of raion soviets, and transferring other functions to the farms; yet, says Kravchuk, collective farms and state farms are different institutions, so cannot perform the same functions. And – a final blow of damnation for the hapless authors – 'such a prospect does not correspond to the prospect marked out by the party' (Kravchuk, 1966, p. 33).

Even so, the question of relations between local soviets and higher state organs requires careful regulation, since the principles of 'democratic centralism' and 'dual subordination' can easily in practice degenerate into domination of lower soviets by higher administrative bodies. V. P. Semin, a deputy minister in the Russian republic, pointed to a major problem that troubled relations between ministries and local soviets: the multiplicity of institutions responsible for providing identical services, and the impossibility for local soviets to coordinate and control them (Semin, 1969, pp. 91–2). A similar point was made by the Moscow *oblispolkom* chairman, who suggested that the central planning organs should listen to the oblast authorities when devising plans, and greater attention should be paid to coordinating the work of different ministries: frequently, a new factory is sited in a town without making adequate provision for housing and all the other services nowadays required (Kozlov,

1968: 5–6) – a problem that has been noted by Western scholars (e.g., Taubman, 1973). At the same time, some problems were not being tackled by anyone (Semin, 1969, p. 92). Kozlov (1968, p. 8) called for new statutes on town and district soviets (which have since been introduced), giving the local soviets the powers needed to sort out such problems where they arise.

Barabashev defines the problem in terms of the concept of 'leadership' (*rukovodstvo*), involving two elements: the allocation and definition of functions among the various levels of soviet; and devising mechanisms for coordinating the activities of the various soviets responsible for a given territory (Kravchuk, 1973, p. 52). This is indeed one of the current concerns of Soviet political science and practitioners of politics and administration, bearing in mind the stream of new legislation relating to local soviets that began in the late 1960s – a point made by Barabashev at a conference in May 1975 (Barabashev, 1975a). It is but one of the areas where changes in definition are accompanying changes in legislation and practice.

THE WORK OF THE SESSIONS

The previous chapter looked at the work of writers concerned with examining the role and performance of deputies, and the effectiveness with which they perform their representative functions. Their approach to the formal sessions of the soviets was to see how far they permitted the deputies to represent their constituents in the debates, and to present their electors' interests in the formal decision-making forum. Other writers have approached the sessions from a different vantage-point. For example, A. V. Moskalev, who is concerned to judge the efficiency of the session as a decision-making unit, presents a list of criteria by which he believes the session should be judged (Moskalev, 1975, pp. 28–48).

First, the deputies: since the success of the soviet as a whole depends largely on the activity and perseverance of the deputy,

Moskalev and other writers argue that greater care must be exercised in selecting deputies with the appropriate inclinations and skills, as well as the formal educational qualifications and social characteristics such as class, party membership, sex, occupation, and 'the moral qualities of promoted candidates, their devotion to the cause of communism, which is taken for granted' (Moskalev, 1975, p. 33, n. 3); the selection process must ensure the choice of individuals who are competent to fulfil the duties of deputy. Selecting deputies as a reward for good work (as is common, he states) lowers the quality of sessions, since these 'honorary deputies' are not very diligent in performing their obligations (p. 34).

Moskalev repeats Leizerov's argument that the number of deputies affects the chances of participation in debates, and he doubts the value of electing councils of 500 and more (1975, p. 34). The economic cost of running large meetings is considerable, and the greater the numbers involved, the less back-up support the executive organs are able to give to each one. A reduction in numbers is indicated for at least the larger soviets, and a balance should be striven for between representativeness and efficiency of operation (Moskalev, 1975, p. 36; also Bezuglov, 1973, p. 21).

The duration of sessions is another of Leizerov's points taken up by Moskalev. At the higher levels, sessions last from 10 am to 6 pm; locally, a single afternoon session is normal, so reports of undue haste and superficial discussion and decision-making are to be found. An argument in favour of this arrangement is that there is a great economic cost involved in taking valuable workers out of production: indeed, occasionally managers refuse to allow indispensable workers time off to attend sessions ('Ne otpustili na sessiyu', 1975). (Soviet deputies at all levels continue their normal job during their term of office, thereby supposedly maintaining their links with their constituents, rather than becoming preoccupied with the formalities of parliamentarianism and their own status as representatives: see, for example, Turajev, n.d., p. 50.) However, the cost of holding longer sessions would partly be balanced by reducing the number of deputies, and Moskalev suggests that legislation should indicate norms for the duration of sessions of various soviets. A start had already been made in Kalinin oblast, where the oblast soviet's standing orders (*reglament*), article 17, state that a session may last two or more days (Moskalev, 1975, pp. 37–8). Other writers too have supported the lengthening of sessions (e.g. Tikhomirov, in Gaidukov and Starovoitov, 1965, p. 151).

A further criterion for judging the efficiency of sessions is the quality of decision-making. Several writers cited by Moskalev have tried to list characteristics required of 'optimal' decisions, including legality, appropriateness, timeliness, party commitment (*partiinost'*, implying conformity with party policy). Moskalev proposes his own list: a *scientific basis*, that is, all factors must be taken into account; *concreteness* – measures to be taken must be spelled out with precision and clarity, in place of the all-too-common general phrases; *legality* – decisions must conform strictly with the law; and *form* – all decisions should be presented in a specific form. Moreover, in order to strengthen the authority of such decisions, and remove any implication that the organs of state power are mere supplicants, the verb 'requests' (*prosit*) must be banished from the texts of decisions (Moskalev, 1975, pp. 39–43).

There has been considerable discussion about raising the level of openness (*glasnost'*) surrounding the work of the soviets, and Moskalev adds his weight to the drive to inform the public about the activities of their representative organs. One way of achieving this – by opening the sessions to participation by non-deputies – was criticized by Leizerov, as we saw, because it adversely affects the deputies' own chances of speaking. Moskalev suggested reducing the number of deputies. Yet he supports the idea, first proposed by Bezuglov in 1960 but 'unfortunately not put into practice', of circulating to factories and other institutions invitations to named workers to attend sessions, or open invitations for any interested worker to come to a session and voice his opinion, albeit without a vote (Moskalev, 1975, pp. 44–8). Moskalev seems unaware that there is a contradiction in his proposals, or that the wide extension of such a practice would counteract the trend towards improving the standing of deputies. Leizerov is surely right in insisting that 'all forms of participation by non-deputies in the work of the sessions must be thoroughly regulated' (Leizerov, 1970a, p. 84). Yet no one, it seems, has suggested the obvious compromise: provide a public gallery, from which interested citizens may observe the proceedings – 'to see justice being done' – without interfering in the business of the session.

Kotok (1963, p. 51) pointed out that article 34 of the Estonian statute on village soviets extended to all electors the right to attend sessions, but the public by and large has tended not to be present at meetings of their representative organs, perhaps for a variety of reasons. One custom that has developed, however, to help overcome this and bring greater openness into local politics, is that of holding sessions in different locations, including farms and factories, thereby bringing government to the people (Shabanov, 1969b, p.102; Barabashev, 1975b, p. 103), a custom that, for Kotok at least, 'has completely justified itself' (1963, p. 53; also Toiganbaev and Dzhekbatyrov, 1971, p. 144). Another recent writer suggests a special role for such sessions: they should be used not simply to publicize the good work of well-run soviets, but rather to serve as a means of consulting the people when problems have arisen that cannot be solved by the deputies alone (Moskalev, 1975, p. 139. For a positive appraisal of this tendency throughout the political system, see Tikhomirov, 1975, pp. 225–6).

Other aspects of the sessions have been given consideration. For example, even though Kotok (1963, p. 50) had argued in favour of the bi-monthly session, saying that monthly sessions had never been adhered to, and were often poorly prepared, Kravchuk (1966, p. 28) supported the proposal for a revision to monthly sessions, which would allow the deputies to keep current issues under closer control. For other writers (e.g., Kozlova, 1967, p. 37; Barabashev, in Karev, 1962, p. 49) regularity, rather than frequency, is the important factor, while

Moskalev (1975, p. 92) argues that six two-day sessions a year are more effective than twelve one-day meetings. Azovkin (1971, pp. 233–5) reported with evident satisfaction that sessions were now being called more frequently and regularly, and that the range of topics discussed had also increased substantially; but he points to some glaring gaps in the present coverage of business, and approvingly cites Nemtsev's proposal to extend the length of each sitting to two or three days, to permit a greater number of issues to be examined (p. 235).

In 1977 two experienced deputies suggested quarterly sessions, on the grounds that this would leave the deputies more time for preparation, and for constituency work in implementing the decisions of the soviet; and it would give the executive branch more time to study the issues that arise, and select those that could be resolved administratively, leaving only weighty matters for discussion by the formal session (Slepneva and Mineeva, 1977). As presented, the argument has a certain logic; but experience of the previous generation might lead one not to risk placing too much discretion at the disposal of the administrators: indeed, the point about much of the reformist trend in the post-Stalin period is that it has been in the opposite direction.

Yet whatever its frequency or duration, the efficiency and fruitfulness of a session is bound to depend on how well it is prepared, and the way it is conducted. If the same 'duty orators' (Safarov, in Vasil'ev, 1968, p. 79) monopolize the discussion; if the majority of deputies are not forewarned of what is to be said in the reports (or even of the draft agenda), and have to react immediately in the session itself (Bezuglov, 1971, p. 59; Postnikov and Selivanov, 1968, p. 89); or if the agenda is overburdened with several major questions, all of which require thorough and time-consuming debate (Burkauskas, 1966, p. 115), then the 'debates' are bound to retain their formalistic character. Azovkin, moreover, points to a further vital element in ensuring the success of the soviet debates: that there be allowed a full discussion (*preniya*) after the reports have been presented to the session. The foreclosing of debate before all deputies wishing to do so have had an opportunity to speak, or even the total failure to open a discussion on such questions as the appointment of officials and officers (practices reported by Azovkin), obviously has the effect of 'narrowing the possibilities for the members of a soviet to influence the course of economic and cultural construction, and increases the share of deputies who conduct themselves passively in the session' (Azovkin, 1971, p. 239).

The 1972 statute on the deputies' status (article 11) requires that deputies be informed in advance of the topics and issues to be discussed. A number of writers (e.g., Kozlova, 1967, pp. 39–40; Gabrichidze, 1968, p. 163) approvingly cite the example of the Daugavpils town soviet (Latvia), which in 1966 organized a session in which the deputies split up into permanent commissions to debate the opening report, and followed this with a plenary session. This form of meeting was tried elsewhere, and its benefit in permitting more speakers to take part was apparently appreciated (see Hill, 1977, pp. 99–100). Gabrichidze (1968, p. 165) and Moskalev (1975, pp. 136–7) report cases where the deputies reviewed evidence on film or tape bearing on the topics under discussion. Evidence suggests that in sessions without an opening speaker up to a third of deputies have a chance to speak (Bannykh, 1974, p. 78): in such an experiment at oblast level in Kazakhstan, 24 deputies spoke (Toiganbaev and Dzhekbatyrov, 1971, p. 142), while in the town of Karaganda, in the same republic, the preliminary discussion of agenda items and draft resolutions by deputies with their constituents at their homes and places of work leads to the executive committee receiving lots of comments and suggestions before the session (Toiganbaev and Dzhekbatyrov, 1971, p. 145; Azovkin, 1971, p. 237). These experiments are commended by Soviet writers as manifestations of greater initiative on the part of local soviets and their deputies.

Finally, the decision-making powers of local soviets have been looked at from a different angle: the number of deputies who form a quorum. With a stipulated quorum of two-thirds, and simple majority decisions, as few as a third of all deputies could pass legislation, so Kravchuk (1966, pp. 28–9) proposed amending this rule to require decisions by a majority of all deputies in the soviet. (In fact, attendance is normally around 80 per cent – Moskalev, 1975, pp. 120–1.) The new statutes on local soviets adopted in 1968 and 1971 do state that decisions are taken 'by a simple majority of the votes in the overall number of deputies in the soviet', but for Moskalev this formulation is too imprecise, and he suggests replacing the term 'simple majority' by the phrase 'absolute majority' (1975, pp. 128–9). However, this is an academic question, since decisions are invariably unanimous.

The Soviets and the Apparatus

In theory, the soviet, as the representative institution, is supposed to wield political power; in practice, the administrative organs – the executive committee and its departments – are generally able to control the work of the soviets. Much of the comment has been aimed at putting the administrative agencies into their proper constitutional place, and encouraging the soviets to reassert their powers. (This problem is by no means new to Soviet politics: when the system was being established, in the 1920s, considerable difficulties were encountered in persuading the new soviets to make full use of their legal powers, a reflection of the ambiguous relationship – which still pertains – between party and state: see Male, 1971, p. 130; also chapter 6 below.)

One approach, adopted by several writers (e.g., Sheremet, 1968a; Kozlova, 1967; Lazarev, 1972), has been to define the areas of competence of the various *types* of unit (in addition to the competence of different *levels*, discussed above). This task is particularly difficult, however, in a political system that has specifically rejected the 'division of powers' that has shaped many Western systems: following Marx's and Lenin's criticisms of bourgeois democracy, the Soviet Union has tried to devise institutions that embody the *unity* of the legislative and executive spheres of government (Shabanov, 1969b, pp. 109–11; Lazarev,

1972, pp. 106–9). The question is complicated by the principles of 'democratic centralism' and 'dual subordination', which render the executive and administrative organs at one level subject to decisions not only of their own soviet, but also of higher soviets and higher executive committees, and their departments subject to the directives of the corresponding ministries (Lazarev, 1972, pp. 115–16, 120–1). In Lazarev's interpretation, the tendency in the latest legislation is to define those areas of competence that are exclusive to the sessions of the soviet (e.g., confirmation of the budget, formation of the permanent commissions, election of the executive committee), and to permit the executive organs to decide all other questions that the soviet has general powers to decide (1972, p. 133); however, on the basis of the existing literature, Lazarev concludes that the soviets have the right to resolve directly any question that their own administrative organs can decide (p. 117; Lazarev seems to have changed his view on this question: see Gabrichidze's comments in Gabrichidze, 1968, pp. 197–8). In practice, however, the opposite often happens: the executive committee usurps powers that are supposedly exclusive to the session of the soviet, such as altering the composition of the executive's membership, even though such a practice is illegal (Gabrichidze, 1968, p. 183).

In view of the complexities involved, the legal and philosophical arguments about defining spheres of competence are likely to occupy the minds of scholars in the future. Others have adopted perhaps a less exalted approach to the question of soviet–executive relations, concerning themselves more with the political aspects, even down to basic issues such as how the sessions should be run. Moskalev, for instance, explains that it is hardly appropriate for members of the executive committee to take the chair or act as secretary at sessions, particularly when the work of the committee or its departments is being discussed – yet this often happens in practice (Moskalev, 1975, p. 121); again, with even somewhat comic simplicity, he advises deputies on how to conduct the sessions in such a way as to imply

superiority on the part of the elected representatives. The following passage illustrates the point well:

> Even in the course of a speech [a deputy] can express the
> same requests quite differently. For example, not 'I request
> ...', but 'I consider it necessary for the executive committee
> to resolve the following questions ...', i.e. formulate one's
> requests more decisively, more firmly, as concrete proposals
> on the question under review. Then the speech will sound
> different. It will be the speech of a deputy who is proprietor in
> the soviet. [Moskalev, 1975, p. 126]

The plain fact is that the executive committee is in a position
to control proceedings: it possesses information about issues
that arise; it calls the meetings; it compiles the agenda, which
has not always been notified to the deputies in advance, and pre-
pares the draft resolutions; in the sessions the officers of the
executive, particularly the chairman, tend to deliver the reports
that form the basis of the discussion: so much so that
Tikhomirov has referred to them as 'monopoly rapporteurs' (in
Gaidukov and Starovoitov, 1965, p. 149). Even the sessions at
which the annual report (*otchët*) of the executive committee is
discussed are controlled in the same way: it is the executive itself
that drafts the official resolution on the report, and this quite
naturally leads to 'formalism' in the discussion of the reports
and in the conduct of the session as a whole (Moskalev, 1975,
p. 81). Furthermore, the administrative *apparatus*, with its
various departments and administrations, has a lot of power in
running society without effective control by the elected
representatives. In practice there simply is not time for the
deputies to scrutinize the work of all departments (Moskalev,
1975, p. 82): occasionally, up to seven commissions report on
their respective departments in a single session, and this too
indicates a 'formal approach' to the question (Burkauskas, 1966,
p. 115).

There is, indeed, an easily appreciated tension between the
administrators – nowadays better trained, better equipped and
possessing information and skills in presenting arguments (and

also bearing personal responsibility for the successful development of their area) – and the *public representatives*, who have in many cases tended to lack those qualities. The result has been a tendency towards 'a technocratic approach', with officials trying to decide matters directly, thereby supplanting the rights of the elective organs (Tikhomirov, 1975, p. 246). This, for Tikhomirov at any rate, is incompatible with socialism, where 'the social basis in government retains its priority'; 'the social basis' (*obshchestvennye nachala*) implies that 'all the most important matters are decided on a broad democratic basis, through the soviets, the mass organizations etc.' (Tikhomirov, 1975, p. 246).

A number of proposals in the literature might help to overcome these problems. For example, the initiative for summoning sessions and fixing the agenda could be given to the soviets themselves (Zhilin, 1966, p. 57; Postnikov and Selivanov, 1968, p. 89; Moskalev, 1975: 96). The executive committees could publish the draft agenda and even draft resolutions, so that interested citizens might discuss the issues with their deputy, and deputies arrive at the sessions better informed of public opinion (Shabanov, 1969b, pp. 100–1; Pigalev, 1970, p. 45). Other writers approach the question in terms of the quality of the personnel in the apparatus, by proposing, for example, that legislation should specify the qualifications required for appointment to specific posts (Chkhikvadze, 1967, pp. 278–9; cited in Shakhnazarov, 1972, p. 157), a suggestion in turn reflected in a call for introducing a statute on servants of the state apparatus as 'an urgent task' (Tikhomirov, 1975, p. 217). The notion of a competitive system in the appointment of specialists and officials has been put forward and favourably commented on (e.g., Tikhomirov, 1975, pp. 131, 218; Piskotin and Tikhomirov, 1965, pp. 5–6; Shakhnazarov, 1972, p. 157). All these proposals, if introduced, would probably help in regulating relations between the apparatus and the elected representatives.

However, two major structural reforms have been given special attention by Soviet writers, and have led to controversy: the abolition of the administrative departments, and their replacement by the permanent commissions; and the election of a presidium for local soviets, comparable with those of the USSR and the republican supreme soviets. Both proposals are intended to raise the significance of the elected body, at the expense of the indirectly elected executive committee and the appointed administration.

The proposal to do away with the departments, and hand over their functions to the commissions, goes back to at least the late 1950s. The idea was strongly in line with Lenin's utopian notions about the whole population participating in the running of the country, and in accord, too, with Khrushchev's attempts to hasten the approach of the millennial society of communist self-government. In Dneprodzerzhinsk, and in L'vov province (Ukraine), the urban borough (raion) soviets achieved this abolition of the departments, as reported by Tikhomirov, who commented that 'the transfer to the commissions of all the functions of the corresponding departments is in principle absolutely correct' (Vasil'ev and Tikhomirov, 1961, pp. 34–8). Half a decade later, the secretary of Gorky oblispolkom was urging that the time for experimentation in this matter was over, and it was time to act by bringing in the appropriate legislation (Zhilin, 1966, p. 60). Nothing was done, and the idea was again given strong support in 1969 by Kudinov, who recommended *gradually* abolishing the departments and administrations 'with some exceptions', and transferring their powers to the permanent commissions, strengthened by established (*shtatnye*) staff workers (Kudinov, 1969, p. 33, quoted in Gabrichidze, 1971, p. 15).

Kudinov's advocacy of this particular cause is the most enthusiastic, however, and other writers all stress caution. Tikhomirov suggested the transfer of powers by clearly defined stages, with the commissions and departments working side by side, and the commissions gradually taking over functions of administration (Tikhomirov, 1963, p. 90). Such a scheme was supported by Aimbetov, who nevertheless warned against haste (Aimbetov *et al.*, 1967, p. 229), while two reviewers of Tikhomirov's book indicated their belief that only some of the powers in question could be transferred to the commissions (Kuznetsov and Savenkov, 1964, p. 154). Shabanov also urges caution, since too forced a pace could damage and weaken the position of the whole state apparatus. The party programme, he points out, speaks of the *gradual* transfer of such powers; however, 'experience has shown that in a number of cases this was done prematurely' (Shabanov, 1969b, pp. 105–6). Gabrichidze, citing Kudinov's enthusiastic comment, also calls it 'a premature proposal', pointing out that, as society becomes more complex and specialized, so there is a need for a comprehensive and specialized administrative apparatus (Gabrichidze, 1971, p. 15). Other writers too have stressed the importance of competent and soundly organized administrative structures (e.g., Tikhomirov, 1970; 1975). The even bolder idea of transferring functions entirely from state institutions to 'public' bodies – likewise highly favoured by Khrushchev – has also been played down subsequently, and Topornin has urged an essentially rational approach to the question: undue haste will lead to less effective fulfilment of the relevant function, so such transfers of responsibilities should be decided on grounds of efficiency and effectiveness of execution (in Tikhomirov, 1975, pp. 144–5). This, indeed, seems to be the current policy.

Meanwhile, much stress has been placed on strengthening the work of the commissions, with masses of literature published, to help the deputies in them to operate with maximum effectiveness. By 1973, these commissions embraced 80.7 per cent of local soviet deputies, and involved almost two and a half million non-deputy activists (Savenkov, 1974: 34). In view of the actual or potential importance of these permanent commissions, the proposal has been made to involve *all* deputies. Barabashev agrees that more deputies should be involved, but thinks it would be a mistake to require all deputies to serve, irrespective of their overall burden of public duties (in Kravchuk, 1966, pp. 123–4).

An important element in ensuring the effectiveness of these commissions obviously is the competence of their members in dealing with the subject, and some attention has been paid to this question. The Yaroslavl conference on the deputy's status urged that care be exercised in allocating deputies to the commissions, taking into account their personal wishes and inclinations, their experience, profession and other factors; it also suggested dividing the larger commissions into sections of four to six members, led by experienced deputies (Gorshenev and Kozlov, 1976, p. 128). As in other fields, however, it is Leizerov who has come up with detailed empirical study of this question, analysing and quantifying the composition of the commissions according to their members' official function or occupation, the degree of correspondence between their experience and the field covered by the commission, and similar questions. He notes that re-elected deputies are strongly represented in the commissions (implying continuity and extended experience of such work), but this is balanced by a high level of switching from one commission to another, particularly at village level, and in certain identified commissions. Moreover, he states, 'a direct dependency was established by the research, between the magnitude of renewal and the effectiveness of the commissions' work: the lesser the renewal ... particularly of chairmen, the better the commission works' (see Leizerov, 1974c). He also deals with the question of executive committee representation in the commissions; pointing out that the law and the scholarly literature are indefinite about the desirability of this practice, he firmly declares that it should be banned (1974c, p. 104).

Soviet writers seem anxious to allot to the permanent commissions a far more active role than they have traditionally played, and some of the proposals cited in the previous chapter would have an impact on the performance of the commissions, in particular Perttsik's proposal of time off work for commission chairmen. Another suggestion is to provide for time off for specialists and others to participate as members of the *aktiv* of persons working with the commissions (Shabalin, 1974, p. 99). In these ways, by modest changes in conventions, occasionally bolstered by legislative provision, scholars now see the future course of development in the role of the commissions. If their level of activity and the competence of their members continues to rise, a time might come when functions could indeed be transferred from the administrative departments. The urgency of the early 1960s has now been removed, however.

Finally, the idea of an elected presidium for local soviets. This too was intended in order to overcome the problem of the lack of correspondence between the rights of the soviets and their executive and administrative organs, which operated to the benefit of the latter (Perttsik, 1967a, pp. 142–3). However, there is a lack of agreement on the precise nature of the suggested presidium. It would be elected by the deputies, like the Supreme Soviet presidium; but it was not agreed whether it would exist alongside the executive committee or replace it, nor whether it would consist of paid, full-time officers or unpaid representatives. G. V. Atamanchuk, for example, wanted a presidium with all the functions of the executive committee, including coordination of the work of the permanent commissions and leadership of the administrative organs (Atamanchuk, 1968, p. 108). Such an institution would clearly have to consist of paid members. Shabanov saw the advantages of such an organ being that it would combine the legislative and executive functions during the period between sessions: the *separation* of powers was a sign of bourgeois parliamentarianism, he said, which had not justified itself (Shabanov, 1969b, pp. 109–11). Barabashev was against retaining the executive committee alongside a presidium, as this 'inevitably will complicate the work of the soviets'; and he cites Tikhomirov (1963, p. 95) in support of this position (in Kravchuk, 1966, p. 130); however, the problem would not be solved, in his opinion, by simply transforming the executive committees into presidiums. Instead, he suggested special organizing commissions, to arrange the work of the soviet, leaving the executive committees to get on with administration (Kravchuk, 1966, p. 130). By contrast, Azovkin (1965, p. 7) supported the idea of a voluntary presidium, while Burkauskas (1966, p. 116) argued against the whole idea.

The fullest and strongest argument in favour of the proposal, however, came from Kotok, Nechitailo and Semënov, in 1966. If such an organ of local soviets were created, 'the permanent commissions, the deputies and deputies' groups would emerge from under the tutelage of the *ispolkom*, which would permit the soviet really to become "a working corporation" that not only takes decisions, but also performs the leading role in their fulfilment, and effectively controls the whole course of practical work' (Kotok *et al.*, 1966, p. 125). Moreover, the executive committees could then concentrate all their effort on administration, instead of having also to service the deputies and the soviet. The latter function would be the main purpose of the presidium; hence its role would be more restricted than at Supreme Soviet level. Its main focus of attention would be the permanent commissions, which would be able to operate far more effectively than at present, and this would permit them to take over some functions of the executive committee and its departments – an interesting introduction of the previous proposal. Finally, they argue that a voluntary presidium would be inadequate: if a presidium is to perform its functions properly, they conclude, then it has to be a professional body (Kotok *et al.*, 1966, p. 126).

This is one reform over which political scientists and politicians have collaborated to take action, by devising experiments in Irkutsk oblast soviet and Semipalatinsk city soviet (Kazakhstan) (Kotok *et al.*, 1966, p. 123; Perttsik, 1967a, p. 143). Separate groups of scholars, working in conjunction with state officials, and with the sanction of the local party committees, devised provisional statutes for governing trial presidiums, and incorporating associated structural and functional reforms. Unfortunately, the deputy director of the Academy of Sciences' Institute of State and Law had cause to complain in 1967 that the experiment had not yet taken place (Lunev, 1967, p. 100); nor, to my knowledge, have local soviet presidiums been formed. The new statutes on various local soviets make no provision for such an organ, and it seems to be accepted that those functions that are carried out by the presidium of the Supreme Soviet are performed at local level by the ispolkom (I. M. Chekharin, 1975, pp. 13–14). Yet hope has apparently not been abandoned: Strashun further supported the notion in 1976, suggesting a division of functions and different principles of recruitment to the two bodies (Strashun, 1976, pp. 205–6).

This episode, apparently indicating failure on the part of Soviet reformers, raises the question of the impact of all the earnest debate among political scientists: this will be discussed in chapter 8.

Meanwhile, the attention of Soviet specialists has turned away from the almost exclusive concentration on institutions to different aspects of the society and its political system. The next chapter reviews the literature on interests and public opinion, and their reflection in the political process.

CHAPTER 5

Interests, Information and Public Opinion

Until recently, most Western analysis of the Soviet political system discounted the importance of public opinion and denied the existence of articulation and aggregation of interests in ways that would be recognizable in a democratic system. The standard Western view has seen the members of Soviet society as essentially the *objects* of the political process, organized from above, in order to achieve certain aims defined in the ideology (Friedrich and Brzezinski, 1966, p. 17 and *passim*), rather than as a force that impinges on the political leaders in the decision-making process. Demands are 'a resource which must be used and structured by the political leadership in order to achieve the goals which it has set for society' (Schwartz, 1974, p. 235), and the political leadership is able to regulate access to the political system (Easton, 1965, p. 93).

Plenty of evidence suggests that this is precisely how opinion and interests have been viewed in the Soviet Union, by scholars, philosophers and politicians alike: indeed, there can be little doubt that this is still the dominant view. Even so, Western scholars in the past decade have argued that there may be scope for public opinion to have some impact on the policy-makers, through the agency of interest groups (see in particular the work of Skilling and his collaborators: Skilling, 1966; Skilling and Griffiths, 1971; also Schwartz and Keech, 1968; Stewart, 1969); it has been argued that there is also scope for articulating and processing individual demands, outside the activities of the 'interest groupings' on which most Western writers have concentrated (Oliver, 1969; also Hough, 1976a; Friedgut, 1978).

The result is that 'one of the most controversial innovations of recent years in the study of Soviet politics' (Brown, 1974, p. 71) has led to the development of a new branch of Soviet political studies by Western scholars.

A perusal of the work of a number of Soviet scholars also reveals an attempt to grapple with the serious questions of what constitutes an interest, and how interests and public opinion can be, and ought to be, taken into account in policy-making. This work falls into two distinct categories: defining the concept; and applying it in analysing the political system and its operation.

DEFINING INTERESTS

Although previous Soviet scholars had expounded on the concept, the starting-point in the present Soviet debate was the article on interest (*interes*) in the second edition of the *Bol'shaya Sovetskaya Entsiklopediya* (*BSE*). This unsigned 300-word article defined the concept as 'the selective, purposeful direction of a person towards the acquisition of certain knowledge or the fulfilment of a certain activity'. In other words, interests were seen predominantly in the sense of phenomena that engage the intellect, including a common 'interest' in building communism, although such a restricted view of the concept was rejected in the late 1920s by S. A. Oranskii, as being essentially a bourgeois, individualistic definition (Aizikovich, 1965, p. 163). Moreover, clashes between individual and social interests were said to be resolved by the principle of the subordination of the private to the public interest: this is viewed as the appropriate ('correct') way in which these two kinds of interest are combined under socialism.

The first major challenge to this 'Stalinist' view ('the first swallow': Aizikovich, 1965, p. 163) appeared in an article by the philosopher G. M. Gak, who criticized that definition for concentrating on the 'spiritual' sphere of knowledge or accomplishments, whereas interests are defined by the individual's social context. Gak argued that 'alongside the development of production and the growth of material culture, ever-new personal interests arise', including, for example, the interests of the individual as a consumer (Gak, 1955, p. 19). Gak defined three types or levels of interests: personal interests (*lichnye interesy*); interests of the personality (*interesy lichnosti*); and social or public interests (*interesy obshchestva, obshchestvennye interesy*). In the first category, Gak included interests defined by the individual's membership of various social categories: he is part of nature, of a society, a class, a nation, a state – all of which inspire in him various aspirations and aims which form his personal interests. The interests of the *personality* are broader, and incorporate a social element: thus, out of a sense of familial duty, a mother may forgo her sleep, peace and quiet, and even food for the sake of her child; a patriotic soldier may die for his country. These 'social interests' are instilled into the individual during his upbringing, and define his moral duty.

This kind of approach is familiar in the West, where the analysis of social and political processes in terms of interests based on group membership is well established. In the context of post-Stalin intellectual life in the Soviet Union, this must have been seen as radically new, with strong political implications in a country emerging from a period in which 'private' interests were explicitly disregarded in favour of an ill-defined public interest or 'the interests of socialism'. Gak gave considerable attention to this question, asking whether it is possible to speak of a 'public interest', common to *all* members of a society. His answer, true to the Soviet tradition, is that the public interest is identified as the development of the forces of production, which in turn is determined by the relations of production, especially property relations. In a socialist society, where there are (supposedly) no antagonistic classes, the notion of common interests is perfectly possible: thus, 'socialist property serves the interests of both the whole society and its individual members' (Kim and Nechitailo, 1970, p. 5).

However, when discussing the question of material interests and economic stimulation as a means of raising efficiency – a topic that has been given increasing attention in the period of economic reform (Lewin, 1975, pp. 180–1) – Gak shows that public and individual interests do not always coincide. Hence the need for the socialist principle of subordinating the personal interest to the public. It is impossible to eliminate all possibility of contradiction, so there is a need to train citizens in 'the spirit of communist ideals'. The 'vestiges of capitalism' also sometimes lead to an anti-social understanding of personal interests, so that 'the combination of public and personal interests by the subordination of the personal to the public is achieved by the workers under the leadership of the communist party' (Gak, 1955, p. 28). This general kind of argument has been maintained as 'official' until the present day, and although he skates over the delicate question of precisely how the 'public interest' will be identified — except by reference to developing the productive forces of society — Gak's implication is surely that determining what is consistent with serving the 'public interest' is one of the party's functions.

Gak's views have been cited at some length because this article was a major step in the Soviet analysis of interests. It is a mixture of Marxist–Leninist orthodoxy and radical importation, and it injected into Soviet interpretations the notion that individuals have a variety of legitimate interests, deriving in large measure from their group affiliations. The problem for the political system — and this view seems unexceptionable — is that of finding the appropriate balance between individual and collective interests; and, given the traditions and views of the Soviet regime, both the educational system and the communist party are given a role to perform in resolving this question.

Another Soviet scholar, G. Ye. Glezerman, remarked in the mid-1960s that there had been a significant growth in interest towards 'interests', adding that 'in the last analysis the motive force for people's actions in all spheres of social life is their interests' (Glezerman, 1966, pp. 15–16). In any more or less developed society, he went on, there is 'a mass' of multifarious interests — personal, group, class, public, etc. — the content of which comprises objective needs arising from the conditions of social existence (pp. 16–18). Moreover, even in class society (presumably including a capitalist system) overriding societal or public interests can exist, and the denial of this is a vulgarization of Marxism: the point is, says Glezerman, that *all* social groups have an interest in developing the productive forces, because therein lies social progress, which is in the interests of all (pp. 22–3). This position appears quite remarkable in view of the Marxist–Leninist insistence on class *antagonisms* in pre-socialist society; it is explicable, however, in terms of the official interpretation of *Soviet* society, which is said to contain classes (workers and peasantry, plus the intelligentsia, a non-class stratum) but no longer class *antagonisms*: all groups supposedly have the fundamental interest of building communism. Within each class, there 'unarguably' exist differences of interest among different strata and groups; however, these are of a secondary character, and do not challenge that class's fundamental interests, which override partial and immediate interests (p. 24). Yet, 'the community of fundamental interests of all members of socialist society by no means excludes a huge variety in their specific interests. To ignore these interests would mean to permit a serious error, which could retard the development of socialist society' (p. 25). True collaboration among all social classes and nations, Glezerman concludes, requires that the specific interests of all groups and all republics be satisfied, by correct combination with all-union interests, the interests of a nationally integrating society (p. 26).

B. M. Lazarev demonstrated a whole range of legitimate interests in Soviet society, and observed that 'the variety of interests already contains within itself the possibility of contradictions among them' (Lazarev, 1971, p. 86). In practice, conflicts of interest can be observed between different branches of the economy, and between their interests and general interests (pp. 89–91). Hence the need to provide for national or central interests to have priority over local or departmental interests in any cases of collision (*kolliziya*): the principle of democratic centralism helps to resolve this issue, by establishing a hierarchy within the spheres of competence of the various decision-making organs (p. 86). Even so, Lazarev argues that the centre cannot effectively express local interests (p. 87).

Still more forthright is Shabanov. 'It is natural', he wrote, 'that under socialism too, personal interests exist. It cannot be contended that public and personal interests completely blend together. There are even certain contradictions between them. . . . In conditions of building socialism and communism the state is still not capable of fully satisfying all the material and spiritual requirements of citizens.' Survivals of attitudes from the past also lead to conflict, and in a society building communism each citizen must take account of social and state interests, as well as his own: 'This is not always readily achieved, sometimes it happens not completely smoothly' (Shabanov, 1969b, p. 261).

Lazarev also explores the impact of personal interests on the work of theoretically neutral functionaries. He calls sociology to his support, saying it has been demonstrated that the study of the problems of government or management suffers if it is forgotten that bureaucrats are people with their own interests, which can both help and hinder the performance of their obligations (Lazarev, 1971, pp. 93–4).

INTERESTS AND POLITICS

Already we can see a recognition by Soviet scholars that a wide range of personal and group interests exist in society. A further strand of analysis has shifted the emphasis from the nature of interests to their relationship with the political system and how they can be accommodated in the policy-making and law-making process. Zav'yalov (1970, p. 101) states forthrightly that 'the effectiveness of government in large measure depends on an understanding of the motives of action of classes, various social strata, population groups and individuals', and he ascribes great significance to the 'correct representation' of class, group and individual interests, and their combination with social interests. Bourgeois writers are wrong, he says, in asserting that all personal interests under socialism are subordinated to social interests. He repeats the point that, following the rapid technological development of the 'scientific and technical revolution', new interests constantly arise which the state, as representative of the interests of society as a whole, must discover through a legal mechanism, and must recognize and realize legally (pp. 101–2).

Zav'yalov's views are particularly striking, as his approach sounds close to the systems analysis or functionalist traditions, with inputs, conversion and the authoritative allocation of values; and he even touches on the problem that may arise if interests ('demands' in the Western model) are not accommodated. While noting that he refers to 'interests that do not contradict the nature and spirit of socialist society' (p. 102, n. 7), he indicates that 'in the presence of newly-arisen interests, the absence of their corresponding expression in law can lead to undesirable consequences.' Moreover, citizens can have *political* interests, and the level of their political activity reflects the extent to which such interests are realized (p. 102). It is not clear whether Zav'yalov means that great satisfaction of demands leads to more political activity, by encouraging a strong sense of political efficacy, or that dissatisfaction encourages more active articulation of interests; Soviet experience suggests that failure to satisfy interests leads, for the majority, to apathy.

This kind of argument has also been expressed by Shakhnazarov, who writes that

> the absence of antagonisms does not signify an identity of the needs of the different social groups. Along with the complete and permanent coincidence of the fundamental interests of all classes and social groups, there may arise, and does arise, a lack of coincidence of specific interests. That is a contradiction of a kind which, while not being antagonistic, can become aggravated unless it is resolved in good time. [Shakhnazarov, 1974, p. 29]

Later he states that 'no political organization can function efficiently without being constantly informed about the aspirations and requirements of all the classes and sections of society and without reacting to them in some form or another' (p. 42).

Other Soviet scholars have made a similar point. B. N. Topornin says that political information must be objective and complete, with no tendency towards colouration or distortion, otherwise 'the basis for adopting correct and clear-cut estimates and decisions is eroded' (in Tikhomirov, 1975, p. 85). This obviously refers to the long-standing custom of feeding glowing reports of the 'successful implementation' of policy decisions, so that subsequent policies were framed for a non-existent situation, and consequently became less and less relevant. Topornin also stresses the need for a two-way flow of information: the masses need to understand the point of decisions if they are to implement them effectively and energetically, while the higher levels need to know how their policies are being received at the grass-roots level (in Tikhomirov, 1975, p. 84; see also Manov, who mentions the possibility of 'conflict situations' arising, also in Tikhomirov, 1975, p. 288).

Moreover, there is a need to take the specific interests of different classes into account:

> So long as class differences remain, the socialist state must in its activity take into account both the general and the specific interests of classes and social groups in society, and resolve the possible non-antagonistic contradictions between them, reconcile them, directing them into the common stream. [Il'inskii *et al.*, 1976, p. 16]

(See also Kim and Nechitailo, 1970, p. 14.) The last phrase is taken from the mouth of Leonid Brezhnev, who told the twenty-fourth CPSU congress (1971) that 'the party's policy brings the required results when it precisely takes into account the interests of the whole people, and also the interests of the classes and social groups that compose it, and directs them into one common stream' (*XXIV s"ezd*, vol. I, p. 97). This formulation is virtually indistinguishable from Western descriptions of 'interest aggregation', and firmly implies recognition by the political authorities of the validity of this area of scholarly analysis.

Some scholars have linked this question with the movement towards 'democratization' of the political system, a trend that has been given much attention in the present decade. Indeed, democratization and the aggregation of interests are intertwined, as V. A. Patyulin noted: 'The development of democratic processes beneficially affects the ever more complete reflection of national, class, collective and individual interests' (in Tikhomirov, 1975, p. 160).

Not all Soviet writers share these views. The more conservative of them stress the role of the communist party in uniting all interests. For example, Ye. I. Kozlova writes: 'The highest form, revealing the content of the will of the Soviet people, correctly reflecting the fundamental interests of the people, and the objective laws of social development, is the ideology formulated by the communist party' (1972, p. 24). She also states that 'the genuine socialist democratism of the Soviet electoral system provides for the correct reflection and expression of the will of the Soviet people in the voting' (p. 25), a statement that seems remarkable in view of the many-pronged attack in the previous decade on the Soviet electoral system by her professional colleagues.

Another writer who takes a similarly orthodox view is M. Kh. Farukshin, whose analysis, expounded at length in a monograph on the CPSU in Soviet society (Farukshin, 1973), can be summarized as follows: 'The CPSU began its existence as the party of the proletariat, acting on behalf of that class's real interests; however, following the successful achievement of socialism, the interests of all other classes now coincide with those of the proletariat, so the party now acts in conformity with the interests of the whole Soviet people; in doing so, it is guided by Marxism–Leninism, whose scientific laws of social development the CPSU is in a unique position to elucidate and protect.' Such an interpretation comes very close to asserting that the party knows what is best for people – a view that finds implied support elsewhere (e.g., M. Imashev, in Aimbetov *et al.*, 1967, p. 82).

Nevertheless, despite these conservative views (which find support in the highest political circles), for perhaps the majority of serious Soviet scholars today, the principle of the existence of legitimate interests, which must be taken into account in policy-making, is an established part of their analysis of society. Furthermore, the political leadership too has begun to appreciate the significance of opinion for the governmental process, as witness Brezhnev's statement at the twenty-fifth congress that the study of public opinion deserves close attention (*XXV s"ezd*, vol. I, p. 98).

APPLICATION OF THE CONCEPT

Having established the validity of interests, and the need for the political system to accommodate them, the next stage is to work out the means of doing so. The concept has been used by writers in analysing different institutions and practices, particularly within the state mechanism. Thus, Kim and Nechitailo (1970) explore ways in which the local soviets, specifically, can and do reflect interests arising in society. These authors examine the question in far greater detail and at considerably greater length than other scholars, although using the concept of 'interest' to organize substantially the same material as other writers, who approach the soviets with such concepts as 'representation' and 'participation'.

Similarly, R. A. Safarov uses the concept of 'public opinion' to organize his material, and enumerates various forms for expressing opinions and interests: voting in elections, presenting 'mandates' to the deputies, addressing suggestions to state organs, turning to them with complaints, discussing draft bills, debating current problems, writing in the press or appearing on radio and television, expressing one's opinion at meetings, participating in street processions and demonstrations, evaluating the results of social experiments, and responding to sociological survey questionnaires (Safarov, 1967, p. 52; 1975a, p. 20). Elsewhere (1975b, p. 83), Safarov has called for legislation to oblige local soviets to consult public opinion in their decision-making procedures, while A. N. Bychek also suggested creating a special organ in the local soviets' apparatus, specifically concerned with sounding opinion: he also stressed the role of the deputy as a provider of information on electors' opinions (in Gorshenev and Kozlov, 1976, pp. 91–3). Another writer, reviewing Safarov's 1975 monograph, refers to this new branch of social science (the study of public opinion) with a new jargon word: 'opinionics' (*opin'onika*) (Shlyapentokh, 1976, p. 149).

To the extent that public opinion reflects interests, needs and wants, all the methods mentioned by Safarov and others are in principle available for feeding such demands and supports into the Soviet political decision-making machinery (although governed by the weight of tradition, reinforced by the stipulation in article 39 of the 1977 Constitution, that 'Enjoyment by citizens of their rights and freedoms must not be to the detriment of the interests of society or the state, or infringe the rights of other citizens'). However, three specific forms of interest articulation have been given particular attention: the mandate (*nakaz*); the referendum; and direct communication.

The mandate (nakaz)

The principle of the electors' mandate is a simple one, and through its operation the deputy's electoral programme is formed. Whereas a Western political party aggregates perceived demands into a programme, which it then frames as a manifesto to place before the electorate for endorsement, in the Soviet Union a deputy is supposed to receive 'mandates' from the electors – specific requests of public or social relevance, given at meetings during an election campaign, which it is his duty to see carried out by the soviet. The legal force and definition of *nakazy* was in doubt for some years (see, e.g., Galesnik, 1957, p. 177; Vasilenkov, 1963, pp. 15–17; Kotok, 1967, pp. 97–8; Bezuglov, 1968b, p. 11; Sukhanov, 1969, p. 78), until partially defined in the 1972 statute on the deputies' status (article 7): subsequently, indeed, Binder (1974, pp. 26–9) and Strashun (1976, p. 48) were still arguing about definitions. The principle, however, goes back to the 'mandat impératif' of the Paris Commune. Lenin saw the mandate as a demand (*trebovanie*), as have modern writers (e.g., Azovkin, 1966, p. 146; Kotok, 1967, p. 7; Moshak, 1971, p. 93). Such demands may, in principle, be introduced at any level in the system, including the Supreme

Soviet (Nudnenko, 1975), although normally they are introduced at the local level, where they are discussed in the full
soviet and steps are taken to implement them, frequently involving reference to higher authorities via the planning mechanism.

If the mandate system were freely and effectively operated, it
could serve as an important form of direct input and feedback
for the government. In the mid-1950s it was pointed out that
'Without criticism there is no forward movement. Electors'
mandates contain both criticisms of deficiencies and positive,
businesslike proposals, which help the soviets to fulfil the tasks
placed upon them' (Galesnik, 1957, pp. 186–7).

In practice, however, a number of problems have been
identified, and the way the mandates system operates sometimes
falls far short of the ideal. For instance, the demands contained
in *nakazy* are somewhat haphazard and narrow, reflecting the
interests of a relatively small group of electors (Binder, 1974,
p. 39); many mandates bear traces of 'subjectivism', and their
implications for the general need are not thought out (Sukhanov,
1969, p. 77); while election meetings are frequently so poorly
attended that the *nakazy* that issue from them cannot be
regarded as reflecting the will of the whole electorate in the constituency.

A particular difficulty arises in relating the mandates to the
economic plan. A certain proportion of mandates can be fulfilled
neither by the soviet into which they are fed by the newly elected
deputies, nor by higher soviets or ministries to which they are
passed on (see, e.g., Kotok, 1967, pp. 51–9; Sukhanov, 1969,
pp. 76–7). There are two distinct, although related, aspects to
the question: first, the planning timetable, and the need to bring
forward mandates at the appropriate stage for incorporation
into the plan; and, second, the question of resource allocation
for fulfilling mandates.

The question of the timetable was well elaborated by N. Ye.
Sukhanov, then secretary of the Chita oblast soviet executive
committee. Every year, whole teams of economists, planners,
engineers, etc. in the state administration put in tremendous
effort to produce a plan and budget (normally presented at the

December meeting of local soviets). Every second year, three or four months after confirmation of the budget, a host of new demands in the form of mandates (939 in Chita oblast in 1967, with a tendency to increase at each election) came in for consideration. Their political importance would demand they be given immediate attention, but that would involve the planners in re-calculating a plan already in operation – clearly, an inefficient use of their valuable time; so, often they were put off to the following year. The electors then grew sceptical, as not many could be fulfilled in the one year that remained before the next elections. In short, mandates had little practical effect on plan formulation (Sukhanov, 1969, p. 79).

The unsatisfactory nature of this situation has been commented on by other writers, including Bezuglov and Karabut, who discuss the second element in the problem: lack of resources. Some mandates can easily be incorporated into the present plan, but 'many proposals of the electors are given "over and above" an already adopted plan', which 'usually envisages the complete utilization of material and manpower resources' (in Tikhomirov and Sheremet, 1974, p. 99). Some 'extra' demands can be met by mobilizing volunteer reserves for, say, housing repairs, street-cleaning, maintaining public order; but some remain which require finance, materials, equipment or labour. These mandates are put off to a later year, or not accepted at all, which makes it difficult to keep track of their fulfilment: they may or may not be incorporated into the global figures of a subsequent plan. Moreover, some mandates are patently unrealistic, because the electors are unaware of the soviet's capacities and because there has been no informed discussion before their spontaneous presentation at a public election meeting (Tikhomirov and Sheremet, 1974, pp. 100–1). Even so, such unrealistic mandates are sometimes accepted, and the deputy later has the embarrassing task of explaining why they were not fulfilled (see, for example, Zrazyuk, 1975). Bezuglov and Karabut suggest a number of ways of solving the problem, including *raising the general level of debate* about public affairs, so that there is constant interaction between the 'stormy initiative of the electors' and the calm, scientific efficiency of economic planning – a task that could give a role to party organizations in the preparation of mandates (in Tikhomirov and Sheremet, 1974, p. 101); moreover, the presence of competent officials at election meetings, capable of explaining how plausible and realistic various demands are, can help the discussion of mandates (Starovoitov, 1975, p. 32).

Starovoitov argues that the whole preparation and nomination of mandates should be made less haphazard:

> Look what often happens: a meeting is in progress, and speakers put forward proposals to build a new school building, to open a departmental store in the village, to acquire allocations for equipping a House of Culture, to pave the streets etc. etc. Sometimes at a single meeting so many requests are made that two annual budgets of the whole district are not enough to satisfy the desires of the inhabitants of one village soviet. [Starovoitov, 1975, pp. 31–2]

Other writers have cited with approval a practice common before 1936: local party committees devised draft composite mandates for the corresponding soviet, which were then discussed and voted on at election meetings in the constituencies. Local proposals from the individual constituencies were also put forward at these meetings, voted on and, if approved, added to the composite mandate as supplements (Bezuglov, 1975, p. 89; also Kotok, 1967, pp. 49–51). Modern experiments along similar lines, carried out in the 1970s, have also been described (Tikhomirov and Sheremet, 1974, pp. 104–10; Starovoitov, 1975, pp. 35–6).

The change in the date of local elections, from March to June, facilitated the incorporation of mandates in the forthcoming plan (Leizerov, 1974a, p. 113; Starovoitov, 1975, p. 47). The possibility of such a change was raised as long ago as 1963, and elections to some soviets were switched to June three years later; this 'significantly relieved the problem of combining mandates with economic plans' (Starovoitov, 1975, p. 47). There still remained a six-month gap, however, between the acceptance of mandates and the confirmation of the subsequent plan at the end of the year, and Starovoitov proposed changing the planning and budgeting year, so that the adoption of plans would take place in July and August (p. 47). However, as frequently happens, events have overtaken scholarship. The 1977 Constitution (article 90) extended the term of office of local soviets to two and a half years, implying elections in June and December, on a thirty-month cycle: on the face of it, this can only complicate the problem of allowing for mandates in the annual plan.

Even if the planning timetable were re-jigged, other problems might remain. Much of the value of the mandates system, in the eyes of Safarov and others, is that it gives the Soviet population an opportunity to express its desires. Yet sometimes so-called mandates do not derive from the electors at all, but are 'imposed' by various officials. This is Kotok's comment on one such example:

> Here are revealed the crudest bureaucratic perversions of this form of direct democracy: if a large part of mandates were not discussed at citizens' meetings, but were the fruit of fantasy on the part of executive committee leaders, then these documents have nothing in common with electors' mandates. [Kotok, 1967, p. 101]

In the mid-1970s, however, Starovoitov reported that the same practice of lower officials sending 'lists of their own desires' was still common (Starovoitov, 1975, p. 33). Another practice, reported with disapproval, is to accept only those mandates for which provision has *already* been made in the current year's plan (Sheremet *et al.*, 1971, p. 97). The reason is perhaps not hard to discern: this provides an excellent way (indeed, perhaps the only way, given the short tenure of office of most deputies) of ensuring that deputies can report success to their constituents, thereby no doubt winning political support for themselves and the system!

This problem was one reason why Kotok added his weight to the calls for legislation at republican level to define what constitutes a mandate and to regulate their position in the political system (Kotok, 1967, p. 96); he called specifically (and was supported nearly a decade later by Strashun) for the new Constitution to establish this institution in the political system (Kotok, 1967, p. 94; Strashun, 1976, p. 48). Further support for a statute came from, among others, Sukhanov (1969, p. 79), who quoted Chkhikvadze's ideas on the content of such a statute. Since then there has been some progress. The 1972 statute on the deputies' status went some way in defining what constitutes a mandate, and in various parts of the country local laws have been introduced to regulate the system (Barabashev, 1975b, p. 101). By 1975 the move towards the legislative regula-tion of mandates reached the republican level: in April the Latvian supreme soviet presidium confirmed a local soviet mandates law, the first at republican level (Starovoitov, 1975, p. 110, n. 1). Two years later, the Constitution for the first time included a firm reference to the *nakaz* (article 102), and Brezhnev, in introducing the new fundamental law, reported that over 700,000 mandates had been fulfilled in the previous two years (Barabashev and Sheremet, 1978, pp. 37–8). All of this strongly suggests the development of a potentially significant part of the Soviet mechanism for interest-articulation, now seen as 'the most effective form of expression of the collective (group) interests and needs of the body of electors' (G. N. Manov, in Tikhomirov, 1978, p. 62).

The referendum

One of the ideas put forward by the twenty-second party con-gress in 1961 was that of a referendum. After suggesting that trade unions, the Komsomol and other mass organizations should be allowed the political initiative of proposing draft bills, the party programme adopted at the congress continued: 'Discussion by the people of draft laws and other decisions of both national and local significance must become the rule. The most important draft laws should be put to a nation-wide referendum' (1961 party programme, in Schapiro, 1963, p. 298; *KPSS v rez.*, vol. 8, p. 275).

Safarov saw the referendum as 'one of the important state–legal institutions, directly expressing the sovereignty of the

Soviet people' (Safarov, 1963, p. 15). Kotok examined the institution of a referendum in a monograph (1964). In informing his readers that the word came from the Latin *re fero*, meaning 'I report' or 'I announce' (p. 4), Kotok betrays the weakness of classical education in the Soviet Union, but his discussion of the proposed new institution is sound enough. A referendum he defined as 'the confirmation of one or another state decision by means of popular voting, which lends it a definitive and obligatory character'. Kotok stresses that in socialist society the referendum merely supplements other institutions for evoking the will and interests of the people (p. 8). In this, he disagrees with Safarov's more conventional concept which, according to Kotok, is little more than a revamped bourgeois referendum (see Safarov, 1963, p. 18; Kotok, 1964, p. 9, n. 11). For Kotok, the representative institutions themselves already consist through and through of 'the people', whose will and interests they really do express: a referendum simply extends this and involves the whole population directly in law-making (Kotok, 1964, p. 11). He calls for a 'Statute on the All-Union Referendum', which would define the kind of legislative acts to be submitted to the voters; on whose initiative a referendum would be held; which draft bills would be subject to wide public discussion; and how the voting would be organized. Similar laws would provide for republican referendums; and another statute could permit local referendums and public meetings (p. 125).

Among questions that might be submitted to a referendum, Kotok suggested the new Constitution, and major constitutional changes (Kotok left open the matter of who should decide what was a *major* change), or questions on which the two chambers of the Supreme Soviet were in disagreement – clearly issues on for universal approbation after their acceptance by the Supreme Soviet (Baitin, 1965, p. 158). Other writers who have commented made for a positive endorsement or rejection (for example, by answering 'Yes' or 'No' to a stated question), and a valid poll must involve a 75 per cent turnout, and a two-thirds majority for or against the proposal (p. 178). Kotok concluded by restating his view that the referendum had an important supplementary role to play, but the representative institutions would remain 'the basic form of the embodiment of the sovereignty and supremacy of the people' (p. 186).

These proposals were favourably received by M. I. Baitin, who, in a review of Kotok's book, envisaged pieces of fundamental legislation (such as the five-year plans) being submitted for universal approbation after their acceptance by the Supreme Soviet (Baitin, 1965, p. 158). Other writers who have commented on the idea include B. M. Gorshenev (in Kerimov, 1965, p. 92) and Shakhnazarov (1972, p. 111).

Nemtsev suggested that a referendum would be appropriate in cases of administrative reorganization. In a reference to some of Khrushchev's 'hare-brained schemes', he urged that before making changes in the administrative structure, a thorough study is required of, among other matters, public opinion: this would prevent a repetition of the hasty and ill thought-out changes of 1962–3, a point echoed by Safarov (Nemtsev, 1967, p. 231; Safarov, 1967, p. 49). Among the means for eliciting that opinion are village meetings, questionnaire surveys, and referendums (Nemtsev, 1967, pp. 236–7).

The point is stressed that soundings of public opinion must take *negative* responses into account (Safarov, 1967, p. 46), and that the public must, through widespread prior discussion, be fully informed of the issues involved (Safarov, 1967, p. 48; Nemtsev, 1967, pp. 236–7). In a similar vein Shakhnazarov, writing of future forms of direct and indirect democracy, stresses that a proper referendum would require 'gigantic and in the highest degree scrupulous work', taking into account the correct formulation of the problem, objective explanations of the probable consequences of various alternative decisions, 'and, of course, the strict adherence to the rules of the referendum, the generalization of the data and the presentation of the results' (Shakhnazarov, 1972, pp. 111–12). Moreover, Safarov – the most enthusiastic Soviet student of public opinion – perhaps with a long-term view towards his projected Institute of Public Opinion (see Safarov, 1975b, p. 92, n. 1), and doubtless feeling a need to create work for it (and himself), argues that 'the logic of democracy demands that, irrespective of the subject of a survey, public opinion be elicited *before and after* the adoption of important political and state decisions' (Safarov, 1967, p. 50; emphasis added). Topornin too sees popular involvement in government as an essential ingredient of pure socialism, and urges that 'the experience and knowledge of the workers be fully taken into account when introducing new institutions or transforming old ones' (in Tikhomirov, 1975, p. 82), while N. P. Farberov stressed the need for maximum freedom of criticism and businesslike discussion if optimal results are to ensue from nationwide debate and referendum (in Tikhomirov, 1975, p. 55).

In the 1960s, therefore, there was a quite enthusiastic response to the party's suggestion at the beginning of the decade; this has continued into the 1970s, and Kotok's and Farberov's views on the referendum were favourably remarked upon by the dissident historian Roy Medvedev (1975, p. 147). In 1964 Kotok asserted his belief that the referendum, 'enriched with new features, which are characteristic of the real democratism of socialist society', would occupy 'a conspicuous position' in the promised new Constitution (Kotok, 1964, p. 4). The Constitution was long delayed, but when finally promulgated, in 1977, the referendum was incorporated in article 5. Whether Kotok considered this to be a suitably 'conspicuous' position for this institution we shall never know: in the meantime he had died.

Direct communication

Apart from the mandate and the referendum, attention has also been paid to less formal contacts between citizens and the political machinery. These can be of two kinds: indirect, through public organizations; and direct, in the form of letters, suggestions and proposals addressed to officials and politicians. This area of political activity has been given significant encouragement by politicians themselves, at the highest level.

There are several types of non-state, non-party organizations in the Soviet Union, ranging from the clearly political, such as trade unions and the Komsomol, through professional bodies, such as the Writers' Union and the Composers' Union, to general, interest-directed societies, such as sports associations, the Society for the Protection of Cultural and Historical Monuments and the Society for Friendship with Foreign Countries (with divisions for friendship with specific countries). The first of these groups (unions and Komsomol) are closely involved with party and state, and have a well established role to play in industrial management, in the provision of leisure facilities, and in instilling the appropriate ideological views in young people and workers (Keizerov *et al.*, 1974, p. 73; Chekharin, 1977, pp. 51–8). The sports, cultural and other associations have a part to play in building communism through helping to form the 'rounded, developed communist man', and giving citizens the experience and habits that come from involvement in social organization (Chekharin, 1977, p. 66): in other words, they are involved in developing the political culture. The role of the professional associations in fostering creative artists is overshadowed in most Western eyes by their role in monitoring the ideological soundness of their members, which is too well known to require further elaboration. This role in supporting the aims of the regime is further emphasized by the consideration, to which virtually all Soviet writers refer, that they function under party leadership.

However, such organizations can also be of immense help to the party as articulators of specific interests (see Friedgut, 1978, p. 475). Over a decade ago, before the concept of 'interest' had become generally accepted by Soviet social scientists, Safarov saw the expression of interests as one of the functions of such organizations (Safarov, 1967, p. 51). More recently, the same author declared that

> The participation of the popular masses in government through the system of public organizations . . . is called upon to reinforce the position of public opinion and create scope for its democratic influence on the organs of government.

After citing a book published in St Petersburg in 1903

(G. Yellinek's *Obshchee uchenie o gosudarstve* – General Teaching on the State), Safarov concludes:

> And if public opinion is not in a position to influence, or if this influence is restricted only to the circle of secondary questions, then one must seek the reasons for this phenomenon in the weakness of the public organizations themselves. [Safarov, 1975b, p. 67]

There may be more than a grain of truth in this argument: weak and ineffectual leadership may be a reflection of a relatively low priority given to these organizations by the party, which deploys its most authoritative members in other, perhaps more significant, positions. If the party wishes to strengthen these institutions it will tend to allocate higher-calibre members to leading positions in them. But it is also true that political leaders, particularly at the local level, have frequently adopted a cavalier attitude and misused their powers, thereby infringing the rights of citizens (Tikhomirov, 1975, p. 183).

Nevertheless, for Safarov and others, there are significant prospects for developing this channel for indirectly feeding interests into the political system.

Turning to the direct articulation of interests, among the various means of expressing opinion listed by Safarov were included addressing suggestions to state organs, and turning to them with complaints. This notion has become an accepted part of the Soviet analysis of interest articulation. V. G. Afanas'ev has written of direct communication as an 'important source of direct and reliable information' (Afanas'ev, 1975, p. 99). Safarov also argued that, in fully taking public opinion into account, 'the organs of state raise their social prestige and strengthen the faith of the workers in their decisions and actions' (Safarov, 1975a, p. 20), implying, perhaps, that one reason for the lack of public confidence in the state apparatus is that it has traditionally not responded to popular demands. (This confirms Shabanov's revelation of a low sense of political efficacy among the population: see Shabanov, 1969b, p. 164; and Hill, 1976a, p. 488, n. 24.)

The value of such direct communications was stressed in 1964 by the then head of the legal department of the Azerbaidzhan supreme soviet presidium. Writing at a time when everyday services scarcely existed, he was trying to give a favourable impression of what had been done by the republican government in the previous two years. His account sounds primitive, even pathetic, by the standards of the late 1970s, but he made the point that letters, complaints and other submissions from citizens to the organs of state were a means of bringing their requirements and everyday needs to the attention of the local soviets (Rasulbekov, 1964, p. 119).

Other writers have extended this analysis from the soviets to the party apparatus. In discussing free speech, Shabanov declares that:

> the communist party and the soviet government constantly listen to the voice of the masses, and study in detail all proposals, observations, letters, statements and complaints of the workers, considering them to be a most important means of expressing public opinion and a rich source of information about life in the country. [Shabanov, 1969b, p. 264]

Looking at various methods of party supervision over administration, he says that letters, newspaper articles and so forth are carefully studied by party organs (1969b, p. 46).

The impact of new technology has also been given some attention, generally with enthusiasm. Tikhomirov, for example, mentions the possible establishment of information banks, and the use of electronic means of sounding out and analysing public opinion, as a way of democratizing planning and government (Tikhomirov, 1975, pp. 256–63). He explicitly rejects the fears of 'bourgeois' social scientists that modern technology might undermine privacy and the status of the individual, since 'such a direction in the use of the computer is incompatible with the aims and principles of socialist democracy and the legal position of Soviet citizens' (p. 260). Quite: but 'infringements of socialist legality' (the stock Soviet euphemism for Stalin's disregard for the law and citizens' rights) have not been entirely unknown within Tikhomirov's own lifetime. Nevertheless, this view is

interesting for the light it sheds on Soviet approaches to the
advent of sophisticated and powerful technology.

In this area, the party and government have been extremely
diligent in issuing statements and legislation, and the Soviet
press has been prolific in its articles, usually under the slogan
'Behind the letter there is a person' – a warning and reminder to
insensitive bureaucrats, and a phrase that has been accepted into
the vocabulary of social science. Afanas'ev, for instance, repeats
it, adding: 'and therefore attention to letters is attention to a
person, which is one of the characteristic features of our socialist
system'. As a rule, each letter contains one point, but by taking
them *en masse* general tendencies can be deduced, 'which is very
important, indeed necessary, in government' (Afanas'ev, 1975,
p. 101). An interesting account of *Pravda*'s postbag follows. In
1973, 425,510 letters were received; 24 pages of them were
published, in fortnightly batches. In comparison with 1972, the
number of critical letters declined: 124 compendiums of such
letters were dispatched to party, soviet and ministerial offices
for action, of which 16 dealt with services and trade, 7 with
housing questions, 10 with economic waste, and 4 with
deficiencies in the work of party and soviet organs; finally in the
same year, 12,655 visits were made to the offices of *Pravda*
(Afanas'ev, 1975, pp. 101–2).

Party officials too have welcomed the trend towards an
increase in such submissions, which are seen as 'one of the
manifestations of the party's link with the masses' and 'an
important form of the expression of public opinion, an
inexhaustible source of information on the state of affairs in
different branches of production and public life' (*Sovetskaya
Moldaviya*, 16 February 1972; 22 July 1972). The point was
further stressed by Leonid Brezhnev at the twenty-fifth party
congress: he referred to such letters as 'one of the important
points of linkage [between] our party and its central committee
and the masses'. He told delegates that the number of such
letters was increasing, and assured them that the central committee 'systematically informs itself about everything deserving
attention in workers' letters. The most important proposals and

opinions', he added, 'are reviewed by the politburo and the central committee secretariat, and are taken into account in working out edicts and statutes' (*XXV s"ezd*, vol. I, p. 92). As *Pravda* noted in June 1975, 'letters are still not everywhere dealt with attentively' (*Pravda*, 5 June 1975, p. 1), but the fact that top party leaders now make a point of encouraging the submission of letters and complaints implies that they see value in receiving these indicators of public needs, demands and opinion. Soviet political scientists, who have been urging this for many years now, may perhaps take some credit for this positive development, because there may be an implication that the party now accepts that it does not always know what is best for people – it needs guidance from the people themselves.

THE COMPETENCE OF PUBLIC OPINION

If the public is to play a greater role in the political life of the country (as the official line says it must), then steps will have to be taken to ensure that it can make an *informed* contribution. After all, particularly with the increasing pace of technological change, the process of running a society smoothly, and guiding it in an appropriate direction, becomes ever more complex, and influence if not power can slip into the hands of those with the technical competence and skills needed in running that society. If the masses are to participate fully, and hold political power, they need to understand the process of government, and have access to much of the information on which the technocrats base their decisions. People need, in other words, to be taught the art of government (Chkhikvadze, 1968; Tikhomirov, 1978, p. 57).

One writer to discuss this question at some length (in one of the most stimulating books of Soviet political science) is Shakhnazarov, who comments that 'it is impossible to take part in deciding matters of state without having a clear idea of the structure of the state mechanism, the contents of the Constitution and the basic branches of law, and without knowing the rudiments of the contemporary science of government' (Shakhnazarov, 1972, p. 132). In other words, there is a need for a highly developed *political culture*, a concept that has been used by other writers (see Brown and Gray, 1977, p. 58, n. 1). Thus, Farberov has written that 'the higher the political consciousness of the masses, and their culture, the more successfully does democracy develop. . . .' (in Tikhomirov, 1975, p. 38). In the same book, Topornin develops the theme of public opinion and its growing importance, pointing out that today's public is better educated and is also much more experienced in the skills of participation in political life (p. 86).

Shakhnazarov, however, has the most clearly called for freedom of information. Arguing that 'knowledge of the facts' is the initial condition both for successful government and for the realization of democratic principles, he proposes the regular publication of statistical and other factual information on demographic trends, economic matters, culture, sociological surveys and so forth, and gives his judgement that 'There can be no doubt that all information of that type must be accessible to the broad masses of the workers – this, in point of fact, is the precondition for active participation by citizens in political life' (Shakhnazarov, 1972, p. 137). Shakhnazarov distinguishes also a second type of information: that generated in the course of specific investigations initiated by the state apparatus, some of which will obviously relate to security and defence matters, and about which secrecy will have to be maintained. Apart from this fairly narrow category, however, 'all other information of this type should be accessible to the representative organs and public organizations of the workers' (p. 137). Not only that: the author proposes a special law, stipulating 'by whom and according to what rules governmental information may be obtained, how the appropriate demand [for it] should be formulated and so on' (p. 138). These ideas find the strong support of Safarov (1975b, p. 126, n. 2), who has also called for press freedom to criticize state officials, as a 'preventive, precautionary' measure, in not only informing the public about cases of maladministration, but also thereby making repetition less likely (p. 203).

Shakhnazarov is at his most striking, however, when he discusses the whole philosophical justification of restricting freedom in the Soviet Union, and goes on to attack the traditional, 'inverted' Soviet view. This went as follows: the socialist state suppresses subversive actions; in doing so, it defends the wellbeing of the whole people; that represents a *strengthening* of freedom in society as a whole, rather than a restriction on freedom. Shakhnazarov's comment is simple: 'For all the obvious logicality of such a judgement, it is essentially untrue.' He explains why:

> When the state imposes specific restrictions and deprives a person of the possibility of acting or not acting according to his own judgement in this or that question, then, no matter in whose interests that restriction might be (in the interests of a minority, the majority, the whole society, including that person himself, who does not understand his real interests), the restriction of freedom remains a fact. It cannot be screened by arguments about the good of society, etc. [Shakhnazarov, 1972, pp. 182–3]

This remarkably liberal statement appeared, surprisingly, not in a dissident, *samizdat*, tract, but in a book published in 17,000 copies and aimed at 'specialists and a wide circle of readers'. Elsewhere (pp. 72–4) Shakhnazarov interestingly challenges the view that monolithic public opinion is desirable, in particular the identity of views between different generations. In arguing in favour of the 'generation gap', the author points out that each generation must find its own answers to the 'eternal questions', and build on the experience of previous generations; otherwise society stagnates.

The attitude behind such writings is obviously far removed from that which has pervaded the Soviet political system for two generations, leading to strict censorship and the withholding of all kinds of information that by no stretch of the imagination could be construed as affecting national security, and that citizens in other types of political system take for granted. There is no doubt that the Soviet public is capable of absorbing the full range of information, and developing an informed and mature political culture. The level of communications technology in the USSR is now such that this could be easily attained. All that is needed is the political will (Shakhnazarov, 1972, p. 137).

But the political will is so far lacking, and only the communist party has the capacity to authorize such a development. The role of the party concerns us in the next chapter.

CHAPTER 6

The Party's Role

The acknowledgement of the legitimacy of specific interests, while at the same time continuing to assert the universality of broad, basic interests – identified as the building of a communist society – is not without its implications for the role and functioning of the communist party in the system (Lewin, 1975, p. 268). Soviet writers have in the past decade paid a significant amount of attention to the party's position, stimulated, I believe, by two circumstances. First, there were the dramatic events in Czechoslovakia in early 1968 when the communist party (as viewed from Moscow) seemed willing to relinquish its monopoly of power-holding, to 'remove the party from leadership' (Kadeikin *et al.*, 1974, p. 9), and to substitute merely as strong a political *influence* as it could achieve. Hence, some of the bitterest Soviet attacks on the Czechoslovak reformers of 1968 related precisely to the question of party leadership. 'The leading role of the communist party', wrote the deputy chief editor of the party journal *Kommunist*, 'is the decisive condition for fulfilling the tasks of the state of the dictatorship of the proletariat and the all-people's state, [and] the guarantee of the victorious construction of socialism and communism'. One of the lessons learnt from 'recent events' (i.e. the 'Prague spring') was that the leading role must be reserved for the communist party when – with an eye trained on Czechoslovakia, and doubtless a glance at Poland, East Germany and elsewhere – there are other political parties in the system (Platkovskii, 1970). For Shakhnazarov (1972, pp. 76–7) the party's leading role in building socialism and communism is a 'general principle', denial of which is tantamount to denying the need for political leadership in general, leading to anarchy and chaos, and seriously threatening the gains of the socialist revolution.

Such a response to Czechoslovakia 1968 was common in Soviet political literature in the early 1970s, and the reaffirmation of the party's central position has been a dominant theme in subsequent writings on the political system of socialism.

The second circumstance that has prompted this development is the promulgation of the concept of 'developed' or 'mature' socialism (*razvitoi sotsializm*; *zrelyi sotsializm*). The two terms are used interchangeably (Babii *et al.*, 1976, p. 9, n. 3), and the concept, which made its appearance in the late 1960s, has now been consolidated in the vocabulary of Soviet writers on politics (Evans, 1977). A great deal of analysis and elaboration of this concept has appeared in the work of Soviet social scientists. One of the areas for analysis is the communist party's role in the system, and its relationship with the formal institutions of state power, and with other organizations in society.

Obviously, the publication of books on the party is not new. What *is* novel is the *manner* of writing about the party, especially the inclusion of the party as a central part of the 'political system'. Formerly a virtually outlawed subject for political scientists and constitutional lawyers, the party and its relationship with the soviets, with other branches of the state apparatus and with non-state institutions has now been accepted as a legitimate topic for investigation, analysis and comment, within certain bounds; the party's own writers, too, have become much more open in the questions they discuss. Shakhnazarov criticizes 'people within the present-day communist movement' – specifically the Chinese leaders, but he may also have in mind persons closer to home – 'for whom the very attempt to discuss the question of relations between party and state borders on sacrilege . . . . Being blind adherents of dogma, they recognize only that order of things where party organizations from bottom to top simply order about the representative organs of state, and even more its executive apparatus,' (Shakhnazarov, 1972, p. 77).

It is symptomatic of the change in Soviet writers' willingness to discuss the position of the party – and, presumably, the party-controlled censorship's willingness to let it be published – that serious books on Soviet government and society nowadays tend to devote at least a section to this question; this is quite apart from books devoted exclusively to the party and its role.

This academic development has accompanied a more open presentation of the party's position in the official literature, including the speeches of politicians, and symbolized most eloquently by the more explicit references to the CPSU in the 1977 Constitution, the direct mention of 'the party of Lenin' in the revised (1977) words of the national anthem, and the assumption by Brezhnev (CPSU secretary-general) on 16 June 1977 of the position of chairman of the Supreme Soviet presidium (see *Pravda*, 12 and 17 June and 8 October 1977).

This development implies a recognition that the previous conceptual framework was inadequate as a tool for analysing Soviet political life. *Pravda* made the point in its discussion of the response to Burlatskii's article of January 1965 that 'political system' is a broader concept than 'state', and the party's role was specifically mentioned as an area in which Soviet political science was deficient. In 1968 and 1970, in the journal *Voprosy istorii KPSS* (Questions of CPSU History), a whole series of articles discussed this question, and it is noteworthy that several contributors to the debate referred to the study of the party structure as a 'discipline', a 'subject', a 'science' (S. A. Smirnov, 1969, p. 67; Yelistratov, 1969, p. 73; Kushnikov and Sopelko, 1971, p. 71).

The study of the party thus appears to have attained a measure of autonomy within 'political science', and its importance and significance has been repeatedly asserted. A speaker at a conference in western Siberia in 1972 was particularly emphatic. After stating that the significance of scientifically based critical analysis and proof (*dokazatel'nost'*) is growing, and urging (albeit indirectly) 'a deep and objective analysis of the real processes of social life', V. G. Istomin declared that 'For historians of the party, that means it is necessary to raise the *quality* of scientific research' (original emphasis). He particularly urged greater conceptual clarity, precision and systematization (Istomin, 1973, pp. 119–20).

Finally, the change in terminology in the new Constitution,

substituting 'political system' for 'state structure', is a conceptual modification that seems to permit the party to be given its proper place in the formal description of the political apparatus. By the same token, this presumably means that the party is accepted as a legitimate object for study by students of the political system.

Clearly, this area of political life has been considerably opened up following the attainment of 'mature socialism'. As V. Ye. Guliev and A. I. Shchiglik put it in 1975:

> the traditional examination of the system of socialist democracy, through the prism of the state and public organizations alone, unjustifiedly narrows its institutional content, and *ipso facto* to a certain degree impoverishes its content . . . [The] general system of socialist democracy . . . includes the party, the state, the mass public organizations and movements, organs of voluntary public activity, and work collectives. [Guliev and Shchiglik, 1975, p. 12]

This obviously reflects a much richer conception of what is 'political'. Their work is part of a virtual flood of studies on the topic of party relations with other institutions, particularly the state. The work of Soviet writers on the party, excluding the output of directly propagandist writers, can be divided into three broad types:

1 analyses of the party's role in the political system of developed socialism, as part of the general elaboration of the concept;
2 more narrowly focused, more detailed analysis of the party's relationship with the state apparatus, including both the soviets and their executive organs; to some extent this pre-dated the general analysis;
3 the development of techniques for measuring the party's performance and general intra-party monitoring, together with proposals for internal development and democratization.

The question of party–state relations will be discussed below; the next chapter is devoted to intra-party democratization.

PARTY AND STATE

The relationship between the party and the Soviet state (the soviets, ministries, executive committees and so on) has been identified by Western and Soviet writers alike as one of the most complicated problems of Soviet political life (Schapiro, 1961, p. 111; Shakhnazarov, 1972, p. 76). Soviet scholars have pointed out that this question has long fascinated Western students of Soviet politics (e.g., Babii *et al.*, 1976, chapter 16; Shapko *et al.*, 1977, chapter 9). Moreover, they have frequently expressed themselves in somewhat intemperate language: 'the apostles of anti-communism pounce with particular fury on the position of the party in the republic of soviets, making it object number one for their slanderous fabrications, their verbal subversions of the foundations of socialist society' (Barabashev and Sheremet, 1967, p. 31).

One reason for this, *not* recorded by Soviet writers, is the custom, until very recently, of ignoring the party's role when analysing the functioning of the state – coupled with infuriating statements to the effect that 'Not a single important political or organizational question is decided by a single state institution in our republic without the guiding directions of the party central committee' (Lenin, quoted in Naida *et al.*, 1967, p. 10, and elsewhere). This is a very neat formula, but it tells us next to nothing about the mechanics of the relationship: *how* the party 'leads and guides' the work of the state institutions and other organizations, and in particular how it achieves this without 'supplanting' them.

This official reticence and obfuscation obviously did nothing to clarify the position, so Western students of Soviet affairs (and Soviet citizens, for that matter) may be forgiven for seeing the state apparatus as largely a façade (Armstrong, 1973, p. 157). In fact, the relationship is hard to disentangle. N. Veselov's assertion – written with a Western readership in mind – that 'The political organisation of socialist society in the USSR is . . . distinguished by the clarity and unambiguousness of relations between the Communist Party, on the one hand, and the state together with the mass organisations of working people, on the other' (Veselov, 1973, pp. 5–6) may reflect the penetrating clarity of his own thinking: but much in the writings of Soviet scholars indicates that they believe the position to be substantially less clear.

It was in the mid-1960s that Soviet writers began to discuss the party's relationship with the state a little more explicitly than hitherto. The party's role and its forms and methods of operation were identified as a legitimate object of study by Lepëshkin in his survey of the state of Soviet political science (1965a, pp. 10–11). The problem of *podmena* (discussed below), leading to a blurring between party and state institutions, functions and roles, was blamed on a failure in many cases to fulfil Lenin's teachings on 'the inadmissibility of mixing the functions of party organs with the functions of the soviets'. There was, therefore, a need to review party–state relations, and Lepëshkin also criticized the specific practice, common under Khrushchev, of issuing joint party–soviet statements relating to matters solely within the legal competence of the soviets, their executive committees or officers. Political scientists, he suggested, should work out scientifically sound recommendations on 'the optimal forms and methods of party leadership, which provide for effective influence by party organs on the life and activity of the soviets'. This was 'the urgent and honourable task of Soviet political scientists and students of administration' (p. 11).

The first significant breach of the wall of discretion on this topic came in an article by Barabashev and Sheremet (1967), entitled simply 'The CPSU and the Soviets', and regarded by some Soviet scholars today as a seminal work (even though the substance of their analysis had already appeared in the first edition of their textbook: 1965a, chapter 3). The authors explicitly identified the relationship between party and soviets as 'the key to understanding the mechanism of popular power' (1967, p. 31), and they introduced a number of concepts, and employed fresh approaches to the question of party–state relations that have subsequently become standard in Soviet discussions of the topic. They attempted, as it were, to delineate the roles of the two sets of institutions, thereby clarifying their places in the political system, and perhaps indicating ways in which long-standing problems might be solved, in particular podmena. This word, literally 'substitution' or 'supplantation', refers to a tendency, on the part of officials and committees of the communist party, to usurp the functions of state bodies, in particular the soviets. It is euphemistically referred to as one of the 'deficiencies' in the way the party plays its role.

Ukrainets (1976) gives a number of reasons, which she calls subjective and objective, for the tenacity of this phenomenon. 'Subjective' reasons refer to the fact that the party and state officials do not understand the appropriate functions of their respective institutions. 'Objective' reasons are the structural imperfections in the state and economy, that oblige the party to take on matters not proper to it; the shifting boundaries between what is considered political and what is economic; and finally, 'the inadequate elaboration of a single, scientifically based approach to marking out the functional obligations of each worker in the party and state apparatuses within their structural subdivisions' (p. 73). M. P. Lebedev places most of the blame on the shoulders of state and economic officials for their lack of responsibility and initiative, but nevertheless concedes that 'it is sometimes connected with distortions in the work of local party organs' (Lebedev, 1970, p. 10).

While there is some substance in these explanations, other factors have probably been equally influential in sustaining this problem: the complexities of governing a huge, diverse and rapidly developing country, with limited degrees of managerial expertise; the fact that, in the party hierarchy, the first secretary at any level has traditionally had superiority over all others in his territory; the overlapping membership between state and party organs, with negative aspects noted by Ukrainets (1976, p. 80); the existence of sometimes severe penalties for incompetence, or indeed for any action that might be construed as 'anti-party'; the custom of drawing leadership in all spheres into and from a single, unified pool (see Hill, 1977, pp. 165–8) — given all this, it is not surprising that overlapping and duplication, not to mention downright interference, should have arisen and become a widespread problem. That is without even considering the possibility that the system was explicitly designed to function in this way (see Fainsod, 1958, p. 93).

Be that as it may, the *effects* of podmena are clear. As explained by P. M. Masherov, first secretary in Belorussia, the party organs burden themselves with business that they are not equipped to deal with, and state organs become dependent on the party organs, passing 'difficult' questions to them to decide, thereby avoiding responsibility (quoted in Ukrainets, 1976, p. 72). These points are further elaborated by Shakhnazarov. Podmena means that the representative institutions are not used to their full potential, and also that the public develops a sceptical attitude towards them. Furthermore, 'such a state of affairs gives rise to a certain disregard for socialist legality on the part of both officials and citizens'. Even when the party's administrative decisions are correct, he argues, they are nevertheless unconstitutional; he adds that the party has plenty of opportunities for acting within constitutional procedures. Finally, as the party takes on such duties, it tends to modify its own structures in order to cope, leading to 'parallelism' between the two institutional structures, and diverting the efforts of the party from its main tasks of training leaders, educating the masses, analysing social processes, and taking political decisions. 'As a result, the leading role of the party not only is not strengthened, but on the contrary, is weakened' (Shakhnazarov, 1972, pp. 80–2).

This is regarded as a serious weakness in the system's functioning. Leonid Brezhnev may assure French television viewers that it does not happen (*Pravda*, 6 October 1976); yet party congresses have *repeatedly* issued firm statements against petty supervision over the work of the state, and attempts by party organs to restrict the initiative of state and other bodies (Petrovichev *et al.*, 1972, p. 434). The constant repetition shows how persistent the problem is, and its very persistence bears further witness to its intractability. As Shakhnazarov notes, somewhat delicately: 'a certain period of time is necessary for old habits in this field to be overcome, and for political directions about the correct relationship between party and state organs to be fully established' (Shakhnazarov, 1972, p. 102). Yet its solution is seen as vital, for the sake of both party and state (Ukrainets, 1976, p. 73). How can the problem be solved?

First, the placement of a better trained, more sophisticated type of local official is expected to help (Ukrainets, 1976, p. 73). Indeed, the tendency under Khrushchev to give technical training to party officials was in part aimed at reducing the tension between them and the state officials (Schapiro, 1961, p. 112). Soviet scholars have stressed two particular lines in approaching the problem: to devise an appropriate line of *demarcation* between the functions of party and state institutions and officials; and to stress that the nature of party leadership is *political*. These two points are not entirely separate; nor, so far, have the issues been successfully and conclusively expounded.

'The system of government is capable of working harmoniously and efficiently', writes Ukrainets (1976, pp. 62–3), 'when the functions of each of its links and of each worker are concretely and clearly defined, when realistically attainable goals are precisely set, and when personnel have sufficient professional qualifications and a high political consciousness.' For V. M. Lesnyi, 'the question of delineating functions is one of the most important' (Lesnyi and Chernogolovkin, 1967, p. 53). This is, indeed, a widely expressed prescription, no doubt reflecting the Soviet vogue for functionalist analysis. While different writers draw up different lists of functions, the overall intention is to allocate *policy-making, leadership and general supervision* to the party, with the functions of *legislation and policy application*, and to some extent *information-gathering*, being assigned to the state, with a secondary role to the so-called 'public organizations'.

Soviet writers nowadays are emphatic that the party has no legislative power. On the basis of Marxism–Leninism, it devises a *political line*, enshrined in the *party programme*, which is in turn 'the initial theoretical basis for action, a kind of *ideological constitution* for the country' (Shakhnazarov, 1972, p. 86; original italics). Using this document (the current programme

was adopted in 1961), party organs issue more specific policy
directives, which are presented as authoritative recommendations for review by the higher state bodies; only after their
approval do they acquire legal force (Shakhnazarov, 1972,
p. 68). Soviet authors stress that such party directives are *not*
orders, that the party does not operate on the basis of 'ordering
about' the state institutions: indeed, 'from the formal and legal
point of view, following the programme, as a party document, is
obligatory only for communists' – although Shakhnazarov
hastily adds that the party's authority commends it for adoption
by all workers and organs of state (p. 86). Shabanov, too,
stresses that the party does not make *laws*: it adopts resolutions,
issues statements, makes decisions, which are then turned into
legal acts by the soviets (Shabanov, 1969b, p. 37); this form of
indirect rule is necessary because 'in Lenin's graphic expression',
communists are 'a drop in the ocean', and even today's multi-
million-strong party cannot decide all questions on its own
(p. 22).

The state apparatus, therefore, gives legal force to the policy
recommendations of the party. How then does the party make
sure that its recommendations are given this endorsement? The
answer given by most writers today is through *persuasion*.

Moshe Lewin, in discussing Shkredov's *Ekonomika i pravo*
(Economics and Law, published 1967), sees that author's
discussion of this question as a tactfully expressed reminder of a
party promise, first made in 1919, that it must act within the
framework of the Constitution and of Soviet legal principles. For
Lewin, this was essentially a 'demand that the party become a
political institution within the framework of the Soviet constitution', and return 'real sovereignty' to the Supreme Soviet, the
modern constitutional equivalent of the Congress of Soviets,
which endorsed the revolution (see Lewin, 1975, p. 243).
Furthermore, the party should act within the prescriptions of its
own statutes; in other words, it must 'stop meddling with the
economy, end its rule of the state administration, and concentrate on formulating general political principles for
reconciliation, coordination, and political leadership' (p. 243).
Lewin's interpretation would certainly not be acknowledged

as accurate in the official Soviet press. However, Shkredov's call was echoed by other writers, more directly concerned with studying the political system. Barabashev and Sheremet, for instance, writing at about the same time, asserted that the party's relationship to any aspect of the work of the soviets bore 'a political character', adding that 'the political leadership of the CPSU is built exclusively on methods of persuasion' (Barabashev and Sheremet, 1967, p. 34). In actual fact, in many (too many) cases, this was not so: but, as so often when the present tense is used in Russian, the sense is one of expressing what ought to be, rather than what is. Developing the theme of 'persuasion', Shabanov claims that the party has never dictated terms to the soviets (Shabanov, 1969b, p. 34), a point also stressed by Paskar', who emphasizes that party leadership is political in character, rather than administrative (Paskar', 1974, p. 79).

The relationship between party and state is political, therefore, and in at least two senses: it relates to *policy*; and it involves relations of *authority*. Policy is the nexus that links the higher party organs with the local soviets and their administrative bodies, through the local party committees and the intermediate soviets and the state apparatus. The functional distinctions between party and state lie, according to Soviet writers, in the different forms of *authority* wielded by the two institutions. The party, with all the authority conferred by the *ideology*, defines the parameters of policy for building communism; that policy is then made law by the state, with the legal authority vested in the soviets by the Constitution. It is up to the party to *persuade* the state bodies to adopt and implement its policies; Soviet writers commonly enumerate the points of contact between party and state institutions, whereby the party can exercise the appropriate pressure. The principal method is through the careful disposition of party members throughout the state apparatus. It is the duty of communist deputies to be the active organizers in carrying out party and state decisions, to carry the non-party deputies with them, and to mobilize the masses; and the role of the party group (involving all communist deputies) is one of explanation, and of persuading its own members and the non-party deputies of the importance and necessity for a particular decision (Ukrainets, 1967, pp 76–7). Only when, following such persuasion, the deputies as a body have formally agreed to a proposition does policy have legal force, and is implemented by the state apparatus, under the supervision of the party; and it is the state (rather than the party) that has the authority to use coercion in the application of policy.

Such is now the accepted view, and is implied in Glezerman's analysis of coercion in the political process: coercion, he asserts, is not one of the party's functions: after all, 'when we are speaking of millions of people, only on the basis of convincing them is it possible to organize them properly' (in Kadeikin *et al.*, 1974, pp. 75, 77). Or, as Ukrainets puts it, quoting another writer, the cPSU *leads* but does not *govern*; still less does it give orders (Ukrainets, 1976, p. 63). Similarly, Lebedev asserts that the party performs its role best when 'it uses not so much the authority of power as the power of authority' (Lebedev, 1970, p. 12).

However, all is not so simple. In many situations no fine distinctions can be drawn, particularly at local level (Ukrainets, 1976, p. 69), and achieving and maintaining the division of functions is more easily said than done (p. 125): moreover, for all party members (including those who are deputies) 'party decisions have the force of law' (p. 65). Shabanov, in a passage distinguished by its frankness, indicates the real nature of the relationship between party and soviets:

> In so far as our communist party is [a] ruling [party], usually the adoption of state-legal acts, involving matters of principle, ... as it were issue from the party organs. The party organs either themselves directly prepare the corresponding draft bills, or appear in the role of directing and controlling organs, which review these drafts in advance from the position of organs of political and organizational leadership. [Shabanov, 1969b, pp. 37–8]

This is comparable with Paskar''s remarkable assertion a few lines further on from his emphatic statement that party leadership is political, rather than administrative: '[This] does not mean, however, that party decisions bear a purely recommendatory character. All decisions of the communist party on the most important questions of public life are obligatory for all state organs, including the soviets' (Paskar', 1974, p. 79). As chairman of the Moldavian council of ministers, Paskar' was well placed to write with authority on this subject! Shabanov swiftly adds that this practice does not contradict democracy, which he defines as a form of class rule (Shabanov, 1969, p. 5; compare Tikhomirov, 1975, pp. 5–14); however, he concedes that it does sometimes reduce the party's role to one of 'petty tutelage' – a problem that is closely akin to podmena (Shabanov, 1969b, p. 38).

Shakhnazarov too, in perhaps the most thoughtful account of these problems, identifies current policy as essentially the province of the state, consisting of (1) formulating specific decisions in accordance with the directions of the political line, and (2) applying these decisions. However, he reserves certain policy areas for direct party decision: foreign policy, where the party 'not only defines the political line, but also together with state organs directly implements it', and international crises and other events that threaten the whole fate of the people and their achievements (Shakhnazarov, 1972, pp. 86–7). Furthermore, in exercising the general function of control or checking on the implementation of policy (for Shakhnazarov, one of the party's main prerogatives), the CPSU has the right of 'authoritative involvement' in current policy-making every time this is necessary, and when there is sufficient basis for this' (p. 88). It is precisely this kind of formulation – as Shakhnazarov *fails* to note – that encourages local party officials to encroach upon the work of non-party officials and institutions: some of the party secretaries in the provinces, particularly those of the less well trained, less sophisticated older generation, may experience little difficulty in identifying a situation that merits direct party intervention (perhaps in the expectation of gaining the credit for the resultant success). This is all the more so if, in the anticipation of such party interference, the relevant state officials have declined to shoulder the responsibility for taking an administrative decision. That, in all its human essence, is what podmena and party–state relations are all about.

Shabanov has also detailed the forms and methods of party involvement in the work of the soviets, in a small book (1969a) that must be virtually without parallel for the amount it reveals about party–state relations in a short space.

From Shabanov's work, corroborated by other writers, we find direct confirmation, with added details, of many assumptions held by Western scholars about the forms and extent of party involvement in the work of the soviets and the state apparatus. What needs to be borne in mind is that his work, and that which has followed in popular format (e.g., Orlov, 1973, pp. 83–9; Il'inskii *et al.*, 1976, pp. 157–65), has spelled out that same detail for Soviet readers in an open, forthright way – a far cry from the utmost secrecy that had been the norm about the party's role in government. The problem of party–state relations is now a legitimate topic of discussion for the public at large, including the problem of podmena and how to solve it. Nevertheless, the arguments about 'persuasion', and the distinctions drawn between 'leading' and 'governing', will doubtless convince few Western readers, when read in the light of firm statements that assert the binding authority of party decisions. Such an analysis is, of course, very convenient for the party authorities, who can use it to exonerate themselves of charges of domination. How many of the Soviet public accept this analysis is impossible to determine, and it is clear that even the most sophisticated Soviet writers on the topic find it virtually impossible to delineate the roles of party and state so precisely that their relationship ceases to generate constant frictions and political problems (Shakhnazarov, 1972, p. 91, n. 1). On this point, Shakhnazarov concludes, rather unsatisfactorily:

> None the less, despite all the inadequacies, such a distinction is necessary, in so far as it permits one more clearly to see the boundary beyond which normal and legitimate organizational work, as a necessary part of policy, begins to become transformed into plain administering. [Shakhnazarov, 1972, p. 91, n. 1]

There is one long-term way of resolving the issue, at least for Ukrainets. As society approaches full communism, she predicts, there will take place a 'closing together' of the forms and methods of party leadership and state administration. As evidence of this, she points to the growing tendency for government and administration to involve methods of 'persuasion and explanation', while party leadership 'more and more becomes enriched by the adoption of the best forms and qualities of the concrete aspects of administration'. 'However', she cautions, 'it is still too early to speak of the identity of party leadership and state administration' (Ukrainets, 1976, p. 71). She does not note the fact that governments around the world in the twentieth century are having more and more to resort to methods of bargaining and persuasion, in place of the now unacceptable command methods of previous generations. Yet behind her formulation may be an implication that the Soviet public, like its counterpart in other advanced countries, does not unquestioningly accept governmental policies, even when they are endowed with the force of law. If that is so, it speaks volumes for the degree of Soviet political development in the quarter-century since the death of Stalin. It may also help to explain the repeated cautioning about the dangers of spontaneity and the need for purposeful leadership on the part of the CPSU (e.g., Shakhnazarov, 1972, p. 92).

Be that as it may, Soviet writers and politicians in the 1970s have argued that the role of the party in Soviet society is to grow and develop; some have also argued that, in order to play that role effectively, the party too will have to change, in the direction of greater democratization.

CHAPTER 7

Intra-Party Democratization

In analysing and interpreting the party's leading role in society, Soviet writers are, in fact, saying little that is new. Such a view has long been party policy, and the many quotations from the speeches and writings of Lenin, cited by Soviet writers in support of their reaffirmation of the line, show that the basic principles – and the likely problems – were identified at the very outset of the regime. However, it was long ago recognized, although now no longer admitted, that the 'norms of party life' were grossly infringed during the Stalin era. Apart from podmena, there are other problems with the way the party has run its own affairs, and dealt with other institutions. Much of the 1970s literature has openly identified certain problems, and pointed to areas where changes are needed if the party is to match up to the task it has set itself. 'Raising the role of the communist party in socialist society', writes Topornin, 'is closely linked with the further development of intra-party democracy' (in Tikhomirov, 1975, p. 100; see also Kulinchenko, in Kadeikin et al., p. 160). In other words, democratization – specifically involving the ordinary membership much more – is the only way in which the party will be capable of achieving the desired development of Soviet society.

As with the critical analysis of the state and its institutions, the basis of Soviet scholars' writings on improving the functioning of the party is the 1961 CPSU programme. That document spoke of the need for 'a new, higher stage in the development of the party itself and of its political, ideological and organizational work', the need to reassert the 'Leninist standards of party life', and the necessity of 'an all-round development of intra-party democracy' (see Schapiro, 1963, p. 311; *KPSS v rez.*, vol. 8, pp. 301–2). Soviet writers were slow to take up these calls in relation to the party, compared with their colleagues, who analysed the programme's implications for developing the Soviet state. However, the question of reform within the party has received increased attention in the past few years, from social scientists working under the party's own auspices (for example, in the central committee's Academy of the Social Sciences), from political scientists examining the political system more broadly, and even in the speeches of politicians themselves. It is understood that the 'democratic' element in the way the party operates is to be delicately balanced by the 'centralist' element in the guiding principle of 'democratic centralism', and they are not arguing on the assumption of 'the more [democracy] the better' (Kadeikin *et al.*, 1974, pp. 160–1). Nevertheless, the 'objective necessity' for greater democracy within the party has been acknowledged (Kadeikin *et al.*, 1974, pp. 141–2, 144–5; Shapko, 1978, p. 95), although this will not appear automatically, and it involves discipline and responsibilities as well as rights to participate in decision-making (Shapko, 1978, p. 95).

In this connection, a range of aspects of the party's structure, recruitment and appointment policies and practices, and methods of rule have been critically examined, and certain reforms suggested. These include modifications to membership recruitment policy; greater care in the appointment of officials, and being more exacting towards them; the development of more effective channels for information within the party; and a much more rigorously devised party structure, with carefully defined roles, functions and responsibilities. In addition, the extensive use of sociological methods has been stressed, as a means of consulting members on policy proposals, and – more interestingly – of assessing the party's performance, and thereby improving the same.

RECRUITMENT

Of all the means available to the party for improving its performance, 'improving the qualitative composition of the party ranks' is regarded as the most important (*Organizatsionno-partiinaya rabota* . . ., 1974, p. 6; Yudin *et al.*, 1973, p. 57), and a great deal of attention has been paid to the question. However, most of the scholarly literature consists of approbatory commentaries and explanations of policy in this area.

The party's essential dilemma can be briefly summed up. As a party of the *working class*, it needs to stress its proletarian element, and not become 'elitist'; as a *ruling* party, it needs to have within its ranks (and under its influence) those whose expertise is indispensable in running a sophisticated modern industrial society; as 'the party of the *whole people*' – self-proclaimed since 1961 – it needs to be representative of all groups in society; as a *vanguard*, it needs to regulate its overall size, otherwise it might turn into 'some amorphous, unscrupulous organization' (Marchenko, 1973, p. 127) – a formulation that is very revealing of Soviet fears of spontaneity. Finding an appropriate admissions and recruitment policy to satisfy all these somewhat conflicting requirements is not an easy task.

Clearly, the party cannot accept everyone who might wish to become a member (Yudin *et al.*, 1973, p. 67; Kadeikin *et al.*, 1974, p. 166; Tikhomirov, 1975, p. 98); admission must therefore be restricted to 'only the foremost, most class-conscious and active representatives of the people, the self-sacrificing builders of communism' (Yudin, 1973, p. 267). In order to avoid the inevitable consequence that this frequently means well-educated managerial and administrative staff, there is a tendency towards stressing the peasant or proletarian *origins* of many of these (Topornin, 1975, p. 61; Chekharin, 1977, p. 27): it scarcely needs to be pointed out that those who attain such positions of authority will not automatically retain their proletarian and peasant values – nor, indeed, would that necessarily be desirable.

Nor can a proletarian profile be maintained by simply bringing in more production workers, many of whom, with low skills and inadequate political awareness, would scarcely constitute 'the best', the 'most progressive', elements in society. So Soviet writers note with satisfaction that the new wave of *proletarian* recruits is drawn from those industries that are likely to be of greatest importance in the future, and where the qualifications of workers are highest (indeed, approaching the role of technician): oil and petrochemicals, gas, chemicals, automobiles, electronics, radio technology, energy, instrument-making and automation equipment-building (Kadeikin *et al.*, 1974, p. 168); attention is also paid to recruiting those *peasants* who are most advanced in terms of training, their use of sophisticated equipment, etc. This is said to foster the union between the working class and the peasantry (Chekharin, 1977, p. 19). Thus, the proletarian element is becoming less like the traditional 'working class', and closer to the 'intelligentsia' in its training and work, and the party thereby gains a means of influencing the work-force in the key economic areas; it is also argued that this gives the proletariat stronger influence within the party (Kadeikin *et al.*, 1974, p. 164).

The possibility of such two-way influence, as an important factor in the party's recruitment of specific social groups, also applies to variables other than occupation, so that the recruitment is not simply on the basis of occupation or class: instead, party organizations 'more minutely study the composition of party entrants within each of these [social class] groups' (Kadeikin *et al.*, 1974, p. 166). In particular, the party's attention towards *women*, *young people*, and representatives of the (non-Russian) *nationalities* has been endorsed (see, e.g., Kadeikin *et al.*, 1974, pp. 172–5; Yudin *et al.*, 1973, pp. 57–67; Kadeikin, 1974, pp. 60–1).

However, the party's capacity to perform its role depends not simply on its new recruits, but on all members, on whom increased demands are now supposedly being made. In this connection, it can decline to confirm unsatisfactory recruits at the end of their year's probation (and Brezhnev has called for a more demanding approach towards probationary members: *XXV s"ezd*, vol. I, p. 89); it can also weed out unsatisfactory established members. Hence, a number of writers discuss not simply recruitment or replenishment (*popolnenie*), but *regulation* of the party ranks, through the judicious combination of recruitment and expulsion policies (Kadeikin *et al.*, 1974, p. 178; Turishchev, 1975, pp. 193–204). Soviet writers are firm in arguing that this 'cleansing' – such as that initiated by the twenty-fourth congress, involving the expulsion of 347,000 members (*XXV s"ezd*, vol. I, p. 89) – is not a purge, although the Russian word *chistka* is translated as such in Soviet dictionaries. 'The basic and only aim of a *chistka*', according to one writer, in a graphic phrase, 'is the release of the party from harmful and impeding ballast' (Marchenko, 1973, p. 129). Certainly, the modern style of 'purge' need not have the harsh overtones that the word acquired in the 1930s; but what becomes of those who are expelled? They would, on the face of it, be thereby deprived of the possibility of further career advancement, since in most cases this depends on the security of party membership. This may have to change, however: if the party restricts its numbers, and continues to stress the importance of proletarian membership, it will have to rely on more managerial personnel outside its own ranks; there is some evidence that this is already happening (see Yudin *et al.*, 1973, pp. 68–9, for one example; also Tikhomirov, 1975, p. 108).

PERSONNEL POLICY

Frederick Barghoorn has noted an interest on the part of Soviet leadership in improving the training of political executives, pointing out that the range of skills now required of leaders at all levels is far wider than the essentially 'political and bureaucratic' ones of the Stalin era (in Farrell, 1970, pp. 75, 63). In this field too, the work of Soviet scholars consists largely of elaborations of official party statements on the subject; in the process, however, they confirm what has long been known openly in the West about Soviet leadership and management styles, and (more significantly) they bring the question into the open for the Soviet public, at the same time putting in strong pleas for the recruitment and training of a very different type of leader for the future.

The reaction is against the generation recruited during and immediately after World War II, given a brief and inadequate training, and dispatched with much authority but little sensitivity to run the country (Yudin *et al.*, 1975, chapter 4, for detailed figures). Weaknesses in the older style of leadership have been pointed out by many writers (e.g., Yudin *et al.*, 1973, p. 198; Tikhomirov, 1975, p. 183), including, for example, the sheer ignorance of the law and its provisions, which contributed to the high level of law infringement that characterized the Stalin era and still lingers on (*Organizatsiya i deyatel'nost'* ..., 1970, p. 165). The party central committee has more than once criticized the widespread tendency to 'pass the buck' (e.g., in January 1967, relating to Estonia, and in February 1972, with reference to Uzbekistan: see Yudin *et al.*, 1975, pp. 167–9).

To replace those leaders, whose expertise and methods of rule do not meet the challenge of today, a new generation is required, possessing both *partiinost'* (ideological and party commitment) and *professional competence*, and a range of other characteristics best summarized by the word 'sophistication': mere enthusiasm is not regarded as sufficient (Makov, 1971, p. 44). Modern management is both a science and an art (*Apparat upravleniya* ... *2*, 1977, p. 181), and society's new leaders must be trained in 'the art of leadership' (Yudin *et al.*, 1973, pp. 184–6; Kadeikin *et al.*, 1974, pp. 211–13). Hence, those recruited to lead society in the future must possess certain personal characteristics: a willingness to use initiative, to accept personal responsibility, to show sensitivity and to respect citizens' rights; each must be 'an honest, conscientious worker, modest and attentive to people' (Kadeikin *et al.*, 1974, pp. 181–2). Indeed, the exercise of leadership involves relationships with people, so that party workers are encouraged to show an interest in the basics of social psychology (Makov, 1971, p. 52), in order to operate more effectively on the basis of persuasion, rather than simply giving orders. These personal characteristics are basic qualifications, in addition to the need for a good general political training, devotion to the cause of communism, plenty of party experience, and a sound understanding of economics (Belyakov and Zolotarev, 1975, p. 171). Once in office, an official needs to pursue his training, instead of relying on his existing 'intellectual baggage', in order to remain on top of the job (Chekharin, 1977, p. 24). Finally, while the 'new' leadership within Soviet society is not to be equated with the 'technocratic elite' with which Western critics charge them (Shakhnazarov, 1972, p. 122; Tikhomirov, 1975, p. 112), a familiarity with modern techniques of management and government is vital, tempered by the personal qualities discussed above. In short, what is required is a quite different style of *leadership culture* from that which has prevailed in the past two generations (see Yu. M. Kozlov, 1978), and in the process of leadership selection today 'the question of questions is how to choose the most worthy among the worthy' (Shakhnazarov, 1972, p. 154).

Whether such paragons of virtue exist anywhere in the world is a moot point, but some writers have raised the possibility of competitive appointment as one means of introducing a greater degree of rationality into appointments, together with statutory regulation of the office of state servant, to control these once appointed (see chapter 4 above). So far, such measures have not been introduced. However, in the USSR old leaders are being removed from office, and replaced by 'promising young workers'; as a reassurance to those who might feel that 'encouraged retirement' – to use a gentle euphemism – is not far away, the party 'treats its old cadres with consideration, tries to make maximum use of their experience and knowledge' (Topornin, 1975, p. 61; the words were originally Brezhnev's: *XXIV s"ezd*, vol. I, p. 125). Nevertheless, there is a significant level of turnover (and not only among the older officials). In selecting their replacements, the party is tightening up on the documentation involved in making appointments, and taking steps to ensure that more consultation is entered into before an appointment is made (Yudin *et al.*, 1973, p. 183).

Other aspects of the party's leadership policy have been discussed, in particular the importance of promoting persons with technical training. Thus, Ye. Z. Razumov complains (and thereby hints that things should be different) that there are few engineers and economists in a number of party town committees, and few highly trained agricultural specialists in rural district committees; he also comments critically on the low representation of women in leading positions (in Kadeikin *et al.*, 1974, pp. 188, 192–3), a point that echoes the central committee's 1967 statement on Estonia (*Spravochnik partiinogo rabotnika*, 1967, no. 7, p. 324).

The nationality question has also been widely considered in this connection, with emphasis on the need for administrators who 'know the life, mores, customs and language of the local population' (Kadeikin *et al.*, 1974, p. 193). This is perhaps an obvious point, but one that has been ignored in the past, when well trained and politically reliable representatives of the indigenous populations and the peripheral areas were simply not available, and Russians and other Slavs were sent to set up industry and administration (Yudin *et al.*, 1975, pp. 127–8; Miller, 1977, p. 9). Brezhnev's appointments as first secretary in Moldavia (1950–2) and Kazakhstan (1954–6) furnish but the most noteworthy example; the apparatus at all levels below him was likewise staffed in large measure by central appointees (see Yudin *et al.*, 1975, pp. 127–37, 163–4). Training facilities now exist in the various republics, as well as the Higher Party School in Moscow; and the training of national cadres is now 'an integral part of the party's nationality policy' (Kadeikin *et al.*, 1974, p. 193). So writers approvingly echo Brezhnev's statement of 1971 (*XXIV s"ezd*, vol. I, p. 124) that it is now official policy to recruit local workers to local positions, and to allocate persons from the centre to fill posts 'only as an exception' (Kadeikin *et al.*, 1974, p. 192; Topornin, 1975, p. 61). John H. Miller, in an illuminating elaboration of the issues surrounding personnel policy in the national areas, points out that Brezhnev's original statement failed to specify whether he referred to first or second secretaryships, or both (Miller, 1977, p. 19). The writings of Soviet commentators refer to leadership in general, implying that it embraces all levels – local, provincial, republican, political and economic. The existence now of an adequate supply of trained local cadres is the reason given for this development in recruitment policy; however, most likely it is also partly a response to known national pressures: in that sense, this is indeed an important aspect of the party's nationality policy. Furthermore, the tendency for *second* secretaries in the major nationality unit party organizations to be recruited from outside the area has also become an established practice in recent years (Miller, 1977, pp. 19–20). Moreover, while applauding the policy of involving local populations more in running their own affairs, Soviet writers also point out (again, echoing the party's line) that the 'internationalization' of personnel is not meant to imply the use of an influential position to foster the interests of individual nationalities (Yudin *et al.*, 1975, p. 165), and the need to retain a significant level of transfer (from one part of the country to another, from one apparatus to another) is emphasized (e.g., Yudin *et al.*, 1975, p. 163).

Seeking a suitable cadres and personnel policy is obviously an extremely complex task. This complexity ensures that, along with membership policy, personnel policy will retain a central position in the party's concern for its internal wellbeing, which directly affects its 'fighting capacity' – its ability to exercise leadership throughout society. That capacity is also affected by other factors: information and structures.

Party Information

We saw that the importance of abundant and accurate information for effective government is now being reflected in the utterances of Soviet politicians. The significance of this for the party is not hard to see. Since it is the party, and specifically its central organs, that has the self-imposed responsibility for formulating policy, obviously the flow of information from the grass roots to the top party bodies is of great value in the process. If the party is to function effectively as a co-ordinator, leader and organizer, then it must have adequate information on which to make judgements about policies, and a sound theoretical framework for evaluating it (Glezerman, in Kadeikin *et al.*, 1974, p. 71). Moreover, if policies once adopted are to be successfully applied, adequate downward communication flows are equally vital, from the party centre to those local levels where policy is implemented; hence writers frequently link upward and downward communication of information as two sides of the same coin that need complementary development (Kadeikin *et al.*, 1974, p. 15).

Even some of the avowedly propagandistic writers acknowledge this point, citing Lenin on the importance of openness, publicity and similar principles of intra-party life (e.g., Verkhovtsev and Malov, 1974, p. 60). Where they differ from their more sophisticated colleagues, however, is in their assumption – which comes over on the page as an assertion – that, because a good flow of information within the party 'forms a firm rule' (Verkhovtsev and Malov, 1974, p. 60), such a rule is therefore firmly applied. Other writers have looked more analytically and more critically at the party's information requirements.

The question of openness (*glasnost'*) in the party's work has been associated with the need for 'a precisely organized system of political and intra-party information': information, that is, dealing specifically with the internal life of the party and its organs and individual members, which is seen as an important method of party leadership and of training for communists (V. A. Kulinchenko, in Kadeikin *et al.*, 1974, p. 158). Such information must measure up to certain criteria: it must comprehensively reveal the workings of the party and its organs and organizations; it must be reliable and objective, but must 'not photograph facts, phenomena and processes, but give them an objective and at the same time party evaluation' (how this criterion can be met without running the risk of introducing harmful distortion is not explained); and these demands can be met by 'information circulating along channels of direct and reverse communication' (V. A. Kulinchenko, in Kadeikin *et al.*, 1974, p. 158). The same author outlines several forms that this intra-party information might take, including the publication of party policy documents and statements, minutes of party committee meetings and conferences, information bulletins relating the experience of various party bodies, and so forth.

This matter was touched upon by Brezhnev at the twenty-fourth party congress, in 1971. He reported that upward communication 'right up to the central committee' had improved signficantly, but said there was still room for improvement, for more widely using information 'as an instrument of leadership, a means of training and control' (*XXIV s"ezd*, vol. I, pp. 119–20). In the wake of that congress, a Leningrad party secretary stated that it is hard to overestimate the role of full and sound information for the party, and he too quoted Lenin in support of this position (Makov, 1971, pp. 44–5). He went on to analyse the various types and sources of information, including that pertaining to intra-party life.

The question has its implications for the degree of democracy within the party, and it is frequently linked with calls for the further development of the hallowed principle of 'criticism and self-criticism'. While firmly rejecting 'bourgeois' arguments about the need for an institutionalized opposition as a 'counterweight' to the ruling party; and rejecting, too, criticism for criticism's sake (since the party is not 'a club of oratorical dilettanti' – Turishchev, 1975, p. 207), the point is made that intra-party criticism is vitally necessary, a means of correcting, and hence avoiding, errors and deficiencies (Tikhomirov, 1975, pp. 102–3). Indeed, for V. A. Kulinchenko, the level of 'creative, constructive criticism' is a measure of the political wellbeing of a party organization (Kadeikin *et al.*, 1974, p. 156), while for Turishchev (1975, p. 206), the capacity to discuss failures and weaknesses, and to organize the masses to overcome them, is a positive feature, signifying a lack of conceit and self-delusion.

In particular – following up Brezhnev's exhortation – there is a need to develop criticism *from below*, as N. A. Petrovichev argues:

Analysis of the work of a number of party committees shows that at plenary sessions ... the basic criticism goes from above, directed towards the lower organizations, and less from below, directed towards the higher organs and workers.

This happens even though 'it is well known that criticism from below reflects the view of affairs of the led, and criticism from above – that of the leaders'; he calls therefore for a 'correct combination' of both forms of criticism (Kadeikin *et al.*, 1974, pp. 14–15). Kadeikin too notes that information coming up from below

> frequently bears a superficial, formal character, does not contain a deep analysis of the facts and phenomena of life; in it, the situation is not always objectively illuminated, and serious deficiencies and omissions are passed over in silence. Some [party] workers ... disapprovingly greet truthful information which reveals deficiencies, and at the same time encourage communications that prettify the true position; [the improvement of party-political information is] one of the most important means of raising the scientific level and the effectiveness of party work. [Kadeikin *et al.*, 1974, pp. 96–8]

Kulinchenko even calls for drawing non-party people more widely into the discussion of party documents, citing the party programme in support (in Kadeikin *et al.*, 1974, p. 147).

The practice almost since the beginning, however, has been to interpret any criticism as subversive, and to eradicate it with all the authority of the 1921 ban on 'fractionalism': so powerful has this ban been for Stalin and his successors that its adoption has been seen as a milestone in the history of the party (Schapiro, 1970, p. 214). Shakhnazarov reiterates the comment that fractionalism contradicts the principle of democracy, perceptively pointing out that, even in Western, bourgeois parties, either opposition groups are made to submit, on pain of expulsion, or they split and form a separate party (Shakhnazarov, 1972, pp. 54–5) – an option that is not, of course, available to critics within the CPSU. After arguing that the persistence of fractionalist activity in the 1920s led Stalin to clamp down on it, and thereby encouraged his personality cult (an interpretation that can be read as both criticism and exoneration of Stalin), Shakhnazarov stresses that intra-party democracy requires open discussion and debate. He quotes a 1924 conference resolution to the effect that leading organs must not regard all criticism as a manifestation of fractionalism, since this simply *encourages* fractionalism (Shakhnazarov, 1972, p. 56) – or it leads to apathy, as recent research has confirmed (Bokarev, 1974a, p. 104). Shakhnazarov spells out the implications of the principle of open discussion: apart from statements that contradict the basic principles of the party programme, points of view expressed prior to the adoption of a decision cannot be used as a basis for accusations of fractionalism, and still less for disciplinary measures; Lenin himself indicated that there would always be argument and struggle in the party (Shakhnazarov, 1972, pp. 56–7).

These observations and criticisms of past and current practices, and suggestions for modifying them, are no doubt perceptive, accurate and sensible. Lacking, however, are *clear* indications of how the situation can be rectified. Broad general statements about the need for certain things to happen give middle-range and local leaderships little concrete assistance in bringing about change. True, the forms and methods of information exchange put forward for use by the state apparatus could be adopted by the party; true, a more sensitive and sophisticated body of party cadres might be expected to appreciate what is required and act accordingly; true, Kadeikin writes approvingly of party press conferences in Kazakhstan, information bulletins circulated to party committees in L'vov oblast and other local practices (Kadeikin *et al.*, 1974, p. 97). Yet the literature reviewed so far remains essentially theoretical, couched in terms of general principles, broad exhortations and – most likely – pious hopes for reform.

I. M. Reutskii and D. V. Yevdokimov have paid closer and more practical attention to the question, in a short monograph on the subject (1974), written with feet firmly on the ground, and based on the experience of Moscow oblast. Specific weaknesses were identified at an obkom meeting in November 1969, seen as a 'notable landmark' in the development of party information in the province: the failure of local secretaries to inform branches of committee decisions, or a tendency to delay doing so; inadequate use of various kinds of meetings at local level as a means of feeding information upwards (deputies' meetings with electors, party branch meetings, Komsomol meetings); failure to study the reports of branch meetings; inadequate attention to letters from the public – these and other concrete means of eliciting and transmitting information were being grossly underutilized. Following this plenum, in 1970–1 new measures were worked out and introduced, amounting to an 'information system', according to which various information bulletins are produced and circulated, reports on the work of the obkom are sent round to local committees and organizations, and in general a much greater exchange of information now apparently takes place, encouraged by seminars on the topic and other measures (Reutskii and Yevdokimov, chapter 2). The book is lacking in theory, yet it is just the kind of work that is of invaluable help to those who are expected to implement the theoretically phrased general exhortations of the scholarly writers and leading politicians.

PARTY STRUCTURE

More than one Soviet writer has pointed out that 'there are no absolutely correct organizational forms and methods of work, valid for all stages of the revolutionary process' (Belyakov and Zolotarev, 1975, p. 4; Ukrainets, 1976, p. 91). The party, in other words, can and must adapt its structures to meet the requirements of a given time and situation (although, when Khrushchev did precisely that – as he thought – in November 1962, in order to cope with the mounting problems of agriculture, he was roundly condemned after his political demise for 'unscientific and groundless reorganizations', which were rapidly undone by his successors).

Belyakov and Zolotarev (1975, chapter 7) discuss many structural modifications made since the mid-1960s, particularly at the primary party organization and party group level, in order to ensure effectiveness in controlling production, and to enable proper coordination of the party organization's work in factories and plants where production is spread among several buildings. The institutional changes in the economy in recent years, with the creation of production associations, trading firms and trusts, has necessitated modifications to the party structure at enterprise level, formally permitted by a change in the party rules at the twenty-fourth congress (see Derbinov *et al.*, 1975, pp. 19–21; *XXIV s"ezd*, vol. II, p. 243). In this connection, Ukrainets argues that changes in the way the party performs its role at town and district level 'may also affect the internal structure of the party apparatus'. In particular, the local committees' organizational departments, responsible for supervising the work of primary party organizations, may develop into the key element in the structure, with special sections, staffed by qualified workers, to deal with primary organizations in different industries or sectors of the economy; she also suggests departments or sectors for socioeconomic analysis and forecasting, necessitated by the growing complexity of society, and the need for the party to base its work on sound, scientific knowledge (Ukrainets, 1976, pp. 93–4).

Kadeikin calls for party legislation, evidently more or less equivalent to the new statutes on the local soviets, setting out the precise functions and fields of competence of various structures associated with party committees – departments, sectors, and various kinds of individual official within the apparatus (Kadeikin *et al.*, 1974, p. 102). Such a measure could help restrict the arbitrary use of powers by local officials, and have a consequent positive impact on the role and performance of state officials, who suffer from *podmena*, resulting from party secretaries expanding their own sphere of authority. In that connection, with a tendency towards greater specialization among local officials, attempts are being made to elaborate a proper functional division, particularly among first and second secretaries; here, the search for 'the best variant' is ongoing (Ukrainets, 1976, pp. 102–3).

Most of the discussion of these matters relates to the *local* level: not surprisingly, since that is where policies decided in the politburo and central committee are ultimately implemented. The ostensible aim of all the changes is to equip the party for more effectively playing its self-appointed role in an ever more complex and sophisticated society, and the proposals and arguments are all directed towards that goal: one searches in vain for critical analysis of the party. All the emphasis is on securing ways for developing the party's traditional role and playing it more effectively.

To that end, the introduction of 'scientific methods' into the organization of party work, including forward planning, is favourably mentioned (Belyakov and Zolotarev, 1975, pp. 172–82). Kadeikin points out, however, that this is a little-studied question, and one that some people believe is inappropriate. He asks the question, 'How can relations with people be scientifically organized?', and his reply boils down to the application of systems analysis, and the appropriate disposition of personnel (Kadeikin, 1974, pp. 129–30). He points out, furthermore, that party work is an extremely complex blend of activities, whose efficacy cannot adequately be judged on the basis of generalized indicators: he cites approvingly the example of the Kazan' mechanical works, whose organization devised an 'evaluation coefficient' embracing production activity, party discipline, political education, lectures, labour discipline and other factors – all of which were relevant in measuring the effectiveness of the works party organization (Kadeikin, 1974, p. 132).

SOCIOLOGICAL METHODS

In the late 1960s there was a heated debate among specialist writers, joined by a few practical workers, about the value of using social science, particularly sociology, for evaluating and improving the work of the party. A decade later, it is accepted that sociological methods are an appropriate means of assessing the party's performance and generally aiding its work, a point made in a Bulgarian monograph, recently published in Moscow in translation (Byrdarov, 1977, p. 117). The debate, indeed, goes back to at least 1967, when *Partiinaya zhizn'* carried an article by the head of the department of organizational and party work of Leningrad city committee, entitled 'Sociological Research in Party Work' (Provotorov, 1967). The author extolled surveys as a means of quickly acquiring information on opinions and on the work of the party organization, and concluded by stressing that, 'in our firm opinion, sociological research, if approached seriously, can become an important means of raising the scientific level of party leadership' (p. 41). At the same time, a paper was read at a conference in Irkutsk on the theme of 'Concrete Sociological Research and Party Propaganda', and sub-titled 'From the experience of the work of the sociological laboratory attached to Irkutsk obkom of the CPSU' (Smol'kov, 1967). Thus, where academic sociologists were available to set up the research units, party committees were willing to use these methods in the mid-1960s. Since then, there has appeared a considerable body of literature on the topic. Even so, the introduction to the Russian edition of Byrdarov's book notes that 'the specific character of sociological research in the sphere of party activity has been insufficiently studied' (Byrdarov, 1977, p. 5).

A regular contributor on this topic, N. N. Bokarev, well described the difficulties in the early days: lack of qualified sociologists, ignorance among party workers and suspicion that it was a passing fad, contrasted with over-eagerness among others, whose enthusiasm might have discredited the whole notion (Bokarev, 1969, p. 48). Like Provotorov, Bokarev also emphasized the need for a serious approach (p. 52). By 1974 he was asserting that the quality of such research had improved substantially, particularly on the theoretical plane, and he gave examples of the kind of research that was being done: analysis of the social composition of party organizations, and comparisons with the population distribution; studies of the levels of activity among party members, and reasons for disparities (including, interestingly, a revelation by one survey that 6.2 per cent of respondents found that no one took any notice of their comments and suggestions); questions more directly associated with work, such as investigations into labour discipline and motivation; and – a reflection of a fashionable form of research at the time – time-budget analysis of party activists and workers, and also of economic leaders: one such study revealed that local party officials spent so much time on meetings that there was little opportunity to organize the implementation of the results of those conferences. Convinced of the value of such work, Bokarev urged greater coordination, and a properly worked-out programme of research, together with more and better trained sociologists (Bokarev, 1974a). Later in the year he published a detailed monograph for party workers, explaining what sociology is all about, describing various research techniques, reporting on his own research in Moscow city and oblast, and reproducing questionnaires used. He concluded that 'this science can make a growing input into the theory and practice of party construction, and into the management of processes that take place in society and in the party' (Bokarev, 1974b, p. 137).

All this work reflects the recognition, differently expressed by other writers but clearly accepted by specialists, that effective policy must be based on sound, 'scientific' information about the state of affairs that the policy is intended to deal with, and also – and this is particularly true of research into the operations of local, especially primary, party organizations – information about the capacity for implementing that policy. Bokarev's stress on *facts* (1974a, p. 102) is echoed by Kadeikin, urging rationality and science:

> In order to understand the trends in party development, to determine the prospects, to select the most successful forms of organization and work methods, it is necessary to use widely an all-round economic analysis, effective and objective information, concrete sociological research and experiments. [Kadeikin, 1974, p. 117]

For Western observers, the point hardly needs to be made, and it seems amazing that Soviet scholars and politicians took so long to recognize the importance of plentiful and sound information. It is an encouraging development, but it must be measured against the occasional call not to overestimate the value of sociological research (e.g., Petrovichev, in Kadeikin *et al.*, 1974, p. 20). Moreover, misgivings are raised by the implementation of the new policy for tapping 'public opinion' since Brezhnev's call for it at the twenty-fifth congress. Already in 1975 and 1976, local newspapers in Belorussia, Moldavia and the Ukraine reported that city committees had set up 'special councils' to study public opinion (Utenkov *et al.*, 1977, p. 109). These moves may turn out to have been an ill thought-out jumping on to a trendy bandwagon (such as that of earlier years, described by Bokarev). Unless these 'councils' contain competent sociologists and are permitted to engage in genuine research, the whole movement could become discredited before it really gets off the ground: indeed, there may be individuals, in positions of authority in the provinces, perhaps, who might pursue such a policy deliberately. Nevertheless, such is the Soviet regime's penchant for claiming continuous success that these reports were interpreted as heralding a significant positive innovation, while other writers (e.g., Shapko, 1978) publish highly laudatory general accounts of the extent to which 'intra-party democratization' has developed in the past decade.

These writings reflect the aim of improving the efficiency of the party apparatus in ruling society effectively. That is the role of Soviet writers on the party, and it largely precludes severely critical analysis and radical proposals for reform. Nothing so much as hints at a questioning of the party's right to decide policy: all is directed towards assisting the party in performing that role with greater efficiency, and to supervise the implementation of policy more effectively. The aim is to make the present system work better.

CHAPTER 8
Political Science and Political Reform

The foregoing chapters have surveyed half a dozen major areas of concern in the writings of Soviet political scientists since the early 1960s. Other points include the crucial question of decentralization of authority, and the rights of lower bodies (including semi-formal ones) to take decisions and make proposals to higher bodies (see, e.g., Sheremet, 1968a, p. 94; Vasil'ev, 1970; Shakhnazarov, 1972, p. 112), and, in particular, the need to reform the planning apparatus, where, on trends of the early 1970s, 80 per cent of the labour force would be swallowed up in planning alone by the year 2000 (Shakhnazarov, 1972, pp. 107–8). In tracing these arguments, one can identify a clear development, beginning with specific institutional analysis and suggestions for changing particular aspects of existing arrangements, and now moving towards broader questions with implications for the whole nature of the system. Conceptual development in Soviet scholarship has led political scientists to discuss issues in terms of culture formation and democratization, concepts and processes that involve the whole of social activity.

A book of this kind has to be selective, and it has concentrated most heavily on those scholars who seem most realistic in their approach to solving the problems of Soviet society. Although they make the appropriate – and frequently just – criticisms of Western writings on the Soviet Union, their main concern is to face up to the difficulties and seek solutions. For example, Shakhnazarov (1972, p. 184) points out that the bourgeois press gleefully picks up evidence of difficulties in the

146

socialist camp and uses it for propaganda purposes; yet for him the benefits derived from the open discussion of problems outweigh any damage. A statement reflecting the 'paranoid' strand in Soviet political thought appears in a book that is itself firmly in the propagandist tradition (entitled *The Organizational Bases of the CPSU and their 'Critics'* – Verkhovtsev and Malov, 1974): citing Z. Brzezinski on the probability of a break with the country's Leninist past, the authors went on: 'This, it turns out, is what our opponents dream of. . . . They would like to rupture this [party] unity by means of fractional struggle, to split and weaken the ranks of the communist party' (p. 60). There is no shortage of such writings, and their purpose is different from that of the serious scholars.

How effective are political scientists in influencing the direction of change? Western literature on this topic contains conflicting views. The totalitarian model left practically no room for such influence. It portrayed a society, essentially isolated from outside influences, where the imposition of strict ideological conformity, through a tightly censored system of communications and education, prevented the generation of critical ideas, and where terror served as the ultimate guarantee against the presentation of challenging interpretations and reformist proposals. Stalin's achievement in establishing orthodoxy in the fields of linguistics and genetics are two well-known examples cited by writers in this school (Friedrich and Brzezinski, 1966, pp. 149–50). The Soviet 'dissident' Andrei Sakharov, too, argues that the censorship causes 'stagnation and dullness' and prevents 'fresh and deep ideas' (Sakharov, 1969, p. 57). Another Soviet critic, the Marxist historian Roy Medvedev, has indicated that the social sciences play 'an extremely insignificant role' in policy formation and in devising methods of government, and this is 'a denial of the principles and ideals of scientific communism' (Medvedev, 1975, p. 37).

In the mid-1960s, however, Henry W. Morton took a somewhat different view, referring to 'an informal sharing of power with ministerial bureaucrats, planners, scientists, economic managers, military leaders, technical experts, social scientists, and cultural authorities', or at least 'a reliance on their advice' (Juviler and Morton, 1967, p. 9). Barghoorn, too, has written of the 'probably . . . increasingly influential advisory role' played by Soviet academic experts in the Academy of Sciences (in Farrell, 1970, p. 63); Skilling has noted public debate, on questions including legal reforms, taking place at conferences and in scholarly and professional publications, as well as in the press (Skilling and Griffiths, 1971, p. 43); and, more recently, Peter H. Solomon has seen participation by experts in the policy-making process as a 'prominent feature' of post-Stalin Soviet politics, so that by the 1970s specialists in criminology (the subject of Solomon's case study) were participating in policy-making 'in a regular and serious way' (in Remnek, 1977, pp. 1, 22). Soviet writers also refer to the 'highly useful links' between organs of the Soviet state and scientific institutions, in particular the Institute of State and Law of the Academy of Sciences (IGPAN), and other specific institutions (e.g., Tikhomirov, 1975, p. 252). Politicians echo such sentiments, as when CPSU central committee secretary M. V. Zimyanin referred to Soviet science taking part, and going to take an ever growing part, in working out programmes of socioeconomic and scientific–technical development for the country; he spoke too of strengthening the role of science in the life of society (*XXV s"ezd KPSS i zadachi kafedr obshchestvennykh nauk*, 1977, pp. 14–15). There seems therefore to be an understanding that the social sciences, including 'political science', are to play a positive role in developing the Soviet system, including the political dimension of society.

We have encountered many proposals for reform of the system, most referring to specific aspects, but some involving changes of potentially radical and wide impact. There is debate, argument, and disagreement among Soviet specialists on the political system (although not, of course, on fundamentals). Their publications are abundant, their conferences frequent. Clearly there are many opportunities for circulating ideas among themselves. As Jerry F. Hough noted at the beginning of the present decade (and this study amplifies Hough's point),

'There has ... been virtually no conceivable proposal for incremental change in party policy in the last five years that has not been aired in the Soviet press'. He went on:

> The proposals must sometimes be carefully phrased, and the more radical ones often have to be published in scholarly journals and books rather than in the pages of *Pravda*, but there is virtually no official policy that is immune from questioning. [Hough, 1972, p. 31]

However, do they have any positive impact on the politicians, who have the power to introduce the reforms?

The fact is that the critical analyses and proposals for reform are presented to the world very often in minute editions: 1100, 700, even a trifling 550 copies. They are sometimes presented as conference papers, and released by publishing houses in Saratov, Minsk, Alma-Ata, Irkutsk, and even more obscure places. They are not available to the general reader, so Soviet political scientists are not likely to build up a groundswell of *popular* support for their proposed reforms: nor, in all likelihood, are they attempting to do so. Their writings are aimed at other specialists, and may even be intended mainly to add to each scholar's *curriculum vitae*. After all, as in the West, Soviet academics are judged by their research output, although many scholars fail to engage in research and publication (*XXV s"ezd KPSS i zadachi kafedr obshchestvennykh nauk*, 1977, p. 17); so one can read in the work of, say, Perttsik or Leizerov the same data, arguments, conclusions and proposals, in different publications under slightly different titles (compare, e.g., Perttsik, 1967a, 1967b, 1968b; Leizerov, 1964, 1974a): this trick is, of course, not unknown among Western scholars! It also indicates tardiness among politicians in adopting the reformist proposals: when the same research results can be re-published after a decade, in support of the same suggestions for reform, then clearly little of consequence has been done in the meantime in that area. Are Soviet political scientists therefore writing for each other? Do they have no impact on the political life about which they write? After all, a factor that inhibited social scientists in the past from putting forward their views was the sense that the politicians were not keen to hear their criticisms and recommendations (Solomon, in Remnek, 1977, p. 7).

THE IMPACT OF POLITICAL SCIENCE

The most obvious place to look for 'impact' is in the outputs of the political system: legislation, government action. If the recommendations of political scientists are incorporated into new legislation, one might reasonably conclude that their ideas have indeed been listened to, and taken up by the politicians. On this scale of measurement, the impact of Soviet political science must be judged as distinctly patchy.

Since the mid-1950s the central authorities have paid increasing attention to the development of the political system, particularly local government (Friedgut, 1978, p. 464). Beginning with a statement on the soviets, dated 22 January 1957, and continuing with further statements and a spate of legislation on local government (still in progress), and including the 1977 Constitution, the authorities have repeatedly turned their attention to various aspects of political life. The legislative programme, part of a much broader process of codification of Soviet legislation, began in 1968, when the USSR Supreme Soviet presidium issued an edict, 'On the basic rights and obligations of village and settlement soviets', which instructed the union republics to introduce legislation conforming with the terms of the central edict; these new laws were introduced in the course of that year (see *Zakony o sel'skikh i poselkovykh Sovetakh...*, 1969). That successfully completed, there followed the turn of the district and urban soviets, for which new laws were introduced in 1971 (see *Zakony o raionnykh Sovetakh...*, 1972, and *Zakony o gorodskikh ... Sovetakh..., 1972*). In 1972 a Statute on the Deputies' Status was introduced (*Zakono statuse deputatov*), and, moving further up the administrative hierarchy, Brezhnev announced at the twenty-fifth party congress that new legislation would be drafted for the provincial and territorial soviets (*XXV s"ezd*, vol. I, p. 107). Following the adoption of the new Constitution, more new legislation is being introduced, as foreseen when Brezhnev introduced the document (Brezhnev, 1977b, p. 54).

As for the party institutions, here too the leadership pays regular attention to deficiencies and overcoming them. A major section of the central committee's congress reports always deals with intra-party developments: party growth and membership policy; personnel recruitment and placement; and other areas of party life (e.g., *XXV s"ezd*, vol. I, pp. 88–97). In addition, the central party authorities regularly review the state of affairs in particular areas, and issue statements drawing the attention of party organizations to the problem, for them to amend their own behaviour accordingly (e.g., *KPSS v rez.*, vol. 10, pp. 101–6, for a statement criticizing the Yaroslavl city party organization).

Politicians thus show concern for those areas of political life that have been the object of political scientists' attention. But how far does the legislative output reflect the opinions and embody the reformist proposals contained in the scholarly literature?

Certain specific measures can be seen in this light: the referendum as a device for tapping public opinion, included in the 1977 Constitution; the requirement that deputies be informed in advance of the agenda of a session, incorporated into the statute on the deputies' status. We have also seen how politicians (including Brezhnev) have accepted the importance of direct popular inputs, in the form of letters to the party authorities, with references to this at party congresses, as well as in oft-repeated formal statements and newspaper editorials on the subject.

Other examples could be given. For instance, in 1971 the USSR council of ministers initiated measures to strengthen the financial position of local soviet executive committees, in part by diverting some of the profits of local industrial enterprises to the local budget, and also part of the turnover tax on goods produced over and above the plan (see 'O merakh. . .', 1971,

p. 31). A suggestion similar to this was made by Atamanchuk in the previous year, that a percentage of the social funds of enterprises should be administered by local soviets (Atamanchuk, 1970, p. 96). At about the same time, a similar proposal was made at a conference in Armenia (Begiyan, 1970, pp. 47–8). And three years earlier, at a conference, the same point was made: after revealing that village soviets, in particular, were heavily subsidized, several speakers suggested that local soviets should be funded in part by local enterprises (Sidorova, 1967, p. 139).

The statute on the deputies' status, which attempted to regularize the position of deputies as 'authorized representatives' in their dealings with public bodies, was proposed by Brezhnev at the twenty-fourth congress in almost casual fashion – its first mention by a political leader, for which he was duly applauded (*XXIV s"ezd*, vol. I, pp. 102–3). While Brezhnev might win the applause of the delegates, and the political benefit that accrued from raising this as a reformist issue, the thinking behind it had been expressed several years earlier, in a paper by A. Ye. Lunev (1967), deputy director of the Institute of State and Law. He argued at a conference in 1967 the need for 'defining in law the position of the deputy as a representative of power in all situations where he is carrying out his deputy's duties. This will', he asserted, using phrases that later accompanied the promulgation of the new statute, 'raise the authority and strengthen the sense of respon- sibility of deputies' (Lunev, 1967, p. 103). It is impossible to be certain that Brezhnev took the idea from political science writings. However, politicians clearly take their ideas from somewhere, and it seems inconceivable that a proposal for a major piece of legislation could be introduced unless its preparation was already fairly advanced. Moreover, we have the testimony of a political figure (the chairman of the Uzbek supreme soviet presidium) that this statute was based on 'a generalization of the achievements of state–legal science and the practice of soviet construction' – meaning a combination of political science prescriptions and the experience of practical administrators and politicians (Matchanov, 1975, p. 3).

It is an open question whether such reforms will be used in the way in which their proposers envisaged they should. For example, it seems highly unlikely that the referendum will be used as a means of repealing legislation, duly passed by the Supreme Soviet, if it proves to diverge from 'the sovereign will of the Soviet people' (Kabyshev, 1969, pp. 130–1). Even so, some Soviet scholars are already trying to encourage movement, thereby giving substance to such reformist measures. Thus, G. N. Manov assures his readers that article 20 of the law on the Supreme Soviet permanent commissions, dealing with the referendum, 'leaves no doubt' that not only constitutional or other basic laws, but 'any other questions of general state importance', may be submitted to nationwide public debate; moreover, these discussions are a significant element in raising political consciousness, and he envisages an act to regulate the holding of referendums (in Tikhomirov, 1978, pp. 67–70).

In other areas, the politicians have apparently been less willing to adopt recommendations for reform. For instance, the idea of a presidium for local soviets has not been adopted; nor has the idea for a statute to regulate the processing of electors' mandates to deputies. The proposal to increase the length of term of local soviets has been only quarter-heartedly incorporated into the new Constitution, extending the term by six months (to two and a half years), instead of by an extra two years. Presumably this will barely solve the problems associated with lack of experience and high turnover levels among deputies, and will have little effect in reducing the cost of running frequent election campaigns, which apparently concerned Bezuglov, Strashun and Starovoitov (see chapter 2). Starovoitov, who favoured the shift in elections from spring to summer, and proposed a further shift to autumn, argued the case for a five-year term for the Supreme Soviet since that would mesh in with the planning timetable, and supported the shift in the electoral season for the same reason: in both cases, the newly elected soviet's plan could incorporate the mandates given during the campaign (in Sheremet, 1976, pp. 94–5). The problem of local elections every two *and a half* years – that is, presumably, in autumn and *spring* – would improve on the present arrangement in one year but revert to the very problem complained of on every second occasion.

The electoral system itself continues as before, despite the various criticisms of the system that have long, and repeatedly, been identified by the specialists, who themselves continue to write works purporting to demonstrate 'the democratism of the Soviet electoral system' (e.g., Pal'gunova, 1977, p. 5). As noted, the 1978 USSR Supreme Soviet election statute did nothing to resolve the major discrepancies between theory and practice identified by Soviet scholars, and in effect confirms the established practice in all its essentials. This mixed reception of the proposals of political scientists parallels that accorded to the research findings and suggestions of sociologists (see Jeffrey W. Hahn, in Remnek, 1977, pp. 52–3).

In view of the reluctance of a cautious leadership to respond, there it is little wonder that some political scientists have shown distinct signs of impatience. We saw how a provincial politician (A. M. Zhilin, secretary of Gorky oblast executive committee) called for an end to experimentation, and its replacement by legislative activity to widen the powers of local soviets' permanent commissions. In 1967, Lunev, with implied disappointment and exasperation, reported that experiments with local soviet presidiums had been drawn up by scholars in collaboration with local party and state workers (as reported in Kotok *et al.*, 1966, p. 123); yet, despite the support of the oblast authorities, the experiment had not yet taken place (Lunev, 1967, p. 100). Moreover, after describing a number of legal and economic experiments that did take place, Lunev adds, somewhat bitterly: 'True, in this matter we did not get by without a racket, without formalism and juridical nihilism' (p. 100). More forthrightly Perttsik, a pioneer in adopting modern research techniques, argued forcefully at a conference in Vilnius in 1970 that the time was ripe for action:

> The results of much research have already been published in our specialist literature, and they have shown the possible ways and directions of constitutional and rule-making activity.

And he concluded:

> Now ... the main thing is that the results and proposals which have been published and presented to the state organs be taken into account in the preparation of state—legislative acts. [Perttsik, 1970, pp. 97–8]

Still more recently, S. V. Solov'ëva (1978, pp. 129–39) examined the reasons for the slow application of specialists' recommendations, pointing out that even to introduce a reformist measure at a very local level requires the sanction of higher authority, and this obviously complicates the problem.

Such statements do not encourage a belief that Soviet political science has any real influence; nor, of course, do the obvious failures – cases where a strong and united body of professional opinion has failed to have its proposals for reform taken up by the Kremlin politicians. Clearly, much depends on the relationship between political scientists and the political leadership.

POLITICAL SCIENTISTS AND POLITICIANS

In a fundamental sense, Soviet political scientists depend on the politicians. The politicians, not the political scientists, have the power to determine the course of society, and to enforce their views. As it happens, their view of society in the last generation has included a general reformist outlook, initiated as part of the movement away from the Stalin personality cult, and continuing today in the development of the mature socialist society. In recent years, and specifically since 1967, the politicians have formally accorded a growing role to the social sciences. Political scientists are therefore sanctioned in their work by the politicians.

Not only are they sanctioned, they are given specific encouragement to work in certain areas. The 1961 party programme raised several issues that political scientists took up and explored, including the electoral system and the institution of a referendum. More recently, the promulgation of the concept of 'developed socialist society' – itself originally a political, rather than theoretical, device – has opened up further areas for academic scrutiny, explanation and theorizing, including in particular relations between the communist party, other institutions and society at large. The central committee's report to the twenty-fourth congress noted a need for 'an ever more decisive turning of the social sciences in the direction of resolving the problems that are topical at present and in the future' (*XXIV s''ezd*, vol. I, p. 112). This call was interpreted by the profession as an encouragement to continue with their work (Shebanov, 1972, p. 3), particularly when the congress had also been told that the party attaches great importance to improving legislation (*XXIV s''ezd*, vol. I, p. 102). Obviously, legislative activity of any sort is grist to the mill of political scientists, many of whom are lawyers. There were 4800 academic lawyers in 1971, including over 360 professors and doctors of legal science and 1400 candidates of science (PhD) (Shebanov, 1972, p. 4). Furthermore, the lawyers themselves have not been backward in stressing the value of legal knowledge among the public at large. 'Legal propaganda', as it is known, had a section of its own at a conference in Ufa in 1975 (Piskotin *et al.*, 1975, pp. 191–208), and the publication of popular journals such as the monthly, pocket-sized, *Chelovek i zakon* (Man and the Law), or popularizing books such as *Zakon obo mne i mne o zakone* (loosely translated 'What the Law Means for You' – Zhogin and Mel'nikova, 1971), are further evidence of a general desire to establish a legal basis to Soviet society (see Hough, 1976b, p. 14). Topornin, in this connection, has written that 'In present-day conditions, the significance of improving the legal regulation of social relations is growing substantially.' Noting that social relations have become more fluid, he states the need for old, outdated laws to be replaced by new ones that reflect current social realities (in Tikhomirov, 1975, pp. 121–2; also Ye. A. Lukasheva, in Tikhomirov, 1978, p. 126).

The codification, systematization and updating of current legislation, embarked on in the late 1950s and early 1960s, is proceeding, and is seen as an important condition for further development (see A. F. Shebanov's contributions to Kerimov, 1965, pp. 140–74, and to Shebanov, 1972, pp. 115–34). Indeed, one writer has called for a long-term legislative programme to be drawn up, embodying the planned development of democracy; this is needed, he claims, in the light of plans in the economic and social field covering the period up to 1990 (Topornin, in Tikhomirov, 1975, p. 82). In view of the Marxist insistence on the interconnection between economics, sociology and politics, this suggestion would appear unassailable on ideological grounds.

That is however an extremely ambitious proposal, and more likely the present programme of piecemeal legislative renewal will continue. In this process, lawyers and other social scientists are claiming a role as professionals. That role is not merely to interpret and popularize the latest legislation (although that forms a significant portion of their work), but also to assess current laws critically, and participate in the framing of new legislation. For instance, scholars in Kazakhstan published in 1977 a collection of essays on the need for changes in the law in a number of fields (Sapargaliev and Sakhipov, 1977). Academic lawyers have been involved in drafting the new local soviet statutes, and also the statute on the deputies' status which, three years later, they wished to amend (see Shebanov, 1972, p. 6; Gorshenev and Kozlov, 1976, p. 129). One example is Professor Georgi Barabashev, whose 1975 election poster, encouraging citizens to vote for him as deputy to Moscow city soviet, announced his participation in elaborating the draft bills on local soviets and on the status of Soviet deputies; he was also said to be a presidium member of the State and Law section of the USSR Ministry of Higher and Secondary Education's scientific and technical council.

Such involvement in the legislative process and in the work of state institutions ostensibly gives lawyers and other political scientists opportunities for bringing their ideas to the attention of those who frame policy. This is but one of several channels open to scholars and other experts in trying to influence policy (see

Churchward, 1973, chapter 7; Remnek, 1977, p. 52). There is no evidence that political scientists are directly involved in *deciding* policy: there were hardly any political scientists or lawyers on the Constitutional Commission, for example (see Skilling and Griffiths, 1971, p. 316). And yet I have been told by one member of the profession that he and some of his colleagues were involved in the work of special advisory committees working on the draft: these were first set up in June 1962 to draft specific sections of the document (Denisov, 1968, p. 105). They were subsequently involved in drafting the constitutions of the union republics, and it is fair to assume that more generally, in this indirect way, specialists are involved in law-making (Skilling and Griffiths, 1971, p. 317). Another Soviet scholar, in discussing the involvement of lawyers in the legislative process, was quite open about this: 'You name any major piece of legislation over the past thirty or forty years,' he said, 'and I could tell you who drafted it.' And, again in 1975, an appointment had to be cancelled because another scholar had a meeting of specialists to discuss what might appear in the central committee's report (to be delivered by Brezhnev) to the twenty-fifth congress six months or so later. 'At this stage we demand the maximum,' he said. 'Later it will be reduced by ten per cent, then another ten per cent, until we find agreement.' No deep secrets of the Kremlin's decision-making or legislative process were being inadvertently disclosed: but this comment reveals an extremely plausible and even sensible account of a political decision-making process, and one that is perhaps not unfamiliar. Such involvement of scholars is even directly encouraged. Yu. Makov, a Leningrad party secretary, urged the drawing-in of scholars into framing decisions dealing with 'the special problems of developing the economy and culture', as one of the preconditions for 'a scientific approach' in party work (Makov, 1971, p. 44). Solomon may be right in contending that unseen involvement of scholars in drafting and editing legislative bills and other governmental statements constitutes their most influential form of activity (see Remnek, 1977, p. 17; also Barry and Berman's judicious analysis and assessment of the impact of jurors on the legislative and political process, in Skilling and Griffiths, 1971, pp. 291–333). Mary McAuley has convincingly argued (1978, pp. 5–6) that the new Constitution represents a compromise among various views and opinions, including those of the specialists whose aspirations for more radical reformist measures, such as those discussed in this study, have been tempered by other, politically relevant, opinions and realities. I would suggest that the same applies to all major pieces of legislation, and possibly also to general policy statements.

Other forms of contact exist between scholars and politicians. In particular, many political figures, particularly from the republican or provincial level of administration, participate in conferences at which papers are presented and discussed by themselves and scholars. For instance, the conference in the Bashkir capital city of Ufa, in May 1975, heard papers from leading scholars (Bezuglov, Starovoitov, Sheremet, Barabashev and others), and also from republican officials and local scholars (Piskotin *et al.*, 1975). Contacts such as these permit scholars to influence the thinking of responsible officials, particularly by bringing to their attention the results of research which may challenge their comfortable and complacent views, thereby possibly stimulating political pressures for assistance to be given by the centre – perhaps in the form of legislative regulation, or of permission to attend to the matter locally.

An even greater opportunity may be afforded by the party central committee's Academy of the Social Sciences, which provides advanced courses for party and state leaders at all levels (Suslov, 1978, pp. 24–5). No doubt much of the Academy's effort will be directed towards ideological training. Nevertheless, work by faculty members and research students produced in recent years (e.g., Kadeikin *et al.*, 1974) shows an awareness of problems and a willingness to discuss them (even if ultimately unsatisfactorily) that would have seemed most improbable a decade ago. If the training given to the country's future leaders matches the capacity of the scholars in the Academy, this can have only a positive impact on the develop-ment of the 'administrative culture' – a concept that has been given increasing attention recently (see, e.g., Yu. M. Kozlov, 1978).

Yet the politicians remain firmly in control. They can impose limits, and there can be little doubt that, in the second half of the 1970s, there has been a tendency to impose greater conformity in the public expression of critical ideas. The repeated attacks on the 'dissident' movement are one obvious and well publicized indicator of this; another is the heightened emphasis on the ideological struggle between two world-views, in which the social sciences are expected to adopt an ideological 'hard line'. Highly revealing is central committee secretary Zimyanin's attack on social science textbooks. Speaking of the criticisms of over-centralization in their preparation and publication, he referred to the circulation of scores of textbooks and teaching aids 'in which were given various interpretations of a number of fundamental theoretical questions, which confused the students and brought positive harm to the learning process'. He gave the example of political economy, where 'there was no book that didn't have its "own" position on goods and money relations, its "own" formulation of a basic law', and where 'there even appeared a peculiar illness: the striving to "discover" ever more new laws'. Zimyanin called for 'stability' in the field of textbooks (*XXV s"ezd KPSS i zadachi kafedr obshchestvennykh nauk*, 1977, pp. 44–5) – an aspiration that fails to recognize that in a rapidly developing field of knowledge textbooks quickly become dated. Symptomatic of the trend is the fact that many books now carry a chapter that purports to 'unmask' the 'false' and 'lying' interpretations of Soviet conditions made by Western scholars (e.g., Shapko *et al.*, 1977, chapter 9; Suvorov *et al.*, 1977, chapter 12; Arnol'dov *et al.*, 1977, chapter 18).

Barghoorn has noted that the Brezhnev–Kosygin leadership has been an 'actively reformist' one in certain important respects, although 'it cannot be said that this leadership has openly or honestly confronted the problems and challenges facing it in a number of important fields' (in Farrell, 1970, p. 76). Indeed, caution, above all, possibly even conservatism, is a characteristic of the Brezhnev era (Nove, 1975, p. 159; Brown and Kaser, 1978, pp. 245, 299). Apart from the early reversals of some of Khrushchev's unsuccessful institutional reorganizations, structural reforms have been very modest (see Brown and Kaser, 1978, pp. 218–21).

Are we to conclude, therefore, that the extensive work of these scholars is ultimately extremely marginal to the political process in the USSR? There are two ways in which I believe Soviet political scientists may be helping to bring about change in the Soviet political system: conceptualization of political processes; and involvement in change at the local level.

POLITICAL SCIENCE CONCEPTUALIZATION

A characteristic feature of Soviet political science is its discriminating use of concepts and vocabulary developed in Western political analysis including, indeed, whole approaches. Thus, the systems approach has been used by at least one Soviet scholar (Marchenko, 1973). So has the structural–functional approach (Lesnyi and Chernogolovkin, 1976). The concept of 'political culture' has been translated into Soviet writings, and the need for its development stressed (Tikhomirov, 1975, *passim*). The literature on public opinion and interests shows clear signs of having adopted concepts and approaches from Western literature: for example, Safarov (1975b, especially p. 25, n. 1) cites many Western writers on public opinion measurement. The vogue for counting and measurement also reflects similar quantitative preoccupations in Western political science in the 1950s and 1960s, facilitated by the introduction of electronic computers; standard deviations, coefficients of variation, correlation coefficients and other basic statistical devices are used alongside other mathematically expressed measures (e.g., Pavlov and Kazimirchuk, 1971, pp. 68–73): this has naturally encouraged the professionalization of political research and analysis.

One effect of de-Stalinization has been the opening-up of the USSR to the outside world, including the world of scholarship.

The free exchange and circulation of information and opinion, called for by, say, Sakharov (1966, pp. 25–6, 62) or, less dramatically yet no less persuasively, Shakhnazarov (1972, pp. 137–8) has not been granted; yet Soviet scholars today have significant opportunities to acquaint themselves with Western thought. Many of them know Western languages; Soviet institutions exchange books and journals with similar institutions abroad, and have modest funds for purchasing Western books (the recent sharp inflation of book prices in Western countries cannot but have harmed the spread of Western ideas to countries with small amounts of available convertible currency, such as the USSR); some Western books are published in Russian translation; and through cultural exchanges with Western states, some social scientists spend extended periods in Western institutions, working alongside Western scholars, purchasing materials, and using libraries; some establish personal contacts which further lead to exchanges of ideas and scholarly materials (on these points, see Churchward, 1973, pp. 57–8; White, 1974, pp. 48–9; Shapiro and Potichnyj, 1976, p. 141). Through all these means, Soviet scholars have been able to become acquainted with Western scholarship, and to adopt approaches and methods where appropriate. Some Soviet scholars appear extremely well informed and widely read in Western political science literature (e.g., Farukshin, 1973; Fedoseev, 1974; Kalenskii, 1977). There may be a fashion to use Western terminology, as Azovkin implies (1973, p. 139), but for many scholars the concepts behind the jargon have proved useful.

It is important to note that these new conceptual frameworks, fresh approaches and novel research methods are not seen as competing with the basic Marxist–Leninist analysis of society. Indeed, a further strand in Soviet political science writing, exemplified by Farukshin (1973) and Fedoseev (1974), sets out directly to challenge and undermine the fundamental assumptions of Western analysis: Fedoseev explicitly calls for a special scholarly institution and journal to serve such a purpose (p. 121). Hence, the selective adoption of such concepts by

Soviet scholars does not imply acceptance of the values that underlie 'bourgeois' conceptual frameworks. Nevertheless, in expounding Western political science concepts, albeit with the intention of immediately demolishing them, such writers are giving them currency in the process; there may also be writers for whom this is a ploy. In general, however, such concepts when adopted serve rather as *techniques* for assessing the effectiveness of society's functioning (see Shakhnazarov, 1976, pp. 108, 111). For this reason, these aspects of 'bourgeois' social science are more acceptable than the ostensibly more appropriate Western writings in the Marxist tradition, which are by and large ignored, or dismissed critically. Mere techniques do not challenge the basic principles on which Soviet society is based, nor the particular interpretation of those principles by the CPSU. On the contrary, they are useful aids in applying them. Many Western Marxist writings, by contrast, or indeed critical east European Marxist writings, obviously challenge the CPSU's own interpretation of Soviet society, of the socialist model, and of Marxism–Leninism itself – as, of course, do Chinese views. Hence, they can be less readily assimilated (White, 1974, p. 49).

Even so, even though Western approaches may be viewed as techniques, the fact is that in adopting and adapting Western methods of analysis Soviet scholars have been led to ask questions of a very different order from those that were common a generation ago. No longer is there simply a preoccupation with outlining constitutional and legal arrangements. Instead, political institutions are judged in terms of their performance in reality, and this has led to far more searching questions about relations between polity and society, about interests and opinions, about the political competence of political actors and the public at large. Inevitably, different questions lead to different answers, which do not permit the complacency that was normal in the past.

Moreover, politicians themselves are being affected by this. They may prefer to talk of the 'selection and allocation of cadres', rather than 'political recruitment', and in this they find support among some scholars (e.g., Farukshin, 1973, pp.

58–61). But one is struck by the attention that politicians, from Brezhnev down, have been paying of late to the question of communication and public opinion. This example indicates that political leaders see value in receiving these signals of public needs, demands and opinion, rather than assuming (as many Western writers in the totalitarian school believed) that the Kremlin knows what is best for people. The stress on electors' mandates is a similar development, and the role of deputies as providers of information on demands and opinions has been recognized (see Gorshenev and Kozlov, 1976, p. 91). The importance of information – indeed, the whole cybernetics approach – has now been widely accepted in the USSR (see Hoffmann, 1977).

Thus, Soviet political scientists, on the basis of solid research, persuasively argue the need for reform. Some politicians now speak in terms unmistakably influenced by new conceptual approaches to society – and the replacement of 'state structure' by 'political system' in the Constitution is perhaps a supreme symbol of the change in perspective. Yet, despite these positive signs, we search in vain for the dramatic evidence that political scientists are listened to, or their work heeded. Possibly the jargon has reached the politicians' ears from a quite different source: the workers in the party's central apparatus, whose summaries of Western analysis and comment on the Soviet Union are phrased with direct translations into Russian of Western terminology. There may be some truth in that conjecture, and we can probably assume that even the writings of Soviet scholars are digested in this way before reaching the politicians.

LOCAL POLITICAL CHANGE

A point that is little understood in the West, where the model of a very highly centralized Soviet political system pervades, is the legislative power of provincial government. In fact, laws (*polozheniya, normativnye akty*, as opposed to statutes, *zakony*, which have wider legal significance and superior force) may be adopted at republican or provincial level, to regulate a specific aspect of political life in that particular territory (Rzhevskii, 1972). Perhaps significantly, Soviet scholars have given increasing attention to this question, and the scholarly literature reveals that local authorities are availing themselves of this power. In the early 1970s, Avak'yan said that such activity had significantly increased in recent years (in Kravchuk, 1973, p. 131; also Tikhomirov, 1978, pp. 141–3); and reports of the kind of local legislation being drafted suggest that it may be used for introducing locally reforms which, perhaps for political reasons, cannot be brought in for the whole country. Such laws do not attract the attention of the outside world, with its eyes firmly fixed on the Kremlin; yet I am convinced that the scale of such activity is significant, even if disappointment has been expressed at the pace of such reform (by, e.g., Solov'ëva, 1978, pp. 129, 133). By this means, slowly and incrementally, reformist change takes place.

A number of examples may be given. As mentioned in chapter 5, there have been many calls in the literature for a statute on electors' mandates. Such a law was adopted in Latvia in April 1975. In the summer of that year, an all-union statute was in draft, but it was not even published, let alone introduced. The Latvian reform nevertheless went ahead, and its results will no doubt be carefully studied before any attempt is made to introduce an all-union statute.

Similarly, there have been calls for giving proper legal status to deputies' groups: that is, semi-formal groupings of deputies who represent broadly the same voters at different levels in the hierarchy of soviets. So far, nothing has been done to implement this proposal at the level of either the USSR or the union republics. Yet by 1969 local soviets and executive committees were themselves adopting such normative acts (Avak'yan, 1969, pp. 81–2); the first such act was apparently adopted in Kuibyshev oblast as early as 1962 (Avak'yan, in Kravchuk, 1973, p. 136). Other provinces have adopted similar laws on deputies' groups, including Kalinin oblast, in June 1971, and Gorky oblast, two years later (*Polozhenie o deputatskikh postakh...*, 1971; *Polozhenie o deputatskikh gruppakh...*, 1973). On the first of these, a footnote explains that the draft was prepared by the oblast soviet executive committee 'jointly with the sector of representative organs of the Institute of State and Law, USSR Academy of Sciences'. Many further instances of local reform could be given.

All of this suggests that a considerable amount of innovation and change may be taking place at levels that are not obvious to most Western specialists, and we have clear evidence, and testimony, that Soviet political scientists are actively involved in this work. The relationship between scholars and politicians of the second and third tiers may be substantially more fruitful than that which exists with top politicians. Obviously this affects the pace and scope of any political reform in Soviet society, and the final chapter deals with the general question of political change.

CHAPTER 9

The Problem of Political Change, and the Future of Soviet Political Science

Leonid Brezhnev's leadership has aimed at greater rationality, as distinct from Stalin's crude and irrational enforced growth and Khrushchev's arbitrariness and unpredictable wilfulness. As has become clear, there is plenty of scope and need for political reform in the USSR, and scholars have been in the forefront in arguing for particular kinds of development and specific changes. Politicians too have acknowledged the need for change. Apart from Brezhnev's reference to 'objective problems in our federal state' (Brezhnev, 1972, p. 3), the Ukrainian party first secretary, V. V. Shcherbitskii, for instance, wrote in a recent book: 'At the XXV CPSU congress it was underlined that not all problems are yet resolved, that *better than all our critics we know our deficiencies, we see the difficulties*, and we are successfully overcoming them' (quoted in Glezerman and Iovchuk, 1978, p. 124; *emphasis added*). The pace of reform is cautious, but much of it is hidden: such as, apart from local reforms already discussed, the widespread turnover in personnel and their replacement by more sophisticated, competent, 'promising young workers'. There is a role in this for political scientists, not only in making specific proposals for institutional reform, but in working out the theoretical background for justifying such positive developments.

Nevertheless, despite signs of change, there is also abundant evidence of a conservative trend in the 1970s. Why are the politicians so shy of adopting some of the sane, sound, sensible

167

(and perhaps necessary) measures put forward in good faith by the social scientists, in response to the party's own calls to examine the political system and devise ways of developing socialist democracy? In short, what is the significance of the materials discussed in this book?

THE PROBLEM OF POLITICAL CHANGE

One's interpretation of the work of Soviet political scientists is bound to depend largely on one's basic assumptions about the nature of the political system. One approach is to assume that the Soviet political system is one in which a relatively small group – essentially the top party leadership – cynically uses power in order to maintain its own privileged lifestyle, by stifling any actual or potential criticism. Plenty of evidence can be adduced to support such an interpretation. The existence of privilege on a substantial scale has been well documented (by, for example, Matthews, 1978), and the treatment of dissidents by forcible psychiatric medication, imprisonment and exile and the general harassment of dissenters has been given so much publicity in the West that it scarcely needs mention as one of the most distasteful aspects of Soviet political life.

Where do the limited forms of criticism and the modest proposals for reform put forward by Soviet scholars fit into such a view? Possibly, as part of an elaborate hoax perpetrated on an innocent Soviet people. The scholars, on this view, become part of 'the system', making quasi-critical utterances in order to add credibility to the official protestations of reformism and democratization, in the eyes of the population (and also of naive and gullible foreign observers such as, perhaps, myself). In that case, one might comment that the mass Soviet public is not likely to be swayed either way by esoteric, heavily footnoted volumes produced in minute editions in provincial cities: such books and scholarly articles are produced by specialists for specialists, and the public is probably not even aware of their existence. In any case, if the political scientists are perpetrators of this hoax, what of Perttsik's cry from the heart in 1970 that it was time the politicians took up some of the ideas and acted? One answer to that question might be that the political scientists are themselves *victims* of the hoax, and are being duped by an ultra-cynical political leadership into believing that their criticisms are being listened to, and that they will have some impact on the policy-makers. This interpretation is more difficult to refute, except by referring again to the evidence – modest though it may be – that the ideas of scholars are sometimes taken up and embodied in legislation, which in some cases is known to have been drafted by, or in collaboration with, lawyers and political scientists.

One might also dismiss the writings of the scholars for their unimaginative repetition and paraphrasing of formal statements and the speeches of politicians, particularly in their more popularly presented writings. However, this does not necessarily disqualify them from serious consideration. This practice greatly facilitates publication (and speeds up writing!), and is a normal and accepted part of the political tradition. As to the *content* of such utterances, politicians in all systems tend to speak quite often in the form of wishfully thinking assertions. So, when Soviet politicians speak of the monolithic unity of the Soviet people in support of the party's policies (e.g., Podgorny in *XXIV s"ezd*, vol. I, p. 5), one may perhaps compare this with the many utterances of British politicians about the 'best police force in the world', the 'mother of parliaments', and other hyperboles that have an exhortative role, rather than being simply factual statements. We know from many sources that the Soviet populace is not overwhelming in its enthusiasm to carry out party policies. When G. N. Manov, for example, writes of passivity, consumerism, selfishness, political indifference and philistinism among some sections of Soviet society, one is inclined to believe him (in Tikhomirov, 1975, pp. 277–8, and Tikhomirov, 1978, p. 58). Presumably other scholars, and Soviet politicians too, are equally aware of these blemishes, which pointedly contradict the official, approved picture. The glowing commentaries may be an example of the Russian characteristic of *vran'yo* (fibbing, leg-pull), wittily elaborated by Ronald Hingley (1978); however, this tendency is not restricted to Russians or the Soviet Union.

Thus, it is impossible to accept the 'official' interpretation, whether expounded by propagandists, politicians or political scientists. But nor need we reject the whole of Soviet political science as a meaningless charade, a deception played on the population by scholars in connivance with the authorities, or on scholars by the authorities. Certainly Soviet scholars themselves do not see their role in that light. As a profession, they do benefit substantially from the system, which rewards competence and academic qualifications generously. They are all party members, which implies a willingness to work within existing arrangements. Yet this does not inhibit them from making critical observations, and Soviet scholars seem sincere in their belief that they are helping the cause of Soviet political development by identifying weaknesses and problems, and suggesting ways to overcome them.

An alternative interpretation of political science and political reform in the USSR can be arrived at by positing a *general desire* to back away from the brutality and exclusiveness of Stalinist methods, at the same time remembering that the Soviet leadership consists of *politicians*, governed by the wise Chinese maxim that 'He who rides on a tiger's back finds it hard to jump off'. There may also exist a partially autonomous security service, over which the political leadership has not complete control. (This is a not entirely implausible factor, given what is known of the freedom of the CIA from United States government control, at least in the past.) Thus, any 'reformist' section in the Soviet leadership may not have the freedom from political pressure that would permit it to introduce more widespread reforms. Medvedev convincingly demonstrates the presence of contrary opinions in influential places (Medvedev, 1975, chapters 3 and 4; also Brzezinski, 1969, pp. 22–3). Philip D. Stewart has argued that there is diversity of opinion on a whole range of issues among the second-level political leaders, the 'next generation' (in Shapiro and Potichnyj, 1976, chapter 2). Nor would the Soviet population necessarily be united in its support for reformist moves.

This feature of Soviet politics may be overlooked by critics of the regime, particularly in the West. There may be a lingering assumption, stemming from the picture of absolute control that characterized the totalitarian model of the system, that the Soviet leadership has the power to impose its will on the country, and that if they wished the Kremlin politicians could reform the system overnight; the corollary is that identified weaknesses exist because the leadership is prepared to tolerate them, or even finds them positively useful. According to this view, Stalinism represented the 'true nature' of the Soviet political system, which the current, essentially conservative leadership attempts to maintain. Any reformist changes are thus forced upon a reluctant leadership by the power of popular, or at least cohesive professional, opinion, or by other 'compelling social pressures' (Johnson, 1970, p. 140), and are interpreted as defeats, or at best concessions (such is the view implied by Chalmers Johnson, 1970, pp. 1–32; see also, for a discussion of such views, William Taubman's challenging survey, in Morton and Tökés, 1974, pp. 369–94).

Yet, as Jeremy Azrael points out, on occasion communist leaders have sponsored and introduced ostensibly resistible changes (in Johnson, 1970, pp. 140–1); and indeed, the situation appears differently if we assume that Stalinism, rather than being the model to be retained by practically any means, represents a model *from which to wean Soviet society*. From the vantage point of a *moderately reformist* political leadership, or of a keenly reformist one faced with political rivals and opponents (including the neo-Stalinists), the problem of reform may look very different.

The basic goal of any political system is to maintain political control and stability, to avoid its own collapse: that, then, is the overall parameter within which the Soviet leaders, as any other political leadership, operate. A second goal, posited at least for the sake of argument, is to *develop* or *reform* the system in the direction of greater democracy. Without going into the possible motivations for such a goal (about which Azrael has made a number of pertinent suggestions: see Johnson, 1970, p. 142), and without claiming that Brezhnev has been the most democratic or radical leader imaginable in Soviet society, let us assume for the purpose of argument that when he speaks of 'the further development of socialist democracy' (*XXIV s"ezd*, vol. I, p. 102), Brezhnev is not engaging in empty rhetoric, but is voicing a desire for changes in the political system, specifically towards greater *rationality*, greater *accountability* on the part of the administrative organs, and greater *involvement* of the population at large in political processes. What difficulties confront a leadership wishing to bring about such changes?

First, there is the sheer size of the country, coupled with an appallingly inadequate system of communications, which vastly reduces the control that the centre can exert over the provinces. The scandals in Georgia that came to light in 1972 (see Brown and Kaser, 1978, pp. 257; 273, n. 79), involving widespread corruption that implicated even a member of the CPSU politburo, are a notorious recent example of the weakness of the centre in controlling the localities. One Soviet scholar has revealed that 'practice bears witness to the fact that excessively large territories are practically not administered' (Nemtsev, 1969, p. 69). The difficulties involved in controlling local politicians and administrators, and inducing them to reform in the desired direction, can be easily appreciated. Moreover, the answer is not necessarily to send trouble-shooters from the centre: their presence may be so resented by those who benefited from the previous carefree arrangements that they will either provoke a reaction, or succumb to the prevailing mores themselves. The special problems of sending Russian administrators into non-Russian areas are an additional factor, implied by Soviet references to the need to build cadres of competent *local* officials. In either case, the reforming leadership fails.

The second major difficulty facing a reformist leadership is the personnel involved, a question of such significance that it merits further elaboration, even at the risk of repetition. There are a number of dimensions. First, those who have benefited

from Stalin's way of running the country are likely to obstruct
attempts to take away their privileged position. The resentful
response of party apparatchiks to Khrushchev's tampering with
the party and state structures in November 1962 has been well
documented (see, e.g., Churchward, 1965; Armstrong, 1966).
This was one of the first elements to be unscrambled by the post-
Khrushchev leadership implying a sensitivity to feelings across
the country, and suggesting a limit beyond which a political
leadership dependent on political peace and economic success
would not now dare to venture. Indeed, it was resistance by local
officials to the economic reform in the 1960s that led to its
failure and virtual abandonment; this testifies to the power of
local leadership to frustrate the reformist intentions of the
Kremlin's politicians (Ryavec, 1975, reviewed by Parrott, 1977,
pp. 57–8).

A second part of this question is the *quality* of party and state
administrative personnel. Many of the incumbents in the 1960s,
at the beginning of the present leadership's period in office, had
been appointed to their posts in the Stalin or Khrushchev eras,
when political reliability and a modest background were positive
assets and the need for competence was played down. Many
writers, faced with accounting for the problems caused by
incompetent management and political leadership, have complained of the poor calibre of local leaders, and, along with
Brezhnev and others, urged that higher standards be demanded
of them. Thus, in 1965 Piskotin and Tikhomirov urged the need
for better staff (*kadry*), and proposed special institutes for training personnel for the administrative apparatus. The quality of
auxiliary staff also needed improvement: the Kazakhstan state
planning commission employed twenty-four shorthand-typists,
yet none of them knew shorthand! (Piskotin and Tikhomirov,
1965: 3–5). A decade or so later, Brezhnev emphasized that

> the present-day leader must within himself organically
> combine party commitment with profound competence,
> discipline with initiative and a creative approach to affairs.
> Alongside that, at every level, the leader is also obliged to take
> into account socio-political and educational aspects, to be

sensitive to people, to their needs and requirements, to serve as an example in work and in his everyday life. [*XXV s"ezd*, vol. I, pp. 95–6]

These sentiments of Brezhnev have been repeated by many writers (e.g., Tikhomirov, 1975, pp. 130–1; Chekharin, 1977, p. 22).

This is obviously a very different type of official from the crude, half-educated, incompetent bully-boys and toadies who found their way into positions of authority in the past; and there has been an apparently serious and continuing attempt to ease those individuals out and replace them by more sophisticated personnel, in what one scholar in conversation referred to as 'a change of generations'. As a result of this and other measures, we find now significant improvement in the educational qualifications of state officers (for figures, see Shapko *et al.*, 1977, p. 20), confirming a trend identified at the beginning of the decade (Harasymiw, 1971, p. 341). But with 405,784 workers employed in the political administration and 1,570,168 in economic administration in 1970 (derived from *Census*, 1973, vol. 6, p. 20), the task of weeding out the unsatisfactory ones and replacing them with well-trained substitutes cannot be rushed.

Soviet scholars do take heart from the trend, however. V. A. Patyulin, for one, argued that recruiting better qualified and educated administrators will lead to a diminishing in the incidence of particular kinds of problems involving illegalities and infringements of citizens' rights. He ascribes these in the majority of cases to 'the still relatively low general educational level of some workers [in the apparatus], their insufficiently high level of legal qualification, and the absence [among them] of the appropriate culture and sense of high civic responsibility for the business entrusted to them'; others simply abuse their powers (in Tikhomirov, 1975, p. 183; also Burkauskas, 1966, p. 118).

Hence, the concept of *culture*, which can be applied in its specifically political orientation as a further explanatory feature in discussing political reform, as Soviet writers have done. The point is this: just as an effectively and efficiently run administration requires highly trained and perceptive civil servants, so, more broadly, the effective running of a participant political system – a democracy – requires a range of political skills and knowledge on the part of the population at large, together with a perception of the political system in which the individual is to play his role (see Pye, 1966: chapter 5). These skills and attitudes are very different from those required in a system dominated from the top, as the Stalinist system was. That is the thrust of Shakhnazarov's argument about creating an informed public opinion (see chapter 5). Obviously, the inculcation of such new skills and attitudes cannot be achieved overnight. It involves a transformation of the political culture, from a *subject* culture to the *participant* culture (see Almond and Verba, 1963, p. 19), and it applies both to the population at large and to their leaders, at all levels. The population needs to develop knowledge of the political system and the positive attitudes that will encourage them to participate, after decades, generations – even centuries – of all but total exclusion from meaningful involvement in politics.

In this connection, it is interesting to note the emphasis being placed on informing people of both their rights and their duties. A book on law for young people, for example, shows in a chatty manner how the law grants rights and imposes duties in various situations, including the work-place and the educational institution, explains certain concepts of citizenship, and discusses the reasons for juvenile crime and delinquency, all with the obvious (and laudable) aim of creating a responsible citizenry (Zhogin and Mel'nikova, 1971). Moreover, the stress on 'participation' under developed socialism may be not simply a propaganda assertion that people participate when in fact they do not, but rather an *exhortation* to participate. One notes also the books in popular format that have appeared in recent years, dealing with some of the questions raised in the scholarly literature. Topornin's exposition of the political system (1975) is one example; another is the collection of essays, reprinted from the journal *Sovety*, significantly entitled *The Organs of Popular Power: Experience and Problems*, with chapters on the importance of public opinion, on problems in applying the statute on the deputies' status, and on the impact of technology on political life, as well as other significant themes (Strepukhov, 1976). These developments appear to be aimed at developing the popular political culture, and not simply at pacifying the population with hollow assertions about the nature of the system.

Among society's leaders, too, certain characteristics are required, suited to operating within ground-rules that assume popular involvement. These will obviously be very different from those governing a system where local leaders are essentially the executors of policy decided on high and simply passed down for implementation. In a participant culture, leaders require those characteristics of competence, knowledge of affairs and of the law, openness and responsiveness in their dealings with the public, that official policy has been promoting in recent years.

Obviously, such an enormous change in outlook, on the part of the whole of society, involving in effect a complete break with tradition going back very many years (and specifically going back on an approach – Stalin's – that was capable of certain dramatic and positive achievements), must take a considerable time. But could not the regime be much more open now? Is it justified in excluding popular participation to the extent that still takes place? Would the system's existence be seriously threatened?

The answer, almost certainly, is that the system would not only *not* be harmed, but would most likely be significantly improved by permitting greater popular involvement, thereby fostering a sense of proprietorship which official propaganda has long stated already exists. The Soviet people may be less experienced than other nations in political matters; but, thanks to the success of the Soviet educational system, they are scarcely less well equipped with the mental skills needed to acquire and assimilate information and exercise discerning judgement (Topornin, in Tikhomirov, 1975, p. 86). Furthermore, the results of sociological surveys are said to indicate a development of precisely that type of civic consciousness: an investigation into the reasons why citizens obey the law revealed that 42.4 per cent did so 'in the common interest', 21.2 per cent did so out of habit, and only 21.5 per cent did so from fear of sanctions for infringement ('Formirovanie...', 1975). In addition, the presence in Soviet society of highly articulate and discriminating individuals – including both dissident intellectuals and loyal scholars – is ample testimony to the capacities of the Soviet population.

It is easy to condemn the Soviet leaders for their failure to reform. Finding adequate explanations for their behaviour is more difficult. However, apart from the general considerations that inhibit reformist political change, there are other features that might help to explain the cautiousness of the Brezhnev leadership specifically. First, as perceived in the Kremlin, the country is faced with a host of potentially massive problems: in the economy, with population dynamics, with the nationalities, with foreign hostilities (both NATO and China). With these and other factors impinging urgently on the consciousness of the leaders, political reform may have to take a back seat. Maintaining the system, keeping the population satisfied, preferably with economic progress and rising living standards: those claim the highest priority, and in comparison with them, institutional reforms take on a relatively minor significance.

Second, the Stalinist system's effectiveness in attaining certain economic goals is no doubt recalled by significant numbers of people, including 'reformists' in the top leadership, who are thus not willing to jettison the system that achieved so much. After all, the present leaders acquired their own political training under that very system that they are being asked to alter. Political tradition and their own training urge them in the direction of toughness, while their experience leads them towards caution in making changes. Dramatic gestures of reform may open up the way to uncontrolled, anarchic spontaneity, threatening the system. That would fly in the face of the traditional view that communism will not develop of its own accord, but has to be planned and worked for, its construction guided and directed; it would also brush up against the fear of spontaneity and chaos that is a deeply ingrained political instinct, and an essential part of the Soviet political culture (Brown and Kaser, 1978, pp. 267–8). In this situation, it would require tremendous political courage to take a truly bold reformist step.

Third, there is the awareness that the present leaders' predecessor, Khrushchev, was prone to indulge in bold, dramatic policy gestures, with singular lack of success: the maize campaign, the virgin lands campaign, the missiles in Cuba, the abolition of ministries, the splitting of the state and party apparatuses – these and other idiosyncratic steps led to confusion at best, and near-disaster at worst, and were an important element in Khrushchev's eventual downfall.

Furthermore (and this can easily be overlooked), no one in the Soviet leadership at any level has direct experience of running a political system that is responsive to popular demands and subject to constant criticism. The likely sense of apprehensiveness on their part is easily appreciated. There is also a large measure of stagnation and inertia which hinders dynamic thinking and inhibits change (Tikhomirov, 1975, p. 245; Arutyunyan, 1970, p. 12), as well as resistance to change on the part of well-entrenched officials across the country.

(Care is needed, however, in evaluating these phenomena. Given the unwillingness of even the British government to change its Official Secrets Act to make government information publicly available (see Cornford, 1978), the unwillingness to reform the electoral system by introducing proportional representation, and the great caution with which the broadcasting of parliamentary proceedings was introduced – not to mention the great misgivings over devolving responsibilities to regional assemblies in Wales and Scotland: given all this lack of eagerness for democratic reform in the United Kingdom, the reluctance of Soviet leaders to embrace wholeheartedly the cause of open government is seen in a somewhat more sober light. Indeed, as Hough argued in a very challenging way (1972), the charge of 'petrification' levelled at the Soviet system can, using similar indicators, be applied to the United States and, indeed, the United Kingdom in the 1970s.)

For these reasons, and others, it is perhaps too much to

expect a firm reformist lead from the top. After all, the present generation of top leaders began their own careers under Stalin, and, quite apart from the danger of revealing their own implication in the abuses of the past, their political instincts have deep roots. Nevertheless, it is equally wrong to interpret the absence of a strong reformist lead as signifying a complete unwillingness to introduce change into the system. The Soviet system *is* changing, slowly, undramatically, but, over the longer term, perceptibly, in a manner and at a pace that permits the regime to keep developments within check, and prevent them from getting out of hand (see Morton and Tökés, pp. xxiv–xxv). In particular, that means that reforms are limited to measures that do not upset the three 'pillars' that characterize the system: the party's 'leading role'; democratic centralism as a means of narrowing debate and ensuring discipline; and censorship (see Brown, 1979, p. 152). Hence, the kinds of change proposed by the Czechoslovak leaders in 1968 are 'out of bounds', since they would lead (as was intended) to a *fundamentally* different system, over such a short time-scale that the outcome could not be predicted, and chaos (it is felt) might ensue.

DIRECTIONS OF CHANGE

In developing the reform of the system, Soviet political scientists have been playing an important part for the past twenty years or so. In that sense, at least, they are part of the system: they examine theoretical and practical questions raised by politicians, and put forward proposals for development that are in turn taken up by politicians. They evidently enjoy greater impact when discussing broad trends than when putting forward specific proposals for institutional reform. Be that as it may, it must be said, on the basis of the work of Soviet scholars, that Soviet society – indeed, more explicitly, the Soviet *system* – has proved itself capable of generating ideas about its own nature other than the glib and superficial formulae of the propagandists; it is capable of identifying and confronting problems that arise, including, for example, new social and political problems posed by advancing sophisticated technology; and it is capable also of working out possible ways of coping with them in the future. It has also demonstrated a broad willingness to develop the system, without, however, either indulging in noisy reformist rhetoric (such as characterized the Dubcek leadership in Czechoslovakia in 1968, with disastrous consequences), or repeating the ill-considered chopping and changing that characterized the Khrushchev regime (or, indeed, permitting the despised 'free play of political forces' that is supposedly a feature of Western societies). The aim is clearly to reform carefully, in a considered fashion, on what they call a 'scientific basis'.

In this connection, the promulgation of the concept of 'developed socialism' may well be a significant reformist development. It no doubt has its specific political overtones. It is useful for establishing Brezhnev as the great leader who has brought the Soviet people to a new stage on the road to communism. The introduction of the 1977 Constitution, signed (significantly) by Brezhnev, symbolically marked this new development, and assured the CPSU secretary-general of a glorious place in the history books. The concept is also valuable on the international plane, by clearly placing the USSR ahead again in the movement towards communism, at a time when other socialist states appeared to be catching up: for instance, the German Democratic Republic also described itself as building a developed socialist state in the prologue to its 1974 Constitution (*Verfassung der DDR. . .* , 1975).

Yet there is a further important aspect of the concept that deserves consideration, namely its value in opening up the way for a thorough examination of the society, and the development of political practices and institutions appropriate for this stage (see, e.g., Guliev and Shchiglik, 1975, p. 10). This is already taking place: again, the 1977 Constitution is the greatest symbol of that, 'serving as the basis for further developing Soviet legislation and improving the whole of law-making activity' (Shafir, 1977, p. 15), and representing 'a powerful means of further developing and deepening socialist democracy'. (Krukhmalev, 1978, p. 19). New laws based on this Constitution are being introduced, although their content has been somewhat disappointing to reformists. Nevertheless, its value should not be underestimated. One problem in the past was that so many areas of social and political life were unregulated by law, so that to make legal provision over a broad field at least establishes a more comprehensive legal framework, and removes some of the very broad scope for malpractice by local officials. Moreover, for the present leaders this development has the obvious political merit of lending a vehicle for political change, without their having either to deny the validity of the Stalin era and its achievements, or to draw attention to its horrors, thereby implying acknowledgement of their own culpability. They can spare themselves political embarrassment, and present themselves as progressive. The distortions of Stalinism can be quietly ignored, as being associated with a former era: one must now look to the future, and build a society on its way to communism.

What kind of society might that be?

A preoccupation of Western students of Soviet politics in recent years, faced with the patent inadequacy of the totalitarian model of Soviet society, has been to see how far the post-Stalin USSR is moving towards the 'pluralist model' (see White, 1977, pp. 101–6). Some seize on evidence of 'group activity', and conclude that such developments signify movement in the direction of 'institutional pluralism' (Hough, 1972, and, most notably, Hough's collection of essays (1977)). Others, while reaching less definite conclusions, nevertheless find the concept of 'pluralism' a useful one in assessing the degree of change in communist systems, including that of the Soviet Union (e.g., Skilling, in Johnson, 1970, pp. 215–34; Burks, in Johnson, 1970, pp. 293–6; Skilling and Griffiths, 1971, p. 44).

Soviet writers reject, sometimes rather contemptuously, such notions. Thus, for Marchenko, pluralism is intended 'to mask the class essence of the capitalist system, to hide the roots of the monopolistic bourgeoisie's rule, to present the struggle of these or those financial and industrial circles for power and profit as the play of "free social forces". . .' (Marchenko, 1973, p. 100). In the Soviet ear the last phrase clearly smacks too much of anarchy and the law of the jungle; and, although Topornin, for one, has recognized the danger of 'over-organization' in society (in Tikhomirov, 1975, p. 141), the consensus view rejects pluralist democracy, along with Western criticisms of the 'standardizing' tendencies of socialism (Topornin, 1975, p. 91). The broad range of 'social organizations', covering the whole spectrum of human activities and interests, and permitting the individual to participate in social life and develop his or her personality in a variety of directions, is cited as evidence of the groundlessness of Western criticisms (Topornin, 1975, p. 91).

I believe we should not reject such ideas out of hand, as writers in the totalitarian tradition did, asserting that such organizations are set up and controlled by the party, and used for organizing the masses (e.g., Scott, 1969, p. 220). Not only do we have the testimony of Soviet writers that these organizations are growing in significance – indeed, their development is formally associated with the mature socialist society – but we also have their claims that they have some impact on the political process. For example, Safarov (1975b, pp. 67–8, 180) sees them as an important element in the development of an informed public, and a means whereby public opinion can influence policy implementation. In principle, too, they can be used as a source of information during the policy-making stage. Therefore, while party sponsorship of and involvement in the whole range of special-interest associations is certainly aimed at lending organization and discipline to the expression of those interests, the party authorities can deploy their members in these organizations both to lead opinion and to sound it out before making policy decisions. The creation of the environmental protection association in the mid-1960s may be a case in point: its establishment must have been in the face of opposition from the heavy industrial lobby, and it might simply have performed the role of pacifying the concerned public and explaining the need for cheaply run, environmentally unconscious big industry. In fact, Safarov has argued that public opinion has enjoyed significant impact in this area (1975b, p. 169), and indeed it is otherwise hard to see why a political leadership so obviously concerned with industrial output and reducing production costs should concern itself with environmental issues, as it has in the past decade (see Perry, 1973).

We thus have a picture of a political system in which a competent and responsive leadership takes into account not only the requirements of the ideology (itself constantly being reinterpreted in the light of current needs and developments), but also the articulated demands and interests of the public, and the considered opinions of specialists. At the same time, the system attempts to develop the political culture by raising the level of political competence, gradually extending the range of information made available, and slowly modifying the institutional forms of participation. This is the glowing picture put forward by scholars in their elaboration of the 'mature socialist society' in which

> collective forms of workers' influence on government have attained all-round and particularly broad development. First, all links in the political system more broadly rely on the experience of the masses in making decisions. Second, the population has begun to inform itself more widely about the basic directions of state activity. Third, all links in the socialist political system have begun more fully to take account of public opinion, which forms around their activity. Fourth, they are all now under more direct and systematic popular control. . . . Alongside this, in the mature socialist society, . . . on all sides are developing various forms of personal participation by individual citizens in the processes of government. [Manov, in Tikhomirov, 1975, p. 277]

There is, of course, a degree of wishful thinking here – as the author betrays when he discusses the difficulties (in Tikhomirov, 1975, p. 277). However, such passages do indicate the values that Soviet political scientists (and, taking up their arguments, some politicians) wish to be embodied in the political system of the immediate and medium-term future, until a new stage on the road to 'communist self-administration' is achieved. It is a very different system from the excessively centralized one of the Stalin era, which was wholly unresponsive to the wishes of the people. It is also very different from the pluralist model against which some Western writers attempt to measure the Soviet polity.

Perhaps such a 'third way' is unattainable, and the system will in any case become recognizably 'pluralist', in one definition or another of that term: in this connection, Hough draws a distinction between 'classical' pluralism and the 'institutional' pluralism that he sees in the Soviet Union (Hough, 1972, pp. 28–9). However, the *institutionalization* of pluralist politics, in the form of competing parties, or the legitimate existence of competing platforms within a single ruling party, is a most unlikely development. Indeed, as Robin Edmonds noted: 'Soviet society is not impervious to change; nor are Soviet political institutions; but they cannot be expected to evolve towards the Western model' (Edmonds, 1975, p. 164).

THE FUTURE OF POLITICAL SCIENCE

Soviet political scientists, I have argued, have played a significant role in political development over the past generation. In responding to the party's invitation to explore ways of developing 'Soviet socialist democracy', they have extensively examined various aspects of political life. In doing so, they have at times made analyses and put forward proposals that match many of those made by 'dissidents'. However, what distinguishes the 'legitimate' political science profession from the overt dissenters is their fundamental loyalty to the system, whose basic tenets (particularly the political supremacy of the communist party) they have not directly challenged. Thanks to this basic loyalty, Soviet scholars have gained a reputation as a 'responsible' profession, not uncritical, but willing to use their skills, techniques and knowledge for the benefit and improvement of society. In return – and this further distinguishes them from dissidents – they have achieved not only a materially privileged position in society, shared with other purveyors of expertise, but also an opportunity to influence the thinking of the politicians, who ultimately have the power to introduce political changes. Their success rate in inducing institutional reforms is in considerable doubt. But in identifying broad weaknesses in political behaviour (matters that can be put right by quiet policy changes, without the necessity of a politically risky identification of reforms) and in their changing the way the political system is viewed – here their impact has been much more vital. It is indeed part of the process of political culture formation.

The signs are that Soviet political scientists, whose profession remains indistinct, are likely to continue in such a role. The concept of 'developed socialism' has presented social scientists of all disciplines with the opportunity of elaborating a fresh analysis of that society, and specifically of working out the appropriate political and institutional arrangements for the future. As one recent book on the theme expressed it:

> The present stage of social development ... raises before legal science a whole complex of most important state–legal problems in the conditions of developed socialism and the building of communist society.... the predictive function of legal science, as of all the social sciences, is acquiring first-degree significance at the present time. [Kozyr' *et al.*, 1977, p. 225]

Among the problems likely to face Soviet political scientists are the political impact of technological change; the development of a more self-conscious and politically self-aware population and the impact of this on personal rights and freedoms; the establishment of new criteria for assessing the competence and general suitability of leadership cadres; and, continually, the institutional forms that embody the principles of public participation (Kozyr' *et al.*, 1977, pp. 226–8). The need for greater awareness of legal and political matters also gives the profession scope for developing its educative role.

Soviet political scientists have a certain interest in continuing the trend, and they can no doubt find plenty of work to justify their existence. However, in the early 1960s it was highly fashionable to emphasize the withering-away of the state; it was also frequently asserted that, not only would state institutions disappear, but so would *law*: it would be replaced as a social regulator by 'communist morality'. This raised the interesting – and, for academic lawyers, alarming – question: What would happen to legal science and scientists? In encouraging the rapid development towards communism, were they sounding their own death-knell?

O. A. Krasavchikov addressed himself optimistically to the question, in an essay in a volume on law and communism (Kerimov, 1965, pp. 175–207). Some writers, particularly certain philosophers, he argued, overestimated the possibility of regulating social relations by moral force alone. There are also in Soviet society certain *conventions* that govern behaviour, which are neither established by legislation, nor form part of any *moral* code: these, he said, will continue under communism. In fact, he argued that the norms that will regulate behaviour under communism 'cannot and should not be reduced simply to moral norms'. Certain relationships cannot be regulated simply by morality – economic and social planning is a case in point: this requires the application of *rational*, rather than moral, norms. Furthermore, as society continues to develop, so the norms required for regulating the society will alter, and a new science will arise: the science of the laws regulating communist social relations. And – probably to the relief of many – this science will develop on the basis of the knowledge gained by present legal science: hence, Krasavchikov writes of 'the process of development ' of legal science into the science of the laws of the social (societal in the proper meaning of this word, and not state-political) regulation of communist relations'. This development will, he says, 'go in parallel with the process of the withering-away of the state and law, as the political essence of the functions of the state changes, and with the transition to forms of social self-administration' (in Kerimov, 1965, p. 183)

In other words (and he uses the Marxist terminology), legal science – the superstructure – will follow changes in the 'substratum', and eventually lead to the 'transfer of powers to its successor'. This new science will be 'synthetic' (or, more properly, eclectic), drawing on such present-day sciences as ethics, social psychology, pedagogy, and so on; indeed, the 'period of synthesis' had, he said, already arrived, and the new science was being created (in Kerimov, 1965, p. 187).

That was in 1965. Since then, legal and political science has continued its own development. Present writers tend to repeat the Marxist teaching that the need for law will eventually die away, as communist morality becomes imbued in people; nevertheless, in the meantime, there is an ever-greater need for a *strengthening* of the legal basis of Soviet society, and it would be a 'mistake' to force the pace of the dying-away process (Pigolkin and Rozhko, 1976, pp. 10, 51, 62; also Kerimov, 1965, p. 134), and it would be 'premature' to seek in the present legal system signs of this withering away of the legal regulation of societal affairs (Tikhomirov, 1978, p. 126).

From this study, I conclude that here is a body of scholars whose works are worthy of our attention; and I reject the contention that 'almost every Soviet work of real social and literary interest since 1965 has been printed only abroad' (Nove, 1975, p. 159). Further: as a profession, political scientists have neither the responsibility of the political leaders, nor the political pressures that bias both their utterances and their policies. Nor have they, as loyal citizens, the same axes to grind as the majority of dissident writers. On those grounds alone, their works should be studied, alongside the works of the politicians and the *samizdat* writings of dissenters. Soviet scholars have access to information and the ability to engage in research that other writers do not enjoy, and which certainly no Western student of Soviet politics can aspire to. We can thus take advantage of their research, much as Shakhnazarov urged Soviet scholars to use Western research results (Shakhnazarov, 1976, p. 111). That is a major and vital benefit stemming from their commitment; furthermore, although that commitment may at times have an inhibiting influence on what they write – and British scholars too have the Official Secrets Act – it also assists them in publishing ideas that,if theycame from a dissident's pen, would lead to severe reprisals. They have their interests as a profession, specifically to advance the cause of political science, by creating a demand for knowledge of legal and political affairs, training new members of the profession to cater for that demand, and trying to persuade the politicians that their professional views and judgements are worth listening to. Another side of their loyal commitment is that the politicians are not naturally biased against them. Thus, *dissent* may not be entirely synonymous with 'the politics for change in the USSR' (Tökés, in Morton and Tökés, 1974, chapter 1), and this second branch of Soviet political thought may be equally significant. Indeed, the development of a critical political science profession also may be regarded as 'a new, and, in the long run, possibly significant dimension' of Soviet politics (Morton and Tökés, 1974, p. 5).

Despite the apparent caution with which scholars' ideas have been accepted, there are three possible lines of development that look promising. First, there is their involvement in *local reform*, discussed above, working together with local state and party authorities in studying problems, applying reformist principles, drafting legislation and monitoring the results. Second, there is the conducting of *experiments*. Although we saw an experiment that was prepared but not allowed to go ahead – that of the local soviet presidium – nevertheless this form of activity has been engaged in on several other occasions. For example, in 1975 Bezuglov reported two experiments in the formulation and aggregation of electors' mandates (Bezuglov, 1975, pp. 89–90); the idea of the 'experimental testing of various methods and ways of working' has been endorsed for application to the party (Kadeikin *et al.*, 1974, p. 106, also pp. 21–2). Two authors even conducted such experiments (Kushnikov and Sopelko, 1971, pp. 78–9; also Andreev and Arzamastsev, 1970, p. 108), and other writers have accorded 'significant importance' to conducting experiments, adding that this was favoured by Lenin (Babii *et al.*, 1976, p. 266; and especially Solov'ëva, 1978, pp. 124–7). This approach has obvious merits from the politicians' point of view. It can save a lot of confusion caused by unstudied reform, such as Khrushchev indulged in (this may explain why the notion of experiments was so widely discussed in the literature in the mid-1960s, shortly after Khrushchev's removal from power), and experience can be acquired on which to judge the likely effects of a particular proposal, without the politicians having to commit themselves to a major legislative innovation, with the political risks which that might involve. Such an approach might therefore provide reform-minded politicians with the evidence needed to convince their colleagues of the value of particular reforms. Morever, the experiment *is* an impeccably scientific device, which should fit well into the ethos of science and rationality and supposedly characterizes 'developed socialism'.

The third possible development, which now seems to be attracting some attention in the Soviet Union, as well as outside it, is the extension of studies in comparative socialism: comparing Soviet institutions and practices with those of other countries in the socialist bloc. The foremost exponent of this branch of Soviet political science is B. A. Strashun, whose work on socialist electoral systems (1973) led him to endorse contested elections. More recently, he has published a broader comparative study of socialist systems, and he explicitly calls for the development of comparative studies of socialist countries (Strashun, 1976, pp. 7–8). Other writers, too, draw parallels and contrasts between Soviet legislation or practice and that of other socialist countries (e.g., Shabanov, in Sheremet, 1976, pp. 212, 214, and, explicitly, p. 216; see also Shakhnazarov, 1972, p. 191). The point here is that, since the regime accepts that other countries' experience in building socialism is legitimate, it may find such experience applicable to Soviet conditions; whereas the experience of 'bourgeois' states, even if similar, would not be acceptable. Reverting to the electoral system, Strashun openly sets out his view that 'in a whole series of cases it seems possible and appropriate to make use of the self-justified experience of foreign socialist countries, with the aim of further improving Soviet electoral law' (Strashun, 1976, p. 202), and elsewhere he draws contrasts between the CPSU's performance of its leading role and that of the party in other countries (pp. 90–102).

There may be an implication that the Soviet Union can learn from other socialist countries, in the words of M. A. Suslov, long-standing member of the politburo, at the opening of the expanded Academy of the Social Sciences of the CPSU central committee. Welcoming the presence of foreign party and state functionaries as future course students, he stated that studying together would permit them all to examine their common experience and adopt what is valuable from each country. 'All this mutually enriches us,' he said, 'and facilitates an acceleration of the pace of development of the countries of the socialist commonwealth' (Suslov, 1978, p. 25). Thus, although the USSR alone claims to have built a 'developed socialist society', and the others have to go through such a stage, nevertheless the assertion is no longer made that the Soviet road must be followed in all its details, and the Soviet Union may itself even follow on specific points.

One final element may augur well for the future of Soviet political science: the change of political generations. The present generation of leaders received its political training and gained its experience in the days of Stalin, a point well argued by Peter Frank (in Brown and Kaser, 1978, pp. 98–111). They are all quite advanced in years, a point also made by many Western scholars (see Brown and Kaser, 1978, pp. 111–12, 262, 306). It is perhaps not to be expected that a group of elderly leaders, obviously reaching the end of their careers, should embark on significant reforms. In this connection, we note with interest Brezhnev's reported wish to be succeeded by a man twenty years younger (Edmonds, 1975, p. 165). If the present leadership's own assertions are correct, concerning the promising, educated, sophisticated younger generation who are being moved into influential positions to replace the 'old guard', then such a generation, when it reaches the positions of real power, may still have the intelligence to appreciate the value of social science in helping to solve problems. Many of them will, presumably, have been educated alongside the present and future political scientists, thus forging personal links which may survive the shift into different careers.

Whether such a development in professionalizing government will represent a move towards 'communism' is debatable. The arguments are complex, and cannot be adequately treated here. The notion of a political leadership advised by 'specialists' and 'experts', and stressing the values of rationality and a scientific approach to running society, may be fundamentally inimical to the development of government by the masses; it is also manifestly contrary to Lenin's views on the need to simplify administration so that the masses can perform the task. Moreover, the idea that the popular political culture needs to be 'developed' implies little faith in the political wisdom and maturity of the masses, and no trust in their capacity to run the society smoothly and harmoniously. Even the calls for officials to display greater competence, professionally and politically, support the continued existence of a stratum of political and economic managers, distinguished from those over whom they have authority, albeit acting with greater sensitivity than hitherto: indeed, the concepts of a 'leadership style' and 'leadership skills' imply that the functions cannot be performed by the average citizen without special training. On the other hand, the modern, technological economy has produced a society so complex and large in the scale of its operations that certain categories of decisions need to be taken on the basis of types of information that the masses are probably not at present competent to handle. For example, such is the scale of state involvement in running the economy and providing welfare, and such is the cost of modern industrial development, that the rational allocation of resources demands sophisticated methods for processing information and reaching policy decisions: the strategy for developing Siberia's wealth is not something that can be decided spontaneously by the masses. There is therefore an objective need for a perceptive leadership to cultivate in the broad masses those skills and values without which such complex goals cannot be attained. The ideological problem posed by this dilemma is that it smacks very much of an elitist society, led by those who know what needs to be done. Hence (perhaps) the repeated calls for leaders at all levels to consult the masses regularly; hence too (perhaps) the trend for drawing more workers into the ranks of the party. Yet the notion of the vanguard, leading the society forward on the correct path, itself implies some significant political distinction between the party and its regime, on the one hand, and the broad non-party masses, on the other. The assumptions underlying this approach can be expressed in more than one way: from one point of view, it accepts the duty of the vanguard to lead; from an alternative political vantage-point, it justifies the rule of a privileged minority or elite (White, 1974, p. 49).

However these ideological dilemmas may be resolved (and the essential point is that they *are* ideological in nature), for the foreseeable future Soviet political scientists are likely to continue their present role. That is, they will continue to play their part in the Soviet system's 'evolutionary change', identifying the problems of an ever more complex and sophisticated society, and proposing solutions that will permit development without stimulating 'major systemic crises' (Morton and Tökés, 1974, p. xxiv). Provided they achieve this, they are likely to retain the general support of the political leadership, and most probably will enhance the authority and prestige of their profession. It is also probable that they will continue to work for recognition as a separate discipline, alongside sociology, economics, psychology and other social sciences. It is not inconceivable that they will eventually succeed.

Bibliography

The following abbreviations of journal titles are used:

APSR	*American Political Science Review*
BJPS	*British Journal of Political Science*
PoC	*Problems of Communism*
SDT	*Sovety Deputatov Trudyashchikhsya* (with the issue of November 1977, the title changed to *Sovety Narodnykh Deputatov*)
SGiP	*Sovetskoe Gosudarstvo i Pravo*
Sov. Studs	*Soviet Studies*
Vop. Fil.	*Voprosy Filosofii*
Vop. Ist. KPSS	*Voprosy Istorii KPSS*

The following abbreviations are used in the names of publishing houses:

Izd.	Izdatel'stvo (publishing house)
Novosti	Novosti Press Agency
Politizdat	Izdatel'stvo Politicheskoi Literatury
Progress	Progress Publishers
UP	University Press (e.g., Oxford UP)
Yur. Lit.	Yuridicheskaya Literatura (formerly known as Gosyurizdat)

AFANAS'EV, V. G. (1975) *Sotsial'naya informatsiya i upravlenie obshchestvom* (Moscow: Politizdat).

AIMBETOV, A., BAIMAKHANOV, M. and IMASHEV, M. (1967) *Problemy sovershenstvovaniya organizatsii i deyatel'nosti mestnykh Sovetov* (Alma-Ata: Nauka).

AIZIKOVICH, A. S. (1965) 'Vazhnaya sotsiologicheskaya problema', *Vop. Fil.*, 1965, no. 11, pp. 163–70.

ALMOND, GABRIEL, A. and VERBA, SIDNEY (1963) *The Civic Culture: Political Attitudes and Democracy in Five Nations* (Princeton, NJ: Princeton UP).

ANDREEV, B. G. and ARZAMASTSEV, A. N. (1970) 'K voprosu o nauchnykh osnovakh partiinogo stroitel'stva', *Vop. Ist. KPSS*, no. 7, pp. 103–9.

Apparat upravleniya sotsialisticheskogo gosudarstva, 2 (1977) (Moscow: Yur. Lit.).

ARMSTRONG, JOHN A. (1966) 'Party Bifurcation and Elite Interests', *Sov. Studs*, vol. XVIII, pp. 417–30.

ARMSTRONG, JOHN A. (1973) *Ideology, Politics and Government in the Soviet Union: An Introduction*, 3rd edn (London: Nelson).

ARNOL'DOV, A. I. *et al.* (eds) (1977) *Dukhovnyi mir razvitogo sotsialisti-cheskogo obshchestva* (Moscow: Nauka).

ARUTYUNYAN, N. KH. (1969) 'Deputat i ego delo', *Izvestiya*, 4 March, pp. 1 and 3.

ARUTYUNYAN, N. KH. (1970) 'Nauchno upravlyat' protsessom sovetskogo stroitel'stva', in *Organizatsiya i deyatel'nost'*, pp. 5–16.

ATAMANCHUK, G. V. (1968) 'Rol' postoyannykh komissii v osushchestvlenii funktsii mestnykh Sovetov', *SGiP*, no. 3, pp. 105–9.

ATAMANCHUK, G. V. (1970) 'Sotsial'noe razvitie i mestnye Sovety', *SGiP*, no. 12, pp. 93–8.

AVAK'YAN, S. A. (1969) 'Pravovoe regulirovanie organizatsionno-massovoi deyatel'nosti mestnykh Sovetov', *SGiP*, no. 4, pp. 78–83.

AZOVKIN, I. A. (1965) 'Mestnye Sovety deputatov trudyashchikhsya na sovremennom etape kommunisticheskogo stroitel'stva', *SGiP*, no. 3, pp. 3–13.

AZOVKIN, I. A. (1966) 'Vzaimootnosheniya deputatov s izbiratelyami v SSSR', in Makhnenko (1966), pp. 141–61.

AZOVKIN, I. A. (1971) *Mestnye Sovety v sisteme organov vlasti* (Moscow: Yur. Lit.).

AZOVKIN, I. A. (1973) Review of V. I. Vasil'ev, *Demokraticheskii tsentralizm v sisteme Sovetov* (Moscow: Yur. Lit., 1973) *SGiP*, no. 12, pp. 137–9.

AZRAEL, JEREMY R. (1970) 'The Legislative Process in the USSR', reprinted in Cornell (1970), pp. 205–17.

BABII, B. M., TARANOV, A. P. and TERLETSKII, B. M. (eds) (1976) *Politi-cheskaya organizatsiya razvitogo sotsialisticheskogo obshchestva (pravovye problemy)* (Kiev: Naukova Dumka).

BAITIN, M. I. (1965) Review of Kotok (1964), *SGiP*, no. 2, pp. 157–8.

BANNYKH, M. P. (1974) *Sessii raionnogo, gorodskogo Soveta* (Moscow: Yur. Lit.).

BARABASHEV, G. V. (1975a) 'Rukovodstvo deyatel'nosti mestnykh Sovetov avtonomnoi respubliki v svete noveishego zakonodatel'stva', in Piskotin *et al.* (1975), pp. 36–9.

BARABASHEV, G. V. (1975b) *Raionnyi, gorodskoi Sovet na sovremennom etape* (Moscow: Yur. Lit.).

BARABASHEV, G. V. and SHEREMET, K. F. (1965a) *Sovetskoe stroitel'stvo*, (2nd edn 1974) (Moscow: Yur. Lit.).

BARABASHEV, G. V. and SHEREMET, K. F. (1965b) 'Mestnye Sovety segod-nya i zavtra', *SGiP*, no. 11, pp. 152–4.

BARABASHEV, G. V. and SHEREMET, K. F. (1967) 'KPSS i Sovety', *SGiP*, no. 11, pp. 31–41.

BARABASHEV, G. V. and SHEREMET, K. F. (1975) 'Razvitie Sovetov i zadachi nauki', *SDT*, no. 8, pp. 9–18.

BARABASHEV, G. V. and SHEREMET, K. F. (1978) *KPSS i Sovety narodnykh deputatov* (Moscow: Znanie).

BEGIYAN, A. Z. (1970) *Sovety Armyanskoi SSR v period stroitel'stva kommunizma*, in *Organizatsiya i deyatel'nost'* . . . (1970), pp. 37–53.

BELYAKOV, V. K. and ZOLOTAREV, N. A. (1975) *Organizatsiya udeseteryaet sily: Razvitie organizatsionnoi struktury KPSS, 1917–1974 gg.* (Moscow: Politizdat).

BERG, A., BIRYUKOV, B. and NOVIK, I. (1971) 'Metodologicheskie aspekty kibernetiki', *Kommunist*, no. 18, pp. 86–95.

BEZUGLOV, A. A. (1968a) 'Otchëty deputatov pered izbiratelyami', *SGiP*, no. 8, pp. 101–5.

BEZUGLOV, A. A. (1968b) *Izbirateli i deputaty strany Sovetov* (Moscow: Znanie).

BEZUGLOV, A. A. (1971) *Sovetskii deputat: gosudarstvennopravovoi status* (Moscow: Yur. Lit.).

BEZUGLOV, A. A. (1973) *Soviet Deputy (Legal Status)* (Moscow: Progress).

BEZUGLOV, A. A. (1975) 'Nakazy izbiratelei i narodnokhozyaistvennyi plan', in Piskotin *et al.* (1975), pp. 87–90.

BINDER, M. A. (ed.) (1974) *Aktual'nye voprosy sovetskogo stroitel'stva* (Alma-Ata: Nauka).

BLONDEL, JEAN (1969) *An Introduction to Comparative Government* (London: Weidenfeld & Nicolson).

BOKAREV, N. N. (1969) 'V interesakh povysheniya urovnya partiinoi raboty', *Partiinaya zhizn'*, no. 4, pp. 47–52.

BOKAREV, N. N. (1974a) 'Sotsiologicheskie issledovaniya problem partiinogo stroitel'stva', *Vop. Ist. KPSS*, no. 1, pp. 102–8.

BOKAREV, N. N. (1974b) *Voprosy sotsiologii v partiinoi rabote* (Moscow: Moskovskii Rabochii).

Bol'shaya Sovetskaya Entsiklopediya (1953) (2nd edn, vol. 18) (Moscow: Sovetskaya Entsiklopediya, article on *Interes*).

'Bol'shoi den' stolitsy' (1975) *Vechernyaya Moskva*, 16 June.

BREZHNEV, L. I. (1972) 'O pyatidesyatiletii Soyuza Sovetskikh Sotsialisticheskikh Respublik' (speech at a jubilee session of the CPSU central committee, the USSR Supreme Soviet, and the RSFSR supreme soviet, 21 December 1972), *Pravda*, 22 December.

BREZHNEV, L. I. (1977a) 'O proekte Konstitutsii Soyuza Sovetskikh Sotsialisticheskikh Respublik' (speech at CPSU central committee plenum, 24 May 1977), *Kommunist*, no. 8, pp. 34–44.

BREZHNEV, L. I. (1977b) 'Zaklyuchitel'noe slovo tovarishcha L. I. Brezhneva' (speech at session of USSR Supreme Soviet, 4 October 1977), *Kommunist*, no. 15, pp. 53–5.

BROWN, A. H. (1974) *Soviet Politics and Political Science* (London: Macmillan).

BROWN, ARCHIE (1979) 'Eastern Europe: 1968, 1978, 1998', *Daedalus*, Winter issue, pp. 151–74.

BROWN, ARCHIE and GRAY, JACK (eds) (1977) *Political Culture and Political Change in Communist States* (London: Macmillan).

BROWN, ARCHIE and KASER, MICHAEL (eds) (1978) *The Soviet Union Since the Fall of Khrushchev*, 2nd edn (London: Macmillan).

BRZEZINSKI, ZBIGNIEW K. (ed.) (1969) *Dilemmas of Change in Soviet Politics* (New York: Columbia UP).

BURKAUSKAS, A. YU. (1966) 'Otchëty ispolkomov na sessiyakh mestnykh Sovetov (po materialam Litovskoi SSR)', *SGiP*, no. 8, pp. 114–19.

BURLATSKII, F. M. (1961) 'Voprosy gosudarstva v proekte Programmy KPSS', *Kommunist*, no. 13, pp. 37–48.

BURLATSKII, F. M. (1965) 'Politika i nauka', *Pravda*, 10 January, p. 4.

BYRDAROV, GEORGII (1977) *Sotsiologiya i partiinaya rabota* (Moscow: Progress; originally published Sofia: Partizdat, 1972).

CARSON, GEORGE BARR, JR (1956) *Electoral Practices in the USSR* (London: Atlantic Press).

CENSUS (1973) *Itogi Vsesoyuznoi perepisi naseleniya 1970 goda*, 7 vols (Moscow: Statistika, 1972–4), vol. 6.

CHEKHARIN, I. M. (1975) *Postoyannye komissii mestnykh Sovetov* (Moscow: Yur. Lit.).

CHEKHARIN, YE. M. (1977) *Razvitie politicheskoi sistemy Sovetskogo obshchestva na sovremennom etape (lektsiya)* (Moscow: Mysl').

CHIRKIN, V. YE. (1967) 'O sistemnom analize politicheskoi organizatsii obshchestva', in Petrov (1967), pp. 107–15.

CHKHIKVADZE, V. M. (1967) *Gosudarstvo, demokratiya, zakonnost'* (Moscow: Yur. Lit.).

CHKHIKVADZE, V. M. (1968) 'Pravovaya nauka sotsializma', *Pravda*, 10 January.

CHURCHWARD, L. G. (1965) 'To Divide or Not to Divide', *Sov. Studs*, vol. XVII, pp. 93–6.

CHURCHWARD, L. G. (1966a) 'Towards a Soviet Political Science', *Australian Journal of Politics and History*, vol. XII, pp. 66–75.

CHURCHWARD, L. G. (1966b) 'Soviet Local Government Today', *Sov. Studs*, vol. XVII, pp. 431–52.

CHURCHWARD, L. G. (1973) *The Soviet Intelligentsia: An Essay on the Social Structure and Roles of Soviet Intellectuals During the 1960s* (London: Routledge & Kegan Paul).

Constitution (Fundamental Law) of the Union of Soviet Socialist Republics (1977) (Moscow: Novosti).

CORNELL, RICHARD (ed.) (1970) *The Soviet Political System: A Book of Readings* (Englewood Cliffs, NJ: Prentice-Hall).

CORNFORD, JAMES (1978) 'The Right to Know Secrets', *The Listener*, 31 August, pp. 258–60.

DENISOV, A. I. (1968) 'Sushchnost'' i znachenie Sovetskoi Konstitutsii', in Kalinychev *et al.* (1968), pp. 91–106.

DERBINOV, YU. V., KUKIN, D. M. and NAZAROV, S. A. (1975) *Pervichnaya partiinaya organizatsiya – avangard trudovogo kollektiva* (Moscow: Mysl').

DIORDITSA, A. F. (1967) *Deyatel'nost' sel'skikh i poselkovykh Sovetov Moldavii – na uroven' novykh zadach* (Kishinev: Kartya Moldovenyaske).

EASTON, DAVID (1965) *A Systems Analysis of Political Life* (New York: John Wiley).

EDMONDS, ROBIN (1975) *Soviet Foreign Policy, 1962–1973: The Paradox of a Super-Power* (London: Oxford UP).

'Effektivnost' deputatskoi deyatel'nosti (opyt konkretnogo sotsiologicheskogo issledovaniya na materialakh Armyanskoi SSR)' (1969) *SGiP*, no. 1, pp. 110–15.

EVANS, ALFRED B., JR (1977) 'Developed Socialism in Soviet Ideology', *Sov. Studs*, vol. XXIX, pp. 409–28.

FAINSOD, MERLE (1958) *Smolensk Under Soviet Rule* (London: Macmillan).

FARBER, I. YE. (ed.) (1969) *Problemy konstitutsionnogo prava* (Saratov: Ministerstvo Vysshego i Srednego Spetsial'nogo Obrazovaniya RSFSR).

FARRELL, R. BARRY (ed.) (1970) *Political Leadership in Eastern Europe and the Soviet Union* (London: Butterworths).

FARUKSHIN, M. KH. (1973) *Partiya v politicheskoi sisteme Sovetskogo obshchestva (Protiv kontseptsii sovremennogo antikommunizma)* (Kazan': Izd. Kazanskogo Universiteta).

FEDOSEEV, A. A. (1974) *Politika kak ob"ekt sotsiologicheskogo issledovaniya (Kritika metodologicheskikh osnov sovremennoi burzhuaznoi politologii)* (Leningrad: Izd. Leningradskogo Universiteta).

'Formirovanie uvazheniya k sotsialisticheskomu pravu (sotsiologicheskie aspekty)' (1975) *SGiP*, no. 4, pp. 37–46 (cited as 'Formirovanie', 1975).

FRIEDGUT, THEODORE H. (1978) 'Citizens and Soviets: Can Ivan Ivanovich Fight City Hall?', *Comparative Politics*, vol. 10, pp. 461–77.

FRIEDRICH, CARL J. and BRZEZINSKI, ZBIGNIEW K. (1966) *Totalitarian Dictatorship and Autocracy*, 2nd edn (New York: Praeger).

FROLIC, B. MICHAEL (1970) 'The Soviet Study of Soviet Cities', *Journal of Politics*, vol. 32, pp. 675–95.

GABRICHIDZE, B. N. (1968) *Gorodskie Sovety deputatov trudyashchikhsya* (Moscow: Yur. Lit.).

GABRICHIDZE, B. N. (1971) *Apparat upravleniya mestnykh Sovetov* (Moscow: Yur. Lit.).

GAIDUKOV, D. A. and STAROVOITOV, N. G. (eds) (1965) *Mestnye Sovety na sovremennom etape* (Moscow: Nauka).

GAK, G. M. (1955) 'Obshchestvennye i lichnye interesy i ikh sochetanie pri sotsializme', *Vop. Fil.*, no. 4, pp. 17–28.

GALESNIK, L. S. (1957) 'O nakazakh sovetskikh izbiratelei', in *Voprosy teorii i istorii gosudarstva i prava i gosudarstvennogo prava, Tom IV* (Sverdlovsk: Sverdlovskoe Knizhnoe Izd.), pp. 162–90.

GÉLARD, PATRICE (1975) *Les Systèmes Politiques des Etats Socialistes: Le Modèle Soviétique* (Paris: Editions Cujas).

GILISON, JEROME M. (1968) 'Soviet Elections as a Measure of Dissent: The Missing One Percent', *APSR*, vol. LXII, pp. 814–26.

GLEZERMAN, G. YE (1966) 'Interes kak sotsiologicheskaya kategoriya', *Vop. Fil.*, no. 10, pp. 14–26.

GLEZERMAN, G. and IOVCHUK, M. (1978) 'Sovetskii obraz zhizni i formirovanie novogo cheloveka', *Kommunist*, no. 4, pp. 119–25.

GOLOVKO, A. A. (1966) 'Nauchnyi eksperiment v gosudarstvennom stroitel'stve (na materialakh istorii Belorusskoi SSR)', *SGiP*, no. 11, pp. 97–101.

GOLOVKO, A. A. (1970) 'Rassirenie prav mestnykh Sovetov – Leninskii demokrati-cheskii tsentralizm v deistvii', in *Problemy* (1970), pp. 6–17.

GONDRYA, M. (1972) 'Slagaemye avtoriteta', *Sovetskaya Moldaviya*, 2 February, p. 2.

GORKIN, A. (1957) 'O Sovetskoi demokratii', *Partiinaya zhizn'*, no. 2, pp. 10–19.

GORSHENEV, V. M. and KOZLOV, B. YE. (eds) (1976) *Zakon o statuse deputata na praktike (materialy nauchno-prakticheskoi konferentsii)* (Yaroslavl: Verkhne-Volzhskoe Knizhnoe Izd.).

GULIEV, V. YE. and SHCHIGLIK, A. I. (1975) 'Partiya i gosudarstvo v sisteme Sovetskoi sotsialisticheskoi demokratii', *SGiP*, no. 4, pp. 10–19.

HARASYMIW, BOHDAN (1971) 'The Qualifications of Local Party and Government Leaders in the Soviet Union and the Development of Pluralism', *Canadian Slavonic Papers*, vol. 13, pp. 314–42.

HILL, RONALD J. (1972) 'Recent Developments in Soviet Local Government', *Community Development Journal*, vol. 7, pp. 169–75.

HILL, RONALD J. (1973) 'Patterns of Deputy Selection to Local Soviets', *Sov. Studs*, vol. XXV, pp. 196–212.

HILL, RONALD J. (1976a) 'Soviet Literature on Electoral Reform: a Review', *Government and Opposition*, vol. 11, pp. 481–96.

HILL, RONALD J. (1976b) 'The CPSU in a Soviet Election Campaign', *Sov. Studs*, vol. XXVIII, pp. 590–8.

HILL, RONALD J. (1977) *Soviet Political Elites: The Case of Tiraspol* (London: Martin Robertson).

HINGLEY, RONALD (1978) *The Russian Mind* (London: Bodley Head).

HOFFMANN, ERIK P. (1977) 'The "Scientific Management" of Soviet Society', *PoC*, vol. XXVI, no. 3, pp. 59–67.

HOUGH, JERRY F. (1972) 'The Soviet System: Petrification or Pluralism?' *PoC*, vol. XXI, no. 2, pp. 25–45.

HOUGH, JERRY F. (1976a) 'Political Participation in the Soviet Union', *Sov. Studs*, vol. XXVIII, pp. 3–20.

HOUGH, JERRY F. (1976b) 'The Brezhnev Era: The Man and the System', *PoC*, vol. XXV, no. 2, pp. 1–17.

HOUGH, JERRY F. (1977) *The Soviet Union and Social Science Theory* (Cambridge, Mass.: Harvard UP).

IL'INSKII, I. P., KERIMOV, D. A. and CHERNOGOLOVKIN, N. V. (eds) (1976) *Sotsialisticheskoe gosudarstvo: sushchnost', funktsii i formy* (Moscow: Mysl').

ISTOMIN, V. G. (1973) 'K voprosu ob osnovnykh funktsiyakh i napravleniyakh partiinogo rukovodstva Sovetami deputatov trudyash-chikhsya', in Orlyanskii *et al.* (1973), pp. 119–23.

JACOBS, EVERETT M. (1970) 'Soviet Local Elections: What They Are, and What They Are Not', *Sov. Studs*, vol. XXII, pp. 61–76.

JACOBS, EVERETT M. (1972) 'The Composition of Local Soviets, 1959–1969', *Government and Opposition*, vol. 7, pp. 503–19.

JOHNSON, CHALMERS (ed.) (1970) *Change in Communist Systems* (Stanford, Calif.: Stanford UP).

JUVILER, PETER H. and MORTON, HENRY W. (eds) (1967) *Soviet Policy-Making: Studies of Communism in Transition* (London: Pall Mall).

KABYSHEV, V. T. (1969) 'Vybory v Sovety i izbiratel'noe pravo', in Farber (1969), pp. 118–37.

KADEIKIN, V. A. (1974) *Problemy nauchnogo podkhoda v partiinoi rabote* (Moscow: Mysl').

KADEIKIN, V. A., PEDOSOV, A. D. and SHAPKO, V. M. (eds) (1974), *Voprosy vnutripartiinoi zhizni i rukovodyashchei deyatel'nosti KPSS na sovremennom etape* (Moscow: Mysl').

KALENSKII, V. G. (1977) *Gosudarstvo kak ob"ekt sotsiologicheskogo analiza (Ocherki istorii i metodologii issledovaniya)* (Moscow: Yur. Lit.).

KALINYCHEV, F. I., KRAVTSOV, B. P., NEDAVNII, A. L. and SOLOV'ËVA, S. V. (eds) (1968) *XXIII s"ezd KPSS i voprosy gosudarstvennogo stroitel'stva* (Moscow: Mysl').

KALITS, I., LAUMETS, A. A. and SHNEIDER, KH. KH. (1965) 'Izuchenie deyatel'nosti deputatov s pomoshch'yu konkretno-sotsiologicheskogo metoda', *SGiP*, no. 9, pp. 65–70.

KARAPETYAN, L. M. and RAZIN, V. I. (1964) *Sovety obshchenarodnogo gosudarstva* (Moscow: Politizdat).

KAREV, D. S. (ed.) (1962) *Yuridicheskii spravochnik deputata mestnogo Soveta* (Moscow: Izd. Moskovskogo Universiteta).

KAZIMIRCHUK, V. P. (1967) 'Sotsiologicheskie issledovaniya v prave: problemy i perspektivy', *SGiP*, no. 10, pp. 37–45.

KAZIMIRCHUK, V. P. and ADAMYAN, N. K. (1970) 'Sotsiologicheskie aspekty sostava deputatov mestnykh Sovetov (na materialakh Armyanskoi SSR)', in *Organizatsiya i deyatel'nost'* (1970), pp. 103–23.

KEIZEROV, N. M., LEBEDEV, M. P. and MAL'TSEV, G. V. (eds) (1974) *Kommunisticheskaya partiya v politicheskoi sisteme sotsialisticheskogo obshchestva* (Moscow: Mysl').

KERIMOV, D. A. (ed.) (1965) *Pravo i kommunizm* (Moscow: Yur. Lit.).

KERIMOV, D. A. (ed.) (1973) *XXIV s"ezd KPSS ob ukreplenii sovetskogo gosudarstva i razvitii sotsialisticheskoi demokratii* (Moscow: Mysl').

KIM, A. I. (1965) *Sovetskoe izbiratel'noe pravo* (Moscow: Yur. Lit.).

KIM, A. I. (1967) 'Teoreticheskie voprosy dal'neishego sovershenstvovaniya Sovetskogo izbiratel'nogo prava', in Petrov (1967), pp. 116–30.

KIM, V. A. and NECHITAILO, G. V. (1970) *Otrazhenie interesov naseleniya v deyatel'nosti mestnykh Sovetov deputatov trudyashchikhsya* (Alma-Ata: Nauka).

KNEEN, PETER (1978) 'Why Natural Scientists are a Problem for the CPSU', *BJPS*, vol. 8, pp. 177–98.

KOTOK, V. F. (1963) *Sovetskaya predstavitel'naya sistema* (Moscow: Yur. Lit.).

KOTOK, V. F. (1964) *Referendum v sisteme sotsialisticheskoi demokratii* (Moscow: Nauka).

KOTOK, V. F. (1967) *Nakazy izbiratelei v sotsialisticheskom gosudarstve (imperativnyi mandat)* (Moscow: Nauka).

KOTOK, V. F. (ed.) (1974). *Problemy gosudarstva i prava na sovremennom etape (trudy nauchnykh sotrudnikov i aspirantov), Vypusk 8* (Moscow: IGPAN SSSR), pp. 99–106.

KOTOK, V. F., NECHITAILO, G. V. and SEMËNOV, P. G. (1966) 'Ob odnoi iz putei povysheniya roli Sovetov', *SGiP*, no. 9, pp. 123–7.

KOZLOV, N. T. (1968) 'Povyshenie roli mestnykh Sovetov na sovremennom etape', *SGiP*, no. 9, pp. 3–10.

KOZLOV, YU. M. (1978) *Kul'tura upravleniya i pravo* (Moscow: Znanie).

KOZLOVA, YE. I. (1967) *Mestnye organy gosudarstvennoi vlasti v SSSR* (Moscow: Mysl').

KOZLOVA, YE. I. (1972) 'Volya Sovetskogo naroda (gosudarstvenno–pravovoi aspekt), *SGiP*, no. 9, pp. 19–25.

KOZYR', M. I., KAZIMIRCHUK, V. P., PISKOTIN, M. I. and SHEREMET, K. F. (eds) (1977) *Kompleksnye sotsial'no-pravovye issledovaniya: opyt i problemy* (Moscow: Nauka).

KPSS v rezolyutsiyakh i resheniyakh s"ezdov, konferentsii i Plenumov TsK (1970–3) 11 vols (Moscow: Politizdat; cited as *KPSS v rez . . .*).

KRAVCHUK, S. S. (ed.) (1966) *Voprosy razvitiya Sovetov na sovremennom etape* (Moscow: Izd. Moskovskogo Universiteta).

KRAVCHUK, S. S. (ed.) (1973) *Pravovye problemy dal'neishego sovershenstvovaniya predstavitel'nykh organov gosudarstvennoi vlasti* (Moscow: Izd. Moskovskogo Universiteta).

KRUKHMALEV, A. (1978) 'Konstitutsiya SSSR i dal'neishee razvitie sotsialisticheskogo demokratizma', *Partiinaya zhizn'*, no. 19, pp. 19–24.

KUDINOV, N. A. (1969) 'Kharakternye cherty Sovetov obshchenarodnogo gosudarstva', in *Revolyutsiya, gosudarstvo i pravo* (Minsk: Izd. Belorusskogo Gosudarstvennogo Universiteta Imeni V. I. Lenina).

KUDINOV, N. A. (1970) 'Politicheskie obychai v SSSR', in *Problemy* (1970), pp. 153–6.

KUSHNIKOV, A. N. and SOPELKO, B. I. (1971) 'Partiinaya rabota kak ob"ekt sotsiologicheskogo issledovaniya', *Vop. Ist. KPSS*, no. 2, pp. 71–80.

KUZNETSOV, I. N. and SAVENKOV, N. T. (1964) Review of Tikhomirov (1963), *SGiP*, no. 9, pp. 153–5.

LASHIN, A. (1975) 'Demokratizm politicheskoi sistemy razvitogo sotsialisticheskogo obshchestva', *Kommunist*, no. 2, pp. 32–42.

LAZAREV, B. M. (1971) 'Sotsial'nye interesy i kompetentsiya organov upravleniya', *SGiP*, no. 10, pp. 86–94.

LAZAREV, B. M. (1972) *Kompetentsiya organov upravleniya* (Moscow: Yur. Lit.).

LEBEDEV, M. P. (1970) 'Partiya v politicheskoi sisteme sotsializma', *SGiP*, no. 2, pp. 3–13.

LEIZEROV, A. T. (1964) 'K voprosu ob uluchshenii poryadka vydvizheniya kandidatov v deputaty mestnykh Sovetov Belorusskoi SSR', in T. S. Gorbunov (ed.), *Materialy k IX konferentsii molodykh uchënykh: obshchestvennye nauki* (Minsk: Akademiya Nauk Belorusskoi SSR), pp. 67–74.

LEIZEROV, A. T. (1970a) 'O vliyanii ryada sub"ektivnykh i ob"ektivnykh faktorov na stepen' uchastiya v rabote mestnykh Sovetov', in *Problemy* (1970), pp. 79–107.

LEIZEROV, A. T. (1970b) 'K voprosu o faktorakh, vliyayushchikh na aktivnost' deputatov', in *Problemy sotsiologii prava* (1970), pp. 99–103.

LEIZEROV ('LEIZERAW'), A. T. (1974a) *Savetskaya vybarchaya sistema* (Minsk: Izd. Belorusskogo Gosudarstvennogo Universiteta Imeni V. I. Lenina).

LEIZEROV, A. T. (1974b) 'Issledovanie effektivnosti deyatel'nosti sel'skikh i raionnykh Sovetov BSSR', *SGiP*, no. 12, pp. 57–62.

LEIZEROV, A. T. (1974c) 'Nekotorye voprosy formirovaniya postoyannykh komissii mestnykh Sovetov', in Kotok (1974), pp. 99–106.

LEIZEROV, A. T. (1977) *Demokraticheskie formy deyatel'nosti mestnykh Sovetov* (Minsk: Izd. Belorusskogo Gosudarstvennogo Universiteta Imeni V. I. Lenina).

LEPËSHKIN, A. I. (1965a) 'Nazrevshie voprosy razvitiya nauki Sovetskogo gosudarstvennogo prava', *SGiP*, no. 2, pp. 5–15.

LEPËSHKIN, A. I. (1965b) 'Slovo o knigakh po Sovetskomu stroitel'stvu i gosudarstvennomu pravu', *SGiP*, no. 12, pp. 131–5.

LEPËSHKIN, A. I. (1967) *Sovety – vlast' naroda, 1936–1967* (Moscow: Yur. Lit.).

LESNYI, V. M. and CHERNOGOLOVKIN, N. V. (eds) (1976) *Politicheskaya organizatsiya razvitogo sotsialisticheskogo obshchestva: struktura i funktsii* (Moscow: Izd. Moskovskogo Universiteta).

LEWIN, MOSHE (1975) *Political Undercurrents in Soviet Economic Debates* (London: Pluto Press).

LOTT, YU. (1964) 'Sovet – shkola gosudarstvennoi deyatel'nosti', *Kommunist Estonii*, no. 12, pp. 87–8.

LUNEV, A. YE. (1967) 'Konkretno-sotsiologicheskie issledovaniya i ikh znachenie dlya razvitiya pravovoi nauki', in Petrov (1967), pp. 95–106.

MAKHNENKO, A. KH. (ed.) (1966) *Voprosy razvitiya i sovershenstvovaniya organov narodnogo predstavitel'stva v SSSR* (Moscow: Ministerstvo Vysshego i Srednego Spetsial'nogo Obrazovaniya RSFSR).

MAKOV, YU. (1971) 'Nauchnyi podkhod v praktike partiinoi raboty', *Kommunist*, no. 11, pp. 43–53.

MALE, DONALD J. (1971) *Russian Peasant Organisation Before Collectivisation: A Study in Commune and Gathering, 1925–30* (Cambridge: Cambridge UP).

MARCHENKO, M. N. (1973) *Politicheskaya organizatsiya Sovetskogo obshchestva i eë burzhuaznye fal'sifikatory* (Moscow: Izd. Moskovskogo Universiteta).

MASLENNIKOV, V. (1977) 'V zerkale konkretnogo issledovaniya', *SDT*, no. 10, pp. 87–8.

MATCHANOV, N. M. (1975) 'Dal'neishee povyshenie aktivnosti deputatov – vazhnoe uslovie uluchsheniya raboty Sovetov', *SGiP*, no. 6, pp. 3–12.

MATTHEWS, MERVYN (1978) *Privilege in the Soviet Union: A Study of Elite Life-Styles Under Communism* (London: Allen & Unwin).

MCAULEY, MARY (1978) 'The Soviet Leadership's Search for Legitimacy' (paper presented to the annual conference of the Political Studies Association of the United Kingdom, March 1978).

MEDVEDEV, ROY A. (1975) *On Socialist Democracy* (London: Macmillan).

MEL'NIKOV, A. (1975) 'Takaya eto professiya', *Sovetskaya Moldaviya*, 3 January, p. 3.

MILLER, JOHN H. (1977) 'Cadres Policy in Nationality Areas: Recruitment of CPSU first and second secretaries in non-Russian republics of the USSR', *Sov. Studs*, vol. XXIX, pp. 3–36.

MORTON, HENRY W. and TÖKÉS, RUDOLF L. (eds) (1974) *Soviet Politics and Society in the 1970s* (New York: The Free Press).

MOSHAK, A. V. (1971) 'Nakazy izbiratelei i status deputata Soveta', *SGiP*, no. 2, pp. 93–6.

MOSKALEV, A. V. (1975) *Sessionnaya deyatel'nost' mestnykh Sovetov* (Moscow: Yur. Lit.).

MOTE, MAX E. (1965) *Soviet Local and Republic Elections* (Stanford: The Hoover Institution).

NAIDA, S. F., *et al.* (1967) *Sovety za 50 let* (Moscow: Mysl').

NEMTSEV, V. A. (1967) 'Ob ispol'zovanii konkretno–sotsiologicheskogo metoda dlya izucheniya problem administrativno–territorial'nogo deleniya', in Petrov (1967), pp. 231–41.

NEMTSEV, V. A. (1968) 'Neskol'ko zamechanii k Polozheniyu o vyborakh v mestnye Sovety deputatov trudyashchikhsya', in *Voprosy gosudarstvennogo prava*, 1968, pp. 22–38.

NEMTSEV, V. A. (1969) 'Raionnyi organ vlasti i ego territoriya', *SGiP*, no. 8, pp. 69–73.

'Ne otpustili na sessiyu' (1975) *SDT*, no. 2, pp. 94–6.

NIKITINSKII, V. I. (1967) 'Znachenie eksperimenta v normotvorcheskoi deyatel'nosti', *SGiP*, 1967, no. 6, pp. 26–34.

NOVE, ALEC (1975) *Stalinism and After* (London: Allen & Unwin).

NUDNENKO, L. A. (1975) 'Poryadok vyrabotki i realizatsii nakazov deputatom Verkhovnogo Soveta SSSR', *Vestnik Moskovskogo universiteta, Seriya 'Pravo'*, 1975, no. 2, pp. 45–51.

'O chëm rasskazala anketa' (1966) *SDT*, no. 10, pp. 41–7.

OLIVER, JAMES H. (1969) 'Citizen Demands and the Soviet Political System', *APSR*, vol. LXIII, pp. 465–75.

'O merakh po ukrepleniyu material'no-finansovoi bazy ispolkomov raionnykh i gorodskikh Sovetov deputatov trudyashchikhsya' (1971) *SDT*, no. 4, pp. 30–1 (cited as 'O merakh . . .', 1971).

'O razrabotke problem politicheskikh nauk: obzor pisem chitatelei' (1965) *Pravda*, 13 June, p. 4 (cited as 'O razrabotke problem . . .', 1965).

Organizatsionno–partiinaya rabota: problemy i opyt (1974) (Moscow: Moskovskii Rabochii).

Organizatsiya i deyatel'nost' Sovetov i organov gosudarstvennogo upravleniya Armyanskoi SSR (1970) (Yerevan: Izd. Adademii Nauk Armyanskoi SSR) (cited as *Organizatsiya i deyatel'nost'*, 1970).

ORLOV, I. M. (1973) *Deyatel'nost KPSS po povysheniyu roli Sovetov v stroitel'stve kommunizma* (Moscow: Vysshaya Shkola).

ORLYANSKII, S. F., BOCHENKOV, K. F. and SHOKEL', V. P. (eds) (1973) *Mestnye Sovety Zapadnoi Sibiri v period stroitel'stva sotsializma, Vypusk I. (Materialy k nauchnoi konferentsii po istorii mestnykh Sovetov, posvyashchennoi 50-letiyu obrazovaniya SSR)* (Prokop'evsk: Izd. Kemerovskogo Pedagogicheskogo Instituta).

PAL'GUNOVA, T. M. (1969) 'Voprosy organizatsii vyborov v mestnye Sovety deputatov trudyashchikhsya', in Farber (1969), pp. 147–58.

PAL'GUNOVA, T. M. (1977) *Vybory v mestnye Sovety* (Moscow: Yur. Lit.).

PAPUTIN, V. (1970) 'Partiinoe rukovodstvo Sovetami', in *Sovershenstvovat' rabotu Sovetov deputatov trudyashchikhsya* (1970), pp. 202–18.

PARROTT, BRUCE (1977) 'Politics and Economics in the USSR', *PoC*, vol. XXVI, no. 3, pp. 54–9.

PASKAR', P. N. (1974) *Sovety deputatov trudyashchikhsya v sisteme politicheskoi organizatsii obshchestva (na materialakh Moldavskoi SSR)* (Kishinev: Shtiintsa).

PAVLOV, I. V. and KAZIMIRCHUK, V. P. (eds) (1971) *Upravlenie, sotsiologiya, pravo* (Moscow: Yur. Lit.).

PERRY, JACK (1973) 'The USSR and the Environment', *PoC*, vol. XXII, no. 3, pp. 52–4.

PERTTSIK, V. A. (1967a) 'O pervykh opytakh sotsiologicheskogo issledovaniya gosudarstvenno-pravovykh otnoshenii (na materialakh Vostochnoi Sibiri)', in Petrov (1967), pp. 131–43.

PERTTSIK, V. A. (1967b) 'Puti sovershenstvovaniya deyatel'nosti deputatov mestnykh Sovetov', *SGiP*, no. 7, pp. 16–21.

PERTTSIK, V. A. (1968a) 'Izbiratel' i deputat', *Izvestiya*, 15 February, p. 3.

PERTTSIK, V. A. (1968b) 'Deputat i izbiratel' (opyt sotsiologicheskikh issledovanii)', in *Voprosy gosudarstvennogo prava . . .* (1968), pp. 3–21.

PERTTSIK, V. A. (1970) 'Sotsiologicheskie issledovaniya gosudarstvenno-pravovykh otnoshenii', in *Problemy sotsiologii prava* (1970), pp. 95–8.

PETROV, L. A. (ed.) (1967) *Nekotorye voprosy sotsiologii i prava (Materialy nauchno-teoreticheskoi konferentsii 'Konkretno-sotsiologicheskie issledovaniya pravovykh otnoshenii')* (Irkutsk: publisher unidentified).

PETROVICHEV, N. A., *et al.* (1972) *Partiinoe stroitel'stvo: uchebnoe posobie*, 3rd edn (Moscow: Politizdat).

PIGALEV, P. F. (1970) 'Sovershenstvovanie deyatel'nosti Sovetov deputatov trudyashchikhsya', *SGiP*, no. 4, pp. 41–9.

PIGOLKIN, A. S. and ROZHKO, I. N. (1976) *Sovetskoe zakonodatel'stvo i ego rol' v kommunisticheskom stroitel'stve* (Moscow: Znanie).

PISKOTIN, M. I. and TIKHOMIROV, YU. A. (1965) 'Sovershenstvovanie organizatsii i metodov deyatel'nosti apparata gosudarstvennogo upravleniya', *SGiP*, no. 9, pp. 3–11.

PISKOTIN, M. I. *et al.* (eds) (1975) *Problemy Sovetskogo stroitel'stva, gosudarstvennogo upravleniya i pravovogo vospitaniya na sovremennom etape (Tezisy dokladov i soobshchenii na nauchno-prakticheskoi konferentsii* (Ufa: Sovet Ministrov Bashkirskoi ASSR).

PLATKOVSKII, V. V. (1970) 'Partiya – rukovodyashchaya sila sotsialisti-cheskogo gosudarstva', *SGiP*, no. 8, pp. 3–12.

Polozhenie o deputatskikh gruppakh gorodskikh, raionnykh v gorodakh, poseklovykh Sovetov deputatov trudyashchikhsya. Utverzhdeno Gor'kovskim oblastnym Sovetom deputatov trudyashchikhsya XIV sozyva na pervoi sessii, 26 iyunya 1973 goda (1973) (Gorky: Gor'kovskii Oblastnoi Sovet Deputatov Trudyashchikhsya).

Polozhenie o deputatskikh postakh mestnykh Sovetov deputatov trudyash-chikhsya. Utverzhdeno resheniem Kalininskogo oblastnogo Soveta ot 15 iyunya 1971 g. (1971) (Kalinin: Kalininskii Oblastnoi Sovet Deputatov Trudyashchikhsya).

Polozhenie o vyborakh v kraevye, oblastnye, okruzhnye, raionnye, gorodskie, sel'skie i poselkovye Sovety deputatov trudyashchikhsya RSFSR (RSFSR electoral law, as amended to 27 October 1966) (1975) (Moscow: Yur. Lit.).

POSTNIKOV, M. A. and SELIVANOV, A. V. (1968) 'KPSS i voprosy sovershenstvovaniya organizatorskoi raboty mestnykh Sovetov', *SGiP*, no. 12, pp. 85–94.

POWELL, DAVID E. and SHOUP, PAUL (1970) 'The Emergence of Political Science in Communist Countries', *APSR*, vol. LXIV, pp. 572–88.

Pravda (daily newspaper of CPSU) (various issues).

Problemy natsional'no-gosudarstvennogo stroitel'stva: Tezisy dokladov na nauchnoi konferentsii yuridicheskogo fakul'teta (14 fevralya 1970g.) (Minsk: Izd. Belorusskogo Gosudarstvennogo Universiteta Imeni V. I. Lenina; cited as *Problemy*, 1970).

Problemy sotsiologii prava, Vypusk I (1970) (Vilnius: publisher unidentified).

PROVOTOROV, V. (1967) 'Sotsiologicheskie issledovaniya v partiinoi rabote', *Partiinaya zhizn'*, no. 19, pp. 36–41.

PYE, LUCIAN W. (1966) *Aspects of Political Development* (Boston, Mass.: Little, Brown).

RASULBEKOV, I. D. (1964) 'Nuzhdy naseleniya – v tsentre vnimaniya mestnykh Sovetov', *SGiP*, no. 7, pp. 117–21.

REMNEK, RICHARD B. (ed.) (1977) *Social Scientists and Policy Making in the USSR* (New York: Praeger).

REUTSKII, I. M. and YEVDOKIMOV, D. V. (1974) *Informatisya – instrument partiinogo rukovodstva* (Moscow: Moskovskii Rabochii).

RYAVEC, KARL W. (1975) *Implementation of Soviet Economic Reforms: Political, Organizational, and Social Processes* (New York: Praeger).

RZHEVSKII, V. A. (1972) 'Soderzhanie i forma pravovykh aktov mestnykh Sovetov', *SGiP*, no. 8, pp. 93–7.

SAFAROV, R. A. (1963) 'Institut referenduma v usloviyakh obshchenarodnogo gosudarstva', *SGiP*, no. 6, pp. 15–25.

SAFAROV, R. A. (1964) 'Sotsial'nyi eksperiment i problemy gosudarstva i prava', *SGiP*, no. 10, pp. 14–22.

SAFAROV, R. A. (1967) 'Vyyavlenie obshchestvennogo mneniya v gosudarstvenno-pravovoi praktike', *SGiP*, no. 10, pp. 46–54.

SAFAROV, R. A. (1975a) 'Organy gosudarstvennogo upravleniya i obshchestvennoe mnenie naseleniya', *SGiP*, no. 1, pp. 20–7.

SAFAROV, R. A. (1975b) *Obshchestvennoe mnenie i gosudarstvennoe upravlenie* (Moscow: Yur. Lit.).

SAKHAROV, ANDREI D. (1969) *Progress, Coexistence and Intellectual Freedom*, Pelican edn (Harmondsworth: Penguin).

SAPARGALIEV, G. S. and SAKHIPOV, M. S. (eds) (1977) *Sovershenstvovanie zakonodatel'stva Kazakhskoi SSR* (Alma-Ata: Nauka).

SAVENKOV, N. T. (1974) *Deputat raionnogo, gorodskogo Soveta* (Moscow: Yur. Lit.).

SCHAPIRO, LEONARD (1961) 'The Party and the State', *Survey*, no. 38, pp. 111–16.

SCHAPIRO, LEONARD B. (ed.) (1963) *The USSR and the Future: An Analysis of the New Program of the CPSU* (New York: Praeger).

SCHAPIRO, LEONARD (1970) *The Communist Party of the Soviet Union*, 2nd edn (London: Methuen).

SCHWARTZ, DONALD V. (1974) 'Information and Administration in the Soviet Union: Some Theoretical Considerations', *Canadian Journal of Political Science*, vol. VII, pp. 228–44.

SCHWARTZ, JOEL J. and KEECH, WILLIAM R. (1968) 'Group Influence and the Policy Process in the Soviet Union', *APSR*, vol. LXII, pp. 840–51.

SCOTT, DEREK J. R. (1969) *Russian Political Institutions*, 4th edn (London: Allen & Unwin).

SEMIN, V. P. (1969) 'Ministerstvo soyuznoi respubliki i mestnye Sovety deputatov trudyashchikhsya', *SGiP*, no. 9, pp. 87–92.

SHABALIN, A. I. (1974) 'Voprosy sovershenstvovaniya deyatel'nosti postoyannykh komissii Verkhovnykh Sovetov avtonomnykh respublik (na materialakh Udmurtskoi ASSR)', in Kotok (1974), pp. 92–100.

SHABANOV, YU. V. (1969a) *Partiinoe rukovodstvo Sovetami deputatov trudyashchikhsya* (Minsk: Belarus').

SHABANOV, YU. V. (1969b) *Problemy Sovetskoi sotsialisticheskoi demokratii v period stroitel'stva kommunizma* (Minsk: Nauka i Tekhnika).

SHAFIR, M. A. (1964) 'Aktual'nye voprosy polozheniya sel'skikh Sovetov i metody ikh izucheniya (po materialam Tul'skoi oblasti)', *SGiP*, no. 10, pp. 23–30.

SHAFIR, M. (1977) 'Etapy razvitiya', *SDT*, no. 10, pp. 7–15.

SHAKHNAZAROV, G. KH. (1972) *Sotsialisticheskaya demokratiya: nekotorye voprosy teorii* (Moscow: Politizdat).

SHAKHNAZAROV, GEORGI (1974) *The Role of the Communist Party in Socialist Society* (Moscow: Novosti).

SHAKHNAZAROV, G. (1976) 'Politika skvoz' prizmu nauki', *Kommunist*, no. 17, pp. 104–14.

SHAPIRO, JANE P. and POTICHNYJ, PETER J. (eds) (1976) *Change and Adaptation in Soviet and East European Politics* (New York: Praeger).

SHAPKO, V. (1978) 'Zakon zhizni KPSS', *Kommunist*, no. 14, pp. 94–104.

SHAPKO, V. M., VINOGRADOV, N. N. and SULEMOV, V. A. (eds) (1977) *KPSS – rukovodyashchee yadro politicheskoi sistemy Sovetskogo obshchestva* (Moscow: Mysl').

SHCHETININ, B. V. (1974) *Sovetskaya izbiratel'naya sistema* (Moscow: Znanie).

SHEBANOV, A. F. (ed.) (1972) *XXIV s"ezd KPSS i voprosy teorii gosudarstva i prava* (Moscow: Yur. Lit.).

SHEREMET, K. F. (1965) 'Voprosy kompetentsii mestnykh Sovetov', *SGiP*, no. 4, pp. 19–27.

SHEREMET, K. F. (1968a) *Kompetentsiya mestnykh Sovetov* (Moscow: Izd. Moskovskogo Universiteta).

SHEREMET, K. F. (1968b) 'Mestnye Sovety v sisteme organov gosudarstva i osobennosti razvitiya ikh funktsii', *SGiP*, no. 8, pp. 90–101.

SHEREMET, K. F. (ed.) (1976) *Sovety deputatov trudyashchikhsya i razvitie sotsialisticheskoi demokratii* (Moscow: Nauka).

SHEREMET, K. F. *et al.* (1971) 'Sovershenstvovanie form deputatskoi deyatel'nosti', *SGiP*, no. 11, pp. 90–9.

SHEREMET, K. F. and KUTAFIN, O. YE. (1976) *Kompetentsiya mestnykh Sovetov deputatov trudyashchikhsya* (Moscow: Znanie).

SHLYAPENTOKH, V. E. (1976) Review of Safarov (1975b), *SGiP*, no. 5, pp. 147–9.

SIDOROVA, O. P. (1967) 'Sovershenstvovat' deyatel'nost' mestnykh Sovetov', *SGiP*, no. 8, pp. 139–40.

SKILLING, H. GORDON (1963) 'In Search of Political Science in the USSR', *Canadian Journal of Economics and Political Science*, vol. XXIX, pp. 519–29.

SKILLING, H. GORDON (1966) 'Interest Groups and Communist Politics', *World Politics*, vol. XVIII, pp. 435–51.

SKILLING, H. GORDON and GRIFFITHS, FRANKLYN (eds) (1971) *Interest Groups in Soviet Politics* (Princeton, NJ: Princeton UP).

SLEPNEVA, T. and MINEEVA, V. (1977) 'A ne luchshe li raz v kvartal?', *SDT*, no. 9, pp. 22–3.

SMIRNOV, I. N. (1976) 'XXV s"ezd KPSS i aktual'nye zadachi obshchestvennykh nauk', *Vop. Fil.*, no. 8, pp. 150–7.

SMIRNOV, S. A. (1969) 'Vazhneishie problemy partiinogo stroitel'stva kak nauki', *Vop. Ist. KPSS*, no. 5, pp. 64–76.

SMOL'KOV, V. G. (1967) 'Konkretno–sotsiologicheskie issledovaniya i partiinaya propaganda (iz opyta sotsiologicheskoi laboratorii pri Irkutskom obkome KPSS)', in Petrov (1967).

SOLOMON, PETER H., JR (1978) *Soviet Criminologists and Criminal Policy: Specialists in Policy-Making* (London: Macmillan).

SOLOV'ËVA, S. V. (1978) *Sovety i nauchno–teknhicheskii progress* (Moscow: Yur. Lit.).

Sovershenstvovat' rabotu Sovetov deputatov trudyashchikhsya (1970) (Moscow: Izvestiya).

Sovetskaya Moldaviya (Moldavian daily newspaper, published in Kishinev) (various issues).

Spravochnik partiinogo rabotniko (1967; 1968), nos 7, 8 (Moscow: Politizdat).

STAROVOITOV, N. G. (1975) *Nakazy izbiratelei* (Moscow: Yur. Lit.).

STEPANOV, I. (1977) 'Problemy narodnogo predstavitel'stva', *SDT*, no. 2, pp. 73–4.

STEWART, PHILIP D. (1969) 'Soviet Interest Groups and the Policy Process: The Repeal of Production Education', *World Politics*, vol. XXII, pp. 29–50.

STRASHUN, B. A. (1973) 'Razvitie izbiratel'nogo prava sotsialisticheskikh stran', *SGiP*, no. 7, pp. 42–9.

STRASHUN, B. A. (1976) *Sotsializm i demokratiya (sotsialisticheskoe narodnoe predstavitel'stvo)* (Moscow: Mezhdunarodnye Otnosheniya).

STREPUKHOV, M. F. (ed.) (1976) *Organy narodnoi vlasti: opyt i problemy* (Moscow: Izvestiya).

SUKHANOV, N. YE. (1969) 'Rabota mestnykh Sovetov s nakazami izbiratelei', *SGiP*, no. 6, pp. 75–9.

SUSLOV, M. A. (1978) 'Rech' ... na torzhestvennom sobranii aspirantov, slushatelei i prepodavatelei Akademii obshchestvennykh nauk pri TsK KPSS, posvyashchennom nachalu raboty Akademii, 1 sentyabrya 1978 goda', *Kommunist*, no. 14, pp. 21–8.

SUVOROV, K. I., KRASNOV, A. V. and SHIRIKOV, L. V. (eds) (1977) *Partiya i intelligentsiya v usloviyakh razvitogo sotsializma: iz opyta raboty partiinykh organizatsii* (Moscow: Mysl').

TADEVOSYAN, E. V. (1965) 'Diskussiya o politicheskoi nauke', *Vop. Fil.*, no. 10, pp. 164–6.

TAUBMAN, WILLIAM (1973) *Governing Soviet Cities: Bureaucratic Politics and Urban Development in the USSR* (New York: Praeger).

THEEN, ROLF H. W. (1971) 'Political Science in the USSR: "To Be, or Not to Be". Some reflections on the implications of a recent Soviet critique of American political science', *World Politics*, vol. XXIII, pp. 684–703.

THEEN, ROLF H. W. (1972) 'Political Science in the USSR', *PoC*, vol. XXI, no. 3, pp. 64–70.

TIKHOMIROV, YU. A. (1963) *Sovety i razvitie gosudarstvennogo upravleniya v period razvërnutogo stroitel'stva kommunizma* (Moscow: Yur. Lit.).

TIKHOMIROV. YU. A. (1970) 'Nauchnaya organizatsiya truda v ispolnitel'nykh organakh mestnykh Sovetov', in *Sovershenstvovat' rabotu Sovetov deputatov trudyashchikhsya* (1970), pp. 183–201.

TIKHOMIROV, YU. A. (ed.) (1975) *Demokratiya razvitogo sotsialisticheskogo obshchestva* (Moscow: Nauka).

TIKHOMIROV, YU. A. (ed.) (1978) *Sovetskoe gosudarstvo v usloviyakh razvitogo sotsialisticheskogo obshchestva* (Moscow: Nauka).

TIKHOMIROV, YU. A. and SHEREMET, K. F. (eds) (1974) *Pravovye voprosy raboty mestnykh Sovetov (organizatsiya deyatel'nosti)* (Moscow: Yur. Lit.).

208   *Soviet Politics, Political Science and Reform*

Time, Space and Politics: Soviet Studies in the Political Sciences (1976) (Moscow: USSR Academy of Sciences).

TOIGANBAEV, A. and DZHEKBATYROV, M. (1971) *Mestnye Sovety Kazakhstana* (Alma-Ata: Kazakhstan).

TOPORNIN, B. N. (1975) *Sovetskaya politicheskaya sistema* (Moscow: Politizdat).

TURAJEV, V. (ed.) (no date) *USSR: Questions and Answers* (Moscow: Novosti; published 1964 or 1965).

TURISHCHEV, YU. G. (1975) *KPSS – zhivoi, razvivayushchiisya politicheskii organizm* (Moscow: Politizdat).

UKRAINETS, P. P. (1976) *Partiinoe rukovodstvo i gosudarstvennoe upravlenie* (Minsk: Belarus').

UTENKOV, A. YA., KULINCHENKO, V. A. and NAZAROV, S. A. (eds) (1977) *Vnutripartiinaya demokratiya i povyshenie aktivnosti kommunistov* (Moscow: Mysl').

VASILENKOV, P. T. (1963) *Deyatel'nost' mestnykh organov vlasti po vypolneniyu nakazov izbiratelei* (Moscow: Izd. Moskovskogo Universiteta).

VASILENKOV, P. T. (1967) *Organy Sovetskogo gosudarstva i ikh sistema na sovremennom etape* (Moscow: Izd. Moskovskogo Universiteta).

VASIL'EV, V. I. (ed.) (1968) *V pomoshch' deputatu mestnogo Soveta (prakticheskoe posobie)* (Moscow: Yur. Lit.).

VASIL'EV, V. I. (1970) 'Razvitie Sovetov kak sotsial'noi sistemy', *SGiP*, no. 11, pp. 92–100.

VASIL'EV, V. I. and TIKHOMIROV, YU. A. (1961) 'Privlechenie mass k rabote Sovetskogo apparata', *SDT*, no. 6, pp. 27–38.

Verfassung der Deutschen Demokratischen Republik von 6 April 1968, amended 7 October 1974 (1975) (Berlin: Staatsverlag).

VERKHOVTSEV, I. P. and MALOV, YU. K. (1974) *Organizatsionnye osnovy KPSS i ikh 'kritiki'* (Moscow: Politizdat).

VESELOV, N. (1973) *The Communist Party and Mass Organizations in the USSR* (Moscow: Novosti).

Voprosy gosudarstvennogo prava i Sovetskogo stroitel'stva, Seriya yuridicheskaya, Vypusk 9, Chast' vtoraya, Tom LVII (1968) (Irkutsk: Izd. Irkutskogo Gosudarstvennogo Universiteta Imeni A. A. Zhdanova).

WEINBERG, ELIZABETH ANN (1974) *The Development of Sociology in the Soviet Union* (London: Routledge & Kegan Paul).

WHITE, STEPHEN (1974) 'Contradiction and Change in State Socialism', *Sov. Studs*, vol. XXVI, pp. 41–55.

WHITE, STEPHEN (1975) 'Political Science as Ideology: The Study of Soviet Politics', in B. Chapman and A. M. Potter (eds) (1975) *W.J.M.M. Political Questions: Essays in Honour of W. J. M. MacKenzie* (Manchester: Manchester UP), pp. 252–68.

WHITE, STEPHEN (1977) 'Communist Systems and the "Iron Law of Pluralism" ', *BJPS*, vol. 8, pp. 101–17.

XXIII s"ezd Kommunisticheskoi partii Sovetskogo Soyuza, 29 marta – 8 aprelya 1966 goda: Stenograficheskii otchët (1966) 2 vols (Moscow: Politizdat; cited as *XXIII s"ezd*).

XXIV s"ezd Kommunisticheskoi partii Sovetskogo Soyuza, 30 marta – 9 aprelya 1971 goda: Stenograficheskii otchët (1971) 2 vols (Moscow: Politizdat; cited as *XXIV s"ezd*).

XXV s"ezd Kommunisticheskoi partii Sovetskogo Soyuza, 24 fevralya – 5 marta 1976 goda: Stenograficheskii otchët (1976) 3 vols (Moscow: Politizdat; cited as *XXV s"ezd*).

XXV s"ezd KPSS i zadachi kafedr obshchestvennykh nauk (1977) (Moscow: Politizdat).

YELISTRATOV, P. M. (1969) 'O nauchnom obobshchenii opyta raboty mestnykh partiinykh organizatsii', *Vop. Ist. KPSS*, no. 12, pp. 69–75.

YUDIN, I. N. (1973) *Sotsial'naya baza rosta KPSS* (Moscow: Politizdat).

YUDIN, I. N. *et al.* (1973) *Nekotorye voprosy organizatsionno-partiinoi raboty* (Moscow: Politizdat).

YUDIN, I. N. *et al.* (1975) *Internatsional'nyi printsip v stroitel'stve i deyatel'nosti KPSS* (Moscow: Politizdat).

Zakon Soyuza Sovetskikh Sotsialisticheskikh Respublik o Statuse deputatov Sovetov deputatov trudyashchikhsya v SSSR (1972) text in *Pravda*, 22 September.

Zakon Soyuza Sovetskikh Sotsialisticheskikh Respublik o Vyborakh v Verkhovnyi Sovet SSSR (1978) text in *Pravda*, 8 July.

Zakony o gorodskikh i raionnykh v gorodakh Sovetakh deputatov trudyash-chikhsya soyuznykh respublik (1972) (Moscow: Izvestiya).

Zakony o raionnykh Sovetakh deputatov trudyashchikhsya soyuznykh respublik (1972) (Moscow: Izvestiya).

Zakony o sel'skikh i poselkovykh Sovetakh deputatov trudyashchikhsya soyuznykh respublik (1969) (Moscow: Izvestiya).

ZAV'YALOV, YU. S. (1970) 'Vyrazhenie interesov v sotsialisticheskom prave', *SGiP*, no. 6, pp. 101–4.

ZHILIN, A. M. (1966) 'Povyshenie roli mestnykh Sovetov i razvitie obshchestvennykh nachal v ikh rabote (po materialam Gor'kovskoi oblasti)', *SGiP*, no. 5, pp. 56–64.

ZHOGIN, N. and MEL'NIKOVA, E. (1971) *Zakon obo mne i mne o zakone: chto dolzhny znat' molodye lyudi o Sovetskikh zakonakh* (Moscow: Molodaya Gvardiya).

ZRAZYUK, M. (1975) 'Pochemu nakaz ne vypolnen', *Sovetskaya Moldaviya*, 9 February, p. 2.

Author Index

211

Subject Index

217